The Myth of the Nuclear Revolution

A VOLUME IN THE SERIES

Cornell Studies in Security Affairs

Edited by Robert J. Art, Robert Jervis, and Stephen M. Walt

A list of titles in this series is available at cornellpress.cornell.edu.

The Myth of the Nuclear Revolution

Power Politics in the Atomic Age

KEIR A. LIEBER AND
DARYL G. PRESS

Cornell University Press

Ithaca and London

First published 2020 by Cornell University Press

Library of Congress Cataloging-in-Publication Data

Names: Lieber, Keir A. (Keir Alexander), 1970– author. ⏐ Press, Daryl Grayson, author.
Title: The myth of the nuclear revolution : power politics in the atomic age / Keir A. Lieber and Daryl G. Press.
Description: Ithaca [New York] : Cornell University Press, 2020. ⏐ Series: Cornell studies in security affairs ⏐ Includes bibliographical references and index.
Identifiers: LCCN 2019046302 (print) ⏐ LCCN 2019046303 (ebook) ⏐ ISBN 9781501749292 (cloth) ⏐ ISBN 9781501749308 (epub) ⏐ ISBN 9781501749315 (pdf)
Subjects: LCSH: Nuclear weapons—Political aspects. ⏐ Deterrence (Strategy) ⏐ Arms race. ⏐ Balance of power. ⏐ World politics—1955–
Classification: LCC JZ5665 .L54 2020 (print) ⏐ LCC JZ5665 (ebook) ⏐ DDC 327.1/747—dc23
LC record available at https://lccn.loc.gov/2019046302
LC ebook record available at https://lccn.loc.gov/2019046303

Contents

Acknowledgments

We are deeply grateful for the support and assistance we received while writing this book. Our terrific colleagues and students at Dartmouth College, Georgetown University, and the University of Notre Dame were invaluable sources of intellectual inspiration, research assistance, and constructive criticism.

Our universities provided generous grants for travel, research, and writing. In particular, we thank the Center for Security Studies, the Graduate School of Arts and Sciences, the Office of Research Services, and the Office of the Provost at Georgetown, as well as the Graduate School Office of Research, Institute for Scholarship in the Liberal Arts, and the Kroc Institute for International Peace Studies at Notre Dame.

The financial support of several foundations and other organizations was also crucial for allowing us to complete this work. That included funding from the Carnegie Corporation of New York, the Project on Advanced Systems and Concepts for Countering Weapons of Mass Destruction, and the Smith Richardson Foundation. An earlier version of chapter 3 ("Escaping Stalemate") was published as Keir A. Lieber and Daryl G. Press, "The New Era of Counterforce: Technological Change and Future of Nuclear Deterrence," *International Security* 41, no. 4 (Spring 2017): 9–49; we are grateful to the journal for permission to use the material here.

Over the years, we have presented our work at countless academic workshops and seminars, government offices, educational programs, think tanks, research institutes, military bases, defense universities, and conferences—both in the United States and abroad. We cannot thank by name every individual who participated in, hosted, or discussed our work at those events, but your comments and criticisms were crucial for the development and clarification of our arguments.

One day-long workshop at the University of Chicago stands out, however, and not just because all such murder boards typically do. As colleagues from several universities gathered to tear apart every chapter of our manuscript, they realized and then slowly convinced us that our book, which we had framed far more narrowly, was actually a critique of the theory of the nuclear revolution—arguably the dominant model for understanding the role of nuclear weapons in international politics. We are deeply grateful to those colleagues for their time, insights, withering critiques, and enormously helpful advice.

Which leads to a related topic: the role of friendship in academic research. It is the friendship of colleagues around the world that led so many of them to read, critique, and try to help us improve our work. And it is the friendship among coauthors that makes the long hours of writing, rewriting, tracking down arcane details and citations, and rewriting yet again not just bearable but worthwhile and fulfilling.

We could not have completed this book, nor balanced our professional and personal lives with any hope of success, without our extraordinary spouses, Meredith Bowers and Jennifer Lind. Occasional eye rolls notwithstanding, their support, patience, and encouragement inspired us every step of the way. We also thank, again, those who supported us from the beginning: Nancy and Robert Lieber, James and Grace Press, and Susan and Joel Bowers.

We dedicate this book to our amazing children: Sophie, Isabel, Lucy, and Delilah Lieber, and Eleanor and Ian Press. Scholars of nuclear deterrence often close such dedications by hoping that their kids might someday live in a world without these horribly destructive weapons. We take a different view. We hope that our children, whom we love more than anything, live in a world in which careful scholarship and smart policies minimize the terror inherent in these weapons while maximizing the prospects for an enduring nuclear peace.

The Myth of the Nuclear Revolution

Introduction

The Nuclear Puzzle

The defining characteristics of the nuclear age are terror and peace. Terror, because the existence of nuclear weapons means that any major war could imperil civilization. Peace, because the nuclear era has coincided with an unprecedented period without war among the world's great powers. Small-scale conflicts still occur, yet major conflicts between the most powerful countries vanished with the dawn of the nuclear era in 1945.

The link between nuclear weapons and peace among the great powers is not mere coincidence. First, nuclear weapons have dramatically raised the potential costs of war. As terrible as conflict was in the prenuclear era, the devastation from nuclear war could be far worse. Second, and more important, nuclear weapons appear to make victory in war impossible. Throughout human history the costs of war—though often staggeringly high—were borne disproportionately by the losing side. Leaders plunged their societies into terrible conflicts because if they won, war could pay. But in the shadow of nuclear weapons, both aggressors and victims face the same fate: devastation. By making war both enormously costly and seemingly futile, nuclear weapons have greatly reduced the incentives for major conflicts.

The logic of the nuclear peace is compelling, but it reveals a central anomaly in international politics. If nuclear weapons are such powerful instruments of deterrence, virtually guaranteeing the core security of countries that possess them, then why do so many aspects of international politics in the nuclear era resemble those of the prenuclear age? Specifically, why is there so much geopolitical competition among the major powers? If nuclear-armed countries are fundamentally secure from attack, why don't they act accordingly?

In the prenuclear era, countries used a familiar playbook to defend themselves and jockey for power. They built powerful alliances, engaged in arms races, competed to control strategic territory, and remained vigilant about shifts in the global balance of power. The tragedy of world politics is that these strategies have often exacerbated fear, distrust, and competition in the international system, leading to devastating wars.

Such wars among the major powers have thankfully been absent in the nuclear age, but the playbook used by those countries otherwise remains largely the same. In the Cold War era, the post–Cold War era, and contemporary international affairs, major power rivals have continued to compete for strategic advantage by building and improving their nuclear and conventional military forces, enlarging alliances, expanding into new strategic territory, and all the while eyeing warily any changes in the balance of power.

To be clear, nuclear weapons have had a huge impact on international relations by helping to prevent great power war. These weapons are the most effective instrument of deterrence ever created. But therein lies the key puzzle of the nuclear era. If these weapons are so good at preventing war, why do the major powers continue to play by the old geopolitical rules? Why does security competition remain so intense?

This book explains the central anomaly of the nuclear age: the continuation of great power competition under the shadow of nuclear weapons. Nuclear weapons *are* the most effective instruments of deterrence ever invented, but they have not eliminated the incentives for countries to compete intensely with each other for greater security, power, and strategic advantage. Understanding why power politics endure in the nuclear age does not merely solve a puzzle for international relations theory; it provides vital insights into the requirements of nuclear deterrence, as well as the trends that may undermine deterrence in the coming decades.

The Nuclear Puzzle

International anarchy is the term used by scholars to describe the lack of a world government. Without a legitimate and powerful global authority—to make laws, enforce rules, and provide protection—countries need to protect their own interests and ensure their national security. Scholars and diplomats have long understood that the anarchic nature of international politics breeds distrust among countries and creates powerful incentives for them to compete with each other. The result, as history and contemporary politics show, is that countries try to expand their power relative to rivals, engage in expensive arms races, encircle each other with alliances, and seek to control strategic territory and scarce natural resources.[1]

Nuclear weapons appear to change this entire calculus. Anarchy no longer seems to force countries to compete with each other because countries can guarantee their own security by building nuclear weapons instead. In this sense, nuclear weapons are not merely excellent tools of deterrence; they seem to be revolutionary, greatly mitigating, if not totally eliminating, the logic behind security competition.[2]

Of course, international competition is not fueled solely by the condition of anarchy. A panoply of ideas, emotions, individual leader characteristics, and other domestic forces deserve plenty of blame. But nuclear weapons appear to override those causes, too. As long as leaders are minimally sensitive to costs, they will be deterred from launching a major war against a nuclear-armed rival. Thus, building a nuclear deterrent seems to be the key to security in the nuclear age. The traditional strategies—creating alliances, engaging in arms races, competing to control strategic territory—no longer seem to make sense.

In theory the nuclear age should be one of diminished geopolitical competition—but the reality has been starkly different. On the one hand, nuclear weapons seem to have served as a formidable deterrent to interstate war. The nuclear age corresponds precisely with the "long peace" among the great powers since World War II.[3] While that could be a remarkable coincidence, the more persuasive argument is that peace among nuclear powers can be significantly attributed to the success of nuclear deterrence.[4]

On the other hand, the expectation that nuclear weapons would dampen international competition has failed to materialize in the real world. Nuclear-armed countries continue to obsess about the relative balance of power. They continue to engage in costly arms races. They continue to recruit and rely on allies. And they continue to compete for control of strategic terrain. In sum, countries do not behave as if their possession of nuclear weapons solves their most salient security concerns; instead, they perceive serious threats from abroad and prepare for conflict in ways remarkably similar to the past.

The persistence of intense security competition in international relations constitutes the central puzzle of the nuclear age. Not surprisingly, many others have sought to understand it. Influential works by Robert Jervis and Kenneth Waltz, in particular, identified the basic discrepancy between the logical implications of nuclear deterrence and the real-world behavior of the nuclear powers.[5]

The title of Jervis's 1984 book, *The Illogic of American Nuclear Strategy*, aptly summarized his view that U.S. policies during the Cold War failed to reflect the changed strategic logic of the nuclear age. Jervis argued that U.S. leaders were misguided in engaging in an intense nuclear arms race with the Soviet Union; building robust "counterforce" capabilities (aimed at destroying the other side's weapons, instead of maintaining the ability to retaliate if attacked); and creating excessive conventional military power— beyond what the U.S.-led alliance needed given the security provided by nuclear weapons.[6] Waltz was unwavering in his criticism of the policies of the United States and the Soviet Union, which he argued were nothing but vestiges of the prenuclear world. In Waltz's view, the Cold War superpowers built excessive nuclear arsenals, clung to unnecessary alliances, needlessly feared each other, and irrationally opposed the spread of nuclear weapons to other states (which, according to Waltz's logic, would result in greater peace and stability).[7]

But despite the critiques of Jervis, Waltz, and others, the foreign policies of the major powers during the nuclear age remain strikingly similar to the policies of the past. Although nuclear weapons are supposed to greatly reduce concerns about relative gains, the United States was gripped by fears of rising Soviet power in the 1950s and 1970s, just as Soviet leaders were deeply alarmed by growing U.S. and allied military power in the 1980s.[8] Whereas nuclear weapons were supposed to make arms racing passé, the terms *Cold War* and *arms race* are nearly synonymous. Similarly, the nuclear revolution should have reduced the salience of the U.S. and Soviet alliances, but those organizations were at the core of the superpowers' national security strategies throughout the Cold War. (Moreover, the United States has spent the post–Cold War era expanding its military ties around the world.) To their credit, scholars such as Jervis and Waltz recognized—and drew attention to—the discrepancies between their theories and the realities of geopolitics in the nuclear age.

Such discrepancies endure today. Relative gains concerns remain especially palpable: as the United States eyes a rapidly rising China, those two nuclear powers are engaged in a major conventional military buildup in East Asia, while India and Pakistan are ramping up their nuclear competition in South Asia.[9] Contrary to the logic of the nuclear revolution, strategic territory remains vital. During the Cold War, the superpowers sought allies with territory that could host major conventional forces and be used as a launching point for nuclear operations. Today, geopolitics still revolves around strategically located territory—such as the Strait of Hormuz, the buffer states of Eastern Europe, and the straits through the Indonesian archipelago—especially if it can be used as a springboard for military power projection.[10] In most respects, international politics in the nuclear age looks like business as usual.

What nuclear weapons have helped change about the world—the long peace since 1945—is enormously important, but they have not transformed international politics more broadly. In fact, given their success at protecting nuclear-armed states from attack, it is all the more puzzling that countries armed with these weapons have not adapted their geopolitical strategies accordingly. In an era in which major wars of conquest have essentially disappeared, why do the familiar patterns of international politics endure?

Explaining the Nuclear Puzzle

Proponents of the view that nuclear weapons should have greatly diminished international security competition typically argue that countries and their leaders have been behaving irrationally.[11] Some analysts explain the discrepancy between theory and policy by turning to domestic-level explanations (such as those based on the idea that policymakers are susceptible to misperceptions or that military organizations are prone to pushing aggressive policies), while others offer normative arguments to help policymakers behave more sensibly.[12]

We are now seventy-five years into the nuclear era, and nuclear-armed states are still competing as if they lived in a prenuclear world. Could it really be that leaders are *still* misperceiving the core strategic factors that allegedly define the nuclear age? Do military organizations and other domestic lobbies have so much power that they are not merely nudging foreign policy in directions they prefer but rather driving countries to structure their foreign policies around concepts that are utterly anachronistic? What else might account for the discrepancy between theory and the real-world behavior of states in international relations? We argue that the discrepancy between theory and decades of reality has a simpler explanation: the theory is wrong.

We argue that nuclear weapons are the most effective instruments of deterrence ever created, but the logic linking nuclear stalemate to pacified international politics is flawed. The reason the nuclear age has remained so competitive—and so similar in key respects to previous eras—stems from the difficult challenges states still face in creating strategic stalemate, maintaining stalemate, and practicing deterrence under stalemate. Nuclear weapons do not automatically produce stalemate between adversaries. Nor is stalemate irreversible. Moreover, even when countries find themselves living in conditions of nuclear stalemate, they still may need to deal with enormous security challenges. To be more precise, intense security competition persists in the shadow of nuclear weapons for at least three reasons:

- Creating stalemate among nuclear-armed adversaries is not as simple as many scholars have assumed. Building nuclear weapons is relatively easy, if one can acquire the necessary materials, but building an arsenal that can reliably survive an enemy, disarming attack and be used in retaliation is arduous work—especially if one's potential adversaries are motivated, powerful, and technologically sophisticated.
- Nuclear stalemate does not lie at the end of a one-way street. Even countries that build survivable arsenals need to keep working, since they will be afraid that an enemy might escape stalemate. They may also be tempted to try to escape stalemate themselves, by building their own war-winning options.
- Nuclear stalemate does not automatically solve a country's deterrence requirements. If countries need to use nuclear threats to deter conventional attacks (not just nuclear ones), then merely building a survivable nuclear arsenal may not be sufficient. Those countries will feel compelled to build large, flexible, and resilient nuclear forces to make the threat of escalation credible. In turn, the conventionally stronger side in such cases will face powerful incentives to build forces capable of neutralizing the adversary's nuclear escalatory arsenal.

These three challenges—getting into stalemate, remaining in stalemate, and achieving conventional deterrence under stalemate—go a long way toward explaining the stubborn persistence of arms racing, alliance competition, relative gains concerns, and competition for strategic territory in the nuclear age.

We adopt a multimethod approach to reach our findings. We explore declassified primary sources and historical accounts of decision making, analyze the doctrines and force postures of contemporary nuclear states, and undertake computational modeling to explore the effects of changing technology on nuclear capabilities. We also seek to build on decades of scholarly insights from international relations theorists; key evidence culled by historians; and our practical knowledge of the mechanics of nuclear targeting, employment, and operations. There is a clear cost to wading into a topic that has absorbed so many others before us—mainly, the constant danger of omitting their important contributions and insights. But our goal is to explain something that has remained elusive: why power politics and security competition endure in the nuclear age.

We believe that our book not only explains a major behavioral puzzle in the field of international relations but also yields important lessons about the conditions for stable nuclear deterrence in the twenty-first century. Scholars and policymakers alike should pay heed, since understanding and navigating those conditions will be crucial to the future of international peace and stability.

Outline of the Book

Chapter 1 describes the unique attributes of nuclear weapons that make them the most effective instruments of deterrence ever created, as well as the intensely competitive nature of international politics that has—puzzlingly—endured despite the nuclear stalemate. Stalemate exists when neither adversary in a war can escape destruction and emerge victorious in any practical sense of the term. If nuclear weapons make victory in war impossible, then such wars cannot serve a rational purpose. Specifically, the Clausewitzian definition of war as an extension of politics by other means becomes an absurdity, since no rational goal of statecraft can entail suicidal destruction.[13] From there the notion that nuclear weapons should pacify international politics seems to follow logically. Strategic stalemate should not only deter war but also allows countries to abandon a wide range of costly and risky policies designed to increase their security. Those behaviors are unnecessary, it would seem, because nuclear weapons already make countries that possess them fundamentally secure.

As chapter 1 shows, a significant amelioration of security competition among nuclear powers has not occurred. Relative gains concerns, conventional and nuclear arms racing, and competition for allies and strategic territory remain the foundation of great power politics today. Chapter 1 concludes by proposing that this discrepancy between theory and practice stems from a problem with the theory, rather than the irrational behavior of states. We explain why the optimistic predictions about international politics in the nuclear age depend on several assumptions about the nature of stalemate—all of which turn out to be wrong. Specifically, the hope that the nuclear age will be much more pacific than the past depends on the belief that stalemate is relatively easy to create with nuclear weapons; that a condition of stalemate once created cannot be escaped; and that stalemate is a powerful deterrent not only to nuclear war but also to conventional attack. Chapters 2, 3, and 4 evaluate each of these beliefs about nuclear stalemate, and explain why power politics endures in the nuclear age.

Chapter 2 asks how much nuclear retaliatory capability must countries build to reliably deter nuclear attack? How easy is it to establish nuclear stalemate? In other words, "how much is enough"? The chapter discusses competing views, explains why the outcome of the debate is crucial for understanding the central puzzle of the nuclear age, and turns to the historical record for answers. One view holds that even minimal nuclear arsenals, which pose just the possibility of retaliation, are "enough" to create stalemate, while another contends that stalemate requires far more robust nuclear forces and the virtual certainty of retaliation. However, only the former explanation—that minimal arsenals are sufficient—would allow countries to abandon a wide range of traditional, competitive policies.

Yet the evidence in chapter 2 shows that minimal arsenals have not been enough. At least during the intense rivalry of the Cold War, the threshold of nuclear capability required to generate deterrence was high—certainly, much higher than the capability to create the mere possibility of retaliation. In fact, when the Soviets had merely a small arsenal, the United States planned to wage war, if it came, by rapidly launching a massive disarming strike. The Soviet Union's small arsenal did not make it more secure; rather, it ensured that any war with the United States would immediately go nuclear on a massive scale. The United States felt compelled to find a new war-fighting strategy only later in the Cold War, once the Soviet Union had acquired a large and survivable arsenal. The deployment of a small Soviet nuclear arsenal in the 1950s did not pacify the U.S.-Soviet rivalry; instead, it energized it, as the Soviets raced to build a secure retaliatory force and the United States strove to keep that small arsenal vulnerable.

Chapter 3 analyzes the durability of stalemate. Once countries reach the point where neither can disarm the other, can such a situation be reversed? For geopolitical competition to be greatly mitigated, the path to stalemate must be a one-way street. If the opposite were true—meaning, if an arsenal that is survivable today can become vulnerable tomorrow—then even the achievement of stalemate would not eliminate competitive dynamics. In short, for nuclear weapons to render countries fundamentally secure and allow them to cease competing with potential adversaries, the condition of stalemate must be enduring.

We show in chapter 3 that the survivability of nuclear arsenals has varied over time. During the later decades of the Cold War, it seemed that the superpowers were permanently locked into stalemate: "counterforce" attacks—those aimed at disarming the enemy's nuclear forces—appeared impossible because the superpower arsenals were enormous and dispersed, and some weapons (such as submarines) seemed impossible to find. Yet, as the chapter explains, we now know that the survivability of the Soviet arsenal fluctuated significantly throughout the Cold War, as Soviet leaders learned at various times to their chagrin. The Soviet Union could not stop competing after they deployed a survivable retaliatory force in the 1960s. In fact, at times they struggled to hold on to their survivable deterrent. Today, technological advances made possible by the computer revolution are rendering nuclear forces around the world more vulnerable than before. We use various methods, evidence, and models to demonstrate the emergence of new capabilities for counterforce disarming strikes. This reversibility of stalemate—during the Cold War and today—helps explain why nuclear-armed states have continued to engage in security competition. Stalemate can be broken.

Chapter 4 explores the ability of nuclear weapons to deter conventional war. For nuclear weapons to mitigate traditional security competition, they must not only render nuclear war unwinnable but also serve as a robust deterrent to major conventional attacks. But how can a potential victim of conventional attack make credible threats to escalate to nuclear war if the attacker can retaliate in kind? How can such a seemingly suicidal strategy be made credible? On the one hand, deterring conventional attack might be relatively straightforward if it turns out that attackers are dissuaded by the mere presence of nuclear weapons and thus the fear of nuclear escalation—regardless of the defender's nuclear doctrine, strategy, and force posture. On the other hand, it could be that credible threats of escalation are necessary for nuclear weapons to reliably deter conventional war, and such credibility could hinge on having nuclear options and capabilities that could be employed once war has begun. If this latter view is correct, the process of building and maintaining such capabilities, as well as the potential attacker's efforts to counter such forces, will ensure that international politics remain highly competitive—even in the shadow of nuclear stalemate.

As we argue in chapter 4, countries facing threats of overwhelming conventional attack have almost always opted to develop nuclear forces that are flexible enough to be used in limited ways. We show that nuclear-armed countries that face dire prospects in conventional war are the same ones that tend to develop nuclear postures tailored to coercive nuclear escalation. These postures, therefore, do not appear to be the result of military organizations competing for budgets, of domestic politics, or of ill-informed leaders; instead, they are rational responses to the challenge of credibly threatening to escalate with nuclear weapons to deter or end a conventional war. In short, countries that use nuclear threats to deter conventional wars tend to build flexible, usable nuclear arsenals—and trigger their enemies to build countervailing capabilities. This back-and-forth dynamic, stemming from the challenge of deterrence under the condition of stalemate, is a powerful catalyst of competition in the nuclear age.

The concluding chapter summarizes our key findings and discusses their implications. Proponents of the "theory of the nuclear revolution" contend that nuclear weapons are transformative because they greatly reduce the need for countries to engage in intense security competition, heretofore the bane of international life. But that is too much to expect of nuclear weapons. Although nuclear weapons are the greatest tools of deterrence ever created, they do not automatically confer national security benefits on their owners, much less guarantee enduring safety from foreign threats. The unfortunate reality of international politics in the shadow of nuclear weapons is that countries must still pay close attention to the balance of power, search for ways to change the balance when they find themselves at a disadvantage, and contemplate and plan for war in order to protect vital national interests. The fears that tragically drove international politics for centuries still exist, and those fears are justified. The nuclear age remains an age of power politics.

Power Politics in the Nuclear Age

The history of world politics is filled with accounts of powerful groups using their military might to conquer and dominate their neighbors. The weak lived in fear of the strong. Yet, this pattern appears to have changed abruptly with the invention of nuclear weapons, which appear to make war prohibitively costly and futile. Even otherwise weak defenders, if armed with nuclear weapons, seem able to deter the strongest aggressors—since the benefits of any attack would likely be greatly outweighed by the costs of nuclear retaliation.[1]

This logic of deterrence suggests not only that countries armed with nuclear weapons can no longer fight each other but also that they can abandon all sorts of other competitive behaviors that have long defined world history. If nuclear weapons make conquest impossible, then nuclear-armed countries can feel fundamentally secure. If they are secure from foreign threats, then these countries no longer need to worry about the economic or military growth of rivals, nor do they need to build powerful alliances, engage in arms races, or compete over strategic territory. Those traditional, balance-of-power strategies aimed at ensuring national survival are no longer necessary when survival is supposedly guaranteed by nuclear weapons. In short, the nuclear era should not merely have fewer major wars, it should be a markedly more peaceful world, free of intense international hostility and competition.

Yet, any observer today can see that nuclear-armed countries have not abandoned security competition. Political tensions and preparations for military conflict continue to exist among all of the nuclear powers: the United States, Russia, Great Britain, France, China, Israel, India, Pakistan, and North Korea. The absence of great power war in the nuclear age is certainly consistent with the logic of nuclear deterrence, but the peaceful transformation of international politics—built on the security provided by nuclear weapons—has failed to materialize.

Given that nuclear weapons are uniquely effective instruments of deterrence, why have they *not* transformed international politics? Why do nuclear-armed countries continue to compete for power, allies, strategic territory, and military superiority in an era in which nuclear weapons provide their core security? Why do power politics endure in the nuclear age?

In this chapter, we analyze the two main explanations for why nuclear weapons deter war so effectively: the immense destructiveness of these weapons and their propensity to create stalemate. Differentiating those two explanations is crucial for understanding the main puzzle of the nuclear age: why geopolitical competition remains so intense. Specifically, a careful analysis of the foundations of nuclear deterrence points to the need to investigate the nature of stalemate: how stalemate is created, how it is maintained, and what behaviors are actually checked by nuclear stalemate.

We then examine the historical record of the nuclear age. We show that the patterns of international relations since 1945 largely contradict the idea that nuclear weapons transform geopolitics. Finally, we outline our explanation for why intense security competition endures despite the shadow of nuclear weapons. The answer stems from the inherent challenge countries face in establishing and maintaining deterrence under nuclear stalemate.

The Logics of Nuclear Deterrence

Throughout history—and to this day—the primary effect of new military technologies has been to make soldiers more effective in battle. But nuclear weapons, it is widely believed, have had a fundamentally different impact on international politics. Rather than offer combatants a better way to fight, nuclear weapons have greatly enhanced deterrence. What is it about nuclear weapons that makes deterrence so robust? Why are nuclear weapons the ultimate instruments of deterrence, rather than just the most potent tools of war?

The most obvious explanation for the unique deterring power of nuclear weapons lies in their vast destructiveness.[2] But this explanation is insufficient. Although the immense destructiveness of nuclear weapons undoubtedly gives leaders pause in a way no military innovation ever has, the fundamental difference between nuclear weapons and all other instruments of war is rooted in their propensity to cause stalemate.

The splitting of the atom marked a dramatic increase in the level of destruction that could be inflicted by a single weapon. At the dawn of the nuclear era, a large conventional bomb could destroy a single building, bunker, or bridge. In contrast, even the most basic atomic weapon—like the one used by the United States against the Japanese city of Hiroshima at the end of World War II—could do vastly greater damage. That "Little Boy" fission bomb destroyed 3 square miles of the city. By the mid-1950s, a typical "thermonuclear" weapon could destroy roughly 75 square miles, an area larger than most cities.[3] Not surprisingly, when analysts seek to understand the unique deterring power of nuclear weapons, they are often drawn to the enormous leap in destructiveness.

The destructiveness logic faces a significant limitation, however, in that war was often staggeringly destructive *before* the nuclear age—yet war was endemic. Kenneth Waltz, in distinguishing the nuclear from the prenuclear era, wrote that "countries armed with conventional weapons [know] that even in defeat their suffering will be limited."[4] But that claim is simply wrong. For most of human history, defeat on the battlefield was often total because it was a prelude to mass enslavement, torture, and slaughter.

Massacres have been an integral part of warfare throughout history.[5] For example, accounts of the Peloponnesian War in the fifth century BC are filled with episodes of brutality against defeated populations. Thucydides's description of the Athenian siege of Melos is notable for the matter-of-fact tone used to describe the final outcome: "The Melians surrendered unconditionally to the Athenians, who put to death all the men of military age . . . and sold the women and children as slaves."[6] For the people of Melos (and those of Aegina and Scione, who were also massacred by Athens) there was nothing limited about defeat. Even in cases in which the Athenians showed mercy after military victory, they still typically sold the women and children of defeated cities into slavery.[7]

The brutality of the Peloponnesian War was unexceptional. Genocide was common in the ancient world.[8] Even when total annihilation did not occur, enslavement often did. Alexander the Great's armies either massacred or enslaved the citizens of defeated cities like Persepolis, Tyre, and Thebes. Rome defeated Carthage, slaughtered its men, burned the city to the ground, and enslaved its women and children. Roman legions routinely massacred the inhabitants of the cities they conquered, a practice that declined only when Rome began to allow its soldiers to keep the proceeds from the sale of seized slaves. The Mongols and other great conquerors broke their enemies' will to resist through relentless brutality, annihilating all the inhabitants of any city that resisted in order to terrorize neighboring peoples into acquiescence.

The crucial point is that although defeat in war was often total, wars continued. Over and over again, risk-acceptant leaders marched their soldiers off to war, knowing that if they failed the consequence could be their total destruction.

In more modern times, war remained staggeringly destructive, yet it continued. In terms of economic costs and lives lost, World War I was the most destructive war in European history, until it was superseded only twenty years later. The horrors of World War II are well known. Nazi Germany carried out mass murder and genocide at home and abroad. Imperial Japan brutalized millions of Chinese, Koreans, and other occupied populations. But then the instigators of war paid for their aggression. The United States and United Kingdom firebombed German cities, and the United States burned down sixty-four of the sixty-six largest cities in Japan—before dropping atomic bombs on Hiroshima and Nagasaki. The Soviet Union unleashed mass vengeance against German civilians in the war's final stages, as the Red Army drove to Berlin and sacked the city. In short, the costs of fighting and losing in the prenuclear era were often horrific. Yet the possibility of suffering such terrible losses did not deter the combatants from going to war.

War in the prenuclear age was total in another sense as well: defeated leaders often personally suffered terrible consequences when their armies were defeated. Melian statesmen were killed alongside ordinary citizens. At the conclusion of the civil wars that ended the Ming dynasty, the emperor had his palace guards murder his own senior advisors, and then hanged himself to avoid a worse fate at the hands of his enemies. Russia's tsar Nicholas paid dearly for his defeat in World War I: he was killed, and to eliminate possible successors, his enemies hunted down and murdered his children and extended family, ending the Romanov dynasty. Not surprisingly, murdering a defeated enemy's children was standard practice among hereditary monarchs. And even when there is no threat of succession, leaders' children are often drawn into war. As Soviet armies closed in on Berlin at the end of World War II, senior Nazi leaders murdered their own families and then committed suicide to escape the retribution they knew would follow defeat. More recently, Iraqi leader Saddam Hussein, stripped of power and with his sons already killed, was hanged on the gallows, surrounded by jeering enemies. Libya's ruler, Muammar Qaddafi, was pulled from a culvert, beaten, reportedly sodomized, and then shot to death.[9]

This ghastly account challenges the notion that nuclear weapons are uniquely effective tools of deterrence because they make war so destructive. In contrast to what Waltz claimed, the consequence of defeat was not "limited" in the prenuclear era; wars were barbaric. And yet—despite these horrors—statesmen sent their legions off to fight, time and again. Compared with the old-fashioned punishment—meted out on the battlefield or on the torture rack—what is worse about a bright flash and a quick death? The Japanese victims at Hiroshima and Nagasaki were not worse off than most of those throughout history who endured slavery, torture, execution, and—worst of all—the knowledge that loved ones faced the same fate.[10]

The claim that nuclear weapons mark a sea change in history—from the era of limited violence to one of mass destruction—is incorrect. For leaders, as well as their children, friends, and fellow citizens, military defeat has often meant complete catastrophe. Yet, despite such terrible consequences, human history reads like a never-ending parade of wars. The "destructiveness" of nuclear weapons, therefore, cannot adequately explain the unique deterrent power of these weapons. There must be another logic at work. That mechanism—the logic of stalemate—is the key to explaining deterrence, and it constitutes the foundation for arguments about a nuclear revolution.

Nuclear weapons are uniquely deterring because they appear to make victory in war impossible. They are the ultimate tools of stalemate. In the past, war was hell—but primarily for the defeated. Melos was razed; Athens was not. Leaders in the prenuclear world could rationally launch wars, even when they knew the consequences of losing would be terrible, because they had a chance to win, and thus might avoid the worst of war's consequences. What is unique about the nuclear age is not that war can now be devastating. Rather, it is that both sides—strong and weak, victor and vanquished—can be destroyed if war occurs. As often described, the defining feature of nuclear deterrence is not "overkill" but "mutual kill."[11]

In the prenuclear era, leaders could rationally embark upon war, despite the horrors recounted above, because victory was possible and could yield enormous rewards. Popular accounts of warfare often depict aggression as senseless, partly because the longest and most destructive wars are the ones that receive the most attention. But highlighting those famous, long conflicts distorts history; many wars—especially the quick, one-sided affairs between unequal opponents—have led to enormous gains. The Roman empire ruled the region around the Mediterranean because it won a series of lopsided battles over small, weak neighbors. Spain and then Britain ruled much of the world because they, too, easily defeated weaker peoples who inhabited valuable lands. The territory of the United States—stretching from the Atlantic to Pacific Oceans—resulted from one of the most successful campaigns of conquest in history. The U.S. expansion is often portrayed as an uncoordinated act, driven by pioneers chasing land, minerals, and markets. It does not seem like a *military* campaign, even though there were plenty of battles, because the fight against Native Americans was so one-sided. But that is the point: war could pay handsomely in the nonnuclear era when battles were unfair fights. Most campaigns that went extremely well for conquerors are not even remembered as "wars."

Although many successful wars were waged against vastly weaker parties, even conventional wars between great powers sometimes resulted in low-cost victories. The British defeated the Spanish Armada at the cost of a few ships, granting London naval supremacy for decades. Tokyo prevailed decisively in the Russo-Japanese War, opening the door to its conquests in Korea and China. Even World War II, one of the most destructive wars in history, might have resulted in a low-cost victory for Germany if it had halted its campaign in the summer of 1940, just after occupying Poland, Norway, Denmark, France, and the Low Countries. That would have been one of the most one-sided great power wars in European history, putting Germany in control of the European continent from Poland to the English Channel.[12]

But the creation of nuclear weapons at the end of World War II undermined the logic of conquest. The terrible consequences of war, which in the prenuclear era were principally borne by the defeated, can now be imposed on the victors as well. Specifically, if both adversaries have deliverable nuclear weapons, even stunning battlefield successes would still leave the victor exposed to devastating retaliation. In this sense, major war between two nuclear powers has not become "unthinkable"—that is, too horrible to contemplate—as much as "unwinnable."

What is it about nuclear weapons that create this condition of mutual kill and the impossibility of victory? The stalemating qualities of nuclear weapons stem from three characteristics. First, nuclear weapons are small. A modern nuclear bomb or missile warhead is only a few feet long.[13] Even a warhead on a road mobile missile launcher is only the size of a tractor trailer. Because of their small size, nuclear weapons are difficult to locate and destroy with a disarming strike. Second, nuclear weapons are unique in the amount of explosive power they pack per weapon. As a result, a disarming strike would need to destroy nearly every target to succeed. An attack that left the victim with "only" a dozen functioning weapons would leave him with the capability to inflict terrible damage in response.[14] Third, nuclear weapons are relatively easy to deliver. Because nuclear weapons are small and relatively lightweight, they can be delivered by a wide range of methods, including ballistic missiles, cruise missiles, aircraft, and artillery. Furthermore, ballistic missiles are difficult to shoot down. And with the combination of radar-evading stealth technologies and computer-controlled low-altitude flight, cruise missiles (and possibly aircraft) will likely remain reliable delivery systems into the future. In the prenuclear era, a country that was losing a war usually could not punish the victor because the losing side typically would have lost control of the air, the seas, and key terrain. But because modern ballistic missiles can reach their target regardless of whose air force controls the skies (and in many cases this is true for stealthy cruise missiles and aircraft, too), countries in the midst of losing a conventional war can still strike back and destroy the prospective victor.

These three attributes of nuclear weapons—their small size, destructive power per unit, and ease of delivery—are the foundations of stalemate. The difference between nuclear weapons and virtually all other instruments of warfare is that they allow the weak and defeated to inflict unbearable pain on the strong and victorious. They therefore make real victory appear impossible.

Clearly, the two logics of deterrence work together. The stalemate logic tells us that in a nuclear war, both sides will suffer. The destructiveness logic tells us that they will suffer a lot. But by focusing on what makes nuclear weapons uniquely deterring—their strong propensity to create stalemate—we can now explore the puzzles of the nuclear age. Has the stalemating effect of nuclear weapons pacified international politics? If not, why not?

The Puzzle of the Nuclear Age

Leaders have always feared attack and conquest. Hence, they have always been concerned about shifts in the balance of economic and military power between their own countries and those of potential adversaries. Similarly, leaders have always been concerned that adversaries might forge new alliances to amplify their power; in response, leaders sought to marshal their own alliances and maneuver diplomatically to weaken opposing blocs. In the age of conventional warfare, leaders worried that their enemies might quickly build or develop weapons to dominate the battlefield, so they engaged in arms races to keep their own military forces at the pinnacle of capability. And in times of both peace and war, countries competed to control strategically vital territory, such as land near key waterways and invasion routes. The resulting competition for economic supremacy, allies, military primacy, and strategic territory frequently exacerbated political tensions and helped bring about war.

The logic of nuclear deterrence suggests that these fears should no longer be salient in a world of nuclear-armed states. For the reasons explained above, nuclear weapons appear to make countries fundamentally secure from attack and conquest. As a result, countries can stop worrying about the relative balance of power, engaging in arms races, or competing for alliance partners and strategic territory. They can remain calm even as others rise economically. They can reduce their dependence on allies for security. They need not obsess about even large changes in the balance of military capabilities. And they need not value territory for its security implications. Neither greater wealth, better allies, mightier conventional forces, nor superior control of waterways and invasion routes are important determinants of victory and defeat when countries are armed with nuclear weapons. Figure 1.1 depicts the causal logic and empirical predictions underpinning the view that nuclear stalemate has transformed international politics. In theory, nuclear weapons produce stalemate, which not only prevents war but also mutes, reduces, and mitigates other behaviors that drive international competition and conflict.

But despite the apparent logic of these predictions, the realities of the nuclear age paint a different picture. Although nuclear weapons have proven to be

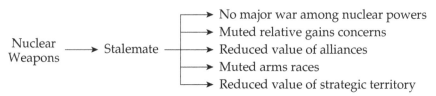

Figure 1.1. The consequences of stalemate?

excellent tools of deterrence—helping to prevent major war—nothing resembling a revolution in international politics has occurred.

NO WAR AMONG NUCLEAR-ARMED COUNTRIES

According to most deterrence experts, nuclear-armed countries are highly unlikely to fight each other.[15] "The probability of major war among states having nuclear weapons approaches zero," according to Waltz.[16] Bernard Brodie argued that nuclear weapons were "a powerful inhibitor to aggression," and that the sole purpose of militaries from that point on would be to avert wars, not fight them.[17] Even limited aggression is thought to be implausible in the shadow of nuclear weapons because the possibility of escalation to nuclear war will deter such provocations.[18] As Waltz writes, "If states can score only small gains, because large ones risk retaliation, they have little incentive to fight."[19] Robert Jervis concurs: "If statesmen are sensible, wars among the great powers should not occur."[20]

The evidence from the nuclear era mostly supports this expectation. No two nuclear-armed states have fought a major war against each other.[21] Most importantly, great power wars—the most destructive types of conflict— disappeared just after nuclear weapons were created. The timing of the disappearance is striking: the world suffered through at least five great power wars (roughly one every twenty years) during the century leading up to the nuclear age, but none in over seven decades since.[22] The abrupt halt to major war is even more telling because the Cold War contained many catalysts for conflict: the superpowers had major ideological differences, held competing universalist visions for the world, demonized each other, and prepared intensely for conflict. Yet peace prevailed—or, to be more precise, major war was prevented. Nuclear deterrence deserves substantial credit for this outcome.[23]

It is worth noting, however, that some evidence raises questions about the reliability of the peace-inducing effects of nuclear weapons. For example, on several occasions nuclear and nonnuclear countries have used limited force against nuclear-weapon states. In 1969, Russian and Chinese ground forces fought over disputed territory, killing hundreds of soldiers. In 1982, Argentina seized the Falkland Islands, a British possession, triggering a significant naval clash in the South Atlantic.[24] During the 1991 Persian Gulf War, Iraq launched forty-two conventionally armed Scud missiles at Israeli cities. In each of those cases, the stakes for the nuclear-armed power were relatively modest, and hence the attacks were unlikely to trigger nuclear escalation. Nevertheless, the cases should not be completely dismissed; even limited attacks on nuclear-armed countries should not occur because they run some risk of catastrophic nuclear escalation. But the attacks did occur.

Two other wars raise bigger puzzles. In 1950, China intervened in the Korean War, launching a major ground offensive that killed thousands of American soldiers in the initial battles. The subsequent fighting over the next two years resulted in more than thirty thousand U.S. fatalities. By inflicting such serious losses on U.S. forces, and lacking a nuclear deterrent of its own, China took a major risk—outside the bounds of caution that the logic of nuclear deterrence suggests.[25] The other notable case occurred in 1973, when Syria and Egypt launched a coordinated surprise attack on nuclear-armed Israel. The Egyptian forces crossed the Suez Canal and advanced into the Sinai Peninsula, while Syrian tanks poured into the Golan Heights on Israel's northern frontier. The Syrian army nearly swept the surprised Israeli defenders from the Heights, and Israel had almost no additional ground forces between the Syrian army and Tel Aviv. The two-pronged attack left Israel exposed to a complete military defeat. The seeming recklessness of the Egyptian-Syrian attack on nuclear-armed Israel belies expectations of caution and restraint when facing nuclear enemies.[26]

To be clear, the idea that nuclear deterrence prevents major wars between nuclear-armed countries is largely supported by the evidence. Given the frequency of great power wars before the nuclear age, this is significant. However, the anomalies raise important questions: Why were China's leaders confident they could inflict tens of thousands of U.S. fatalities without triggering a U.S. nuclear response? And why did Egypt and Syria think it was safe to launch a major, two-pronged surprise attack on Israel without risking escalation? Most importantly, if countries are willing to take such large risks when confronting nuclear-armed enemies, should nuclear-armed countries feel fundamentally safe? If not, why should one expect countries to abandon other competitive behaviors that they have historically adopted to protect themselves?

REDUCED CONCERN ABOUT RELATIVE GAINS

One of the most pernicious consequences of international anarchy is the concern it generates among countries about the relative balance of power. Leaders worry about the growth of military capabilities of other states because that power might someday be turned against them. Even increases in other countries' economic power is a major concern, since wealth is the building block of military might. As a result, shifts in the distribution of power—especially the rise of a new major power—tend to trigger fear, suspicion, and rivalry.

One would expect the invention of nuclear weapons to greatly mitigate relative-gains concerns.[27] If nuclear weapons make war unlikely and conquest nearly impossible, nuclear-armed adversaries no longer need to worry about shifts in the military or economic balance of power, because one side's "gain" cannot undermine the fundamental security of the other. In fact, prominent scholars of deterrence made this point. As Waltz argues, "Nuclear weapons eliminate the thorny problems of estimating the present and future strengths of competing states and of trying to anticipate their strategies."[28] McGeorge Bundy emphasized that what matters most in the nuclear age is not military superiority or the exact state of the nuclear balance, but simply the nuclear danger.[29] According to Jervis, in the nuclear age "there should be only tenuous links between the details of the military balance and political outcomes."[30] And if relative power balances do not matter, then neither should any miscalculations about them.[31] In short, the security afforded by nuclear weapons should significantly diminish the importance of relative power.

In reality, countries have remained keenly concerned about relative gains throughout the nuclear age. During the Cold War, U.S. leaders tracked trends in the Soviet economy and worried greatly when there were signs that Soviet power was growing. In the early 1950s, fears about the growth in Soviet power led the United States to seriously consider preventive war against the Soviet Union.[32] Later in the decade, Soviet achievements in space exploration caused panic in the United States, rooted in the feeling that the United States was "falling behind" in science and technology. By the late 1960s U.S. intelligence and Western economic experts began to realize that the Soviet economy was running out of steam, and that there was little that Soviet leaders could do to prevent such stagnation and decline.[33] Yet, rather than be content with such a shift in the balance of power, the American response was to extend its gains. Leaders in Moscow recognized their inability to keep up with the West.[34] Soviet worries about the balance of relative power eventually played a major role in triggering *perestroika* and *glasnost*, the end of the Cold War, and the collapse of the Soviet Union.[35]

Relative-gains concerns were not limited to the Cold War competition between the superpowers. In the 1980s, the United States grew alarmed about the economic growth of its ally Japan and began to wonder if it might pose a strategic threat to U.S. interests in the Pacific.[36] Nuclear weapons have not prevented India from fearing China's economic rise, or Pakistan from worrying about India's growth. Israel is far ahead of its neighbors in terms of economic and military might, but its strategic planners worry about long-term demographic trends in the Middle East. Russia is concerned about the relative economic growth of potential adversaries to the west (NATO) and east (China); and, of course, the United States is very concerned about the rise of China.

The persistence of relative-gains concerns in the nuclear age is a puzzle. The possession of nuclear weapons is supposed to ensure countries' security in the present and the future. But those states continue to behave as if their core security concerns depend on a favorable balance of power.

REDUCED ARMS RACING

The same logic that links nuclear weapons to reduced concerns about relative gains also suggests that arms races should be muted in the nuclear era. If nuclear weapons make those who possess them secure, then there is little reason for countries to engage in costly competitions for greater military capability. "Nuclear weapons make it possible for states to escape the dynamics of arms racing," according to Waltz.[37] Nuclear-armed states do not need to match each improvement in an adversary's arsenal, or ensure their stockpiles are equal in size. "Numbers are not very important," according to Waltz. "To have second-strike forces, states do not need large numbers of weapons. Small numbers do quite nicely."[38] Jervis is more cautious than Waltz about the requirements for a secure second-strike arsenal, but he shares the same skepticism about the need for countries to arms race once they have built such a retaliatory force. Jervis writes, "When security comes from the absolute capability to annihilate one's enemy, then each side can gain it simultaneously. Neither side need acquire more than a second-strike capability and, if either does, the other need not respond since its security is not threatened."[39] Nuclear weapons should diminish the need for conventional arms races as well. If a nuclear deterrent provides the ultimate protection against defeat in war, then that arsenal should deter, whether the threat comes in the form of nuclear or conventional attack. A world of nuclear-armed countries, in short, should be one with highly muted arms racing.

The history of the nuclear age does not support these predictions. In fact, the nuclear arms race during the Cold War was one of the most intense military competitions in history, as the superpowers spent trillions of dollars expanding their arsenals and improving their weapons in reaction to the moves of their adversary. Many prominent scholars of deterrence were puzzled by this anomaly at the time, and criticized the arms race as unnecessary and illogical. As Charles Glaser argues, "The nuclear arms race should have ground to a halt and the full spectrum of the most threatening nuclear forces should have been limited."[40] But the struggle for nuclear supremacy continued through the last days of the Cold War.[41] Similarly, in *The Illogic of American Nuclear Strategy*, Jervis argued that U.S. leaders' willingness to build excessive amounts of conventional and nuclear power, including robust counterforce capabilities, must have reflected ignorance of the nuclear revolution's implication for arms racing.

No other nuclear dyad has produced the relentless competition of the Cold War, but arms-race dynamics are unfolding in other nuclear standoffs as well. Pakistan and India have been much more restrained than the Cold War antagonists. And, despite its fraught relationship with the United States, China still fields a relatively modest nuclear arsenal—what it calls a "lean and effective" deterrent.[42] Nevertheless, arms racing is brewing in those relationships too. China is modernizing its nuclear arsenal in ways specifically designed to bolster its survivability in the face of growing U.S. offensive capabilities. As U.S. capabilities continue to grow—in nuclear-delivery systems, conventional strike capabilities, and advanced sensors—China will be forced to continue to react. For their part, India and Pakistan are expanding their nuclear arsenals with more warheads, delivery systems, and fissile material production capability. While some analysts are hopeful that the South Asian arms race might level off after the current round of weapons systems are deployed, India is increasingly putting emphasis on its strategic competition with China, which could result in significantly new nuclear capabilities being deployed over the next decade. This, in turn, would likely provoke an even faster nuclear buildup by Pakistan.[43]

The history of conventional arms racing during the nuclear era also contradicts the expectations that nuclear weapons would ensure their owners' security. To be sure, scholars have long debated how to define and measure the intensity of "arms racing," but by any account the Cold War entailed the greatest conventional arms race in history. NATO spent approximately $20 trillion on conventional forces, while the Soviets and their Warsaw Pact allies raced to field a massive military force to oppose NATO. But the Cold War race is hardly unique. China is currently engaged in a major military competition with the United States for superiority in the Western Pacific. The ongoing conventional arms race pits Beijing's anti-access capabilities against U.S. power-projection forces. For its part, China is developing better ways to locate U.S. air and naval forces in East Asia and strike them with long-range weapons. The United States is countering with better ways to blind China's sensors, disrupt its command and control, and destroy its long-range strike platforms.[44] The United States–China relationship does not appear to be the sort of calm, mutually secure one that nuclear weapons are supposed to produce.

In sum, nuclear weapons have not eliminated arms races, and it is not even clear that they have dampened them. For many years the phrases "nuclear weapons" and "arms race" were nearly synonymous. Other nuclear dyads have not reached the same intensity as the Cold War competition, but even those relationships reveal serious concerns among the antagonists about the survivability of their nuclear forces. And competitions in conventional military power continue among nuclear armed states. With respect to arms racing, international politics appears to be business as usual.

REDUCED VALUE OF ALLIANCES

The same logic that posits the end of relative-gains concerns and decline in arms racing predicts the withering of alliances in the nuclear age. Before nuclear weapons, international alliances were crucial, as they allowed states that faced common threats to pool their resources. Although relying on allies entailed other risks (for example, the risks of entrapment or abandonment),[45] confronting threats without allies was often far costlier and dangerous. With nuclear weapons, countries can seemingly ensure their own security without taking on commitments to others or depending on pledges of assistance from abroad. "Since nuclear states easily generate second-strike forces," Waltz explains, "they do not need one another's help at the strategic level. Strategically, nuclear weapons make alliances obsolete."[46] Jervis seems to agree, noting that alliances are less important in the nuclear age: "Defections by allies are therefore less damaging," and nuclear states "should not permit their allies to drag them into excessively dangerous situations."[47]

In reality, alliances appear to be just as relevant in the nuclear era as before. Throughout the Cold War, both the United States and Soviet Union relied heavily on their allies. U.S. and Soviet allies provided a large number of conventional forces, supplying manpower and, in the case of NATO, substantial financial contributions. Washington's key allies in Europe, East Asia, and the Persian Gulf also provided valuable geography, including the forward bases, airfields, and ports that the United States needed to project power around the world. The logic behind those alliances was clear. Conventional war was still possible, so alliances were still necessary for all the reasons they always were—to share costs, pool resources, and provide access to strategically crucial territory.

This pattern continues today. In fact, U.S. alliances have grown since the Cold War, creeping eastward in Europe toward Russia; expanding throughout the Persian Gulf region; and spreading into new locations in East Asia. The United States is not alone in seeing strategic advantage in alliances; indeed, Russia clearly sees the expansion of NATO eastward as a threat to its security.[48] China has warned neighboring states like Vietnam about the perils of aligning with the United States, and appears to be trying to weaken or end the United States–Japan military alliance. In fact, Russia and China have taken steps to increase their cooperation in response to perceived U.S. and Western encroachment on their spheres of interest, evidence that alignment (and perhaps in the future, alliance) is still valuable in the nuclear era.[49] The United States uses its close military ties throughout the Persian Gulf to station military forces, military headquarters, and intelligence assets throughout the region. There is no indication that alliances are becoming less relevant in the nuclear era.

Had nuclear weapons actually ended the practice of countries aligning with strategic partners, the change would be "revolutionary" given just how big a role alliances have played in international relations throughout history. But that change has not occurred. The practice of seeking security and power through alliances is still going strong in the nuclear era.

REDUCED COMPETITION FOR STRATEGIC TERRITORY

Nuclear weapons should reduce the fierce competition over strategic territory that was so common in the prenuclear era. Groups have always competed for territory, to control it for their own advantage and deny it to their adversaries. Some lands were valued for what lay within: fertile soil or valuable minerals. Other territory was deemed "strategic" because it sat astride key transport routes, or because of its proximity to enemies or suitability for hosting military forces. Seizing those lands—to create buffer room or military bases—and denying them to one's adversaries has been a core strategy in international politics.

By creating stalemate, nuclear weapons seem to greatly reduce the value of strategic territory, because the gain or loss of such territory (or resources tied to geography) has little effect on the balance of power. In an era in which nuclear weapons make countries fundamentally secure, countries no longer need to control the natural resources that permit them to sustain large military forces.[50] Whatever natural resources are necessary for economic purposes can be acquired on the global market, and need not be fought over on the battlefield. Controlling key transport routes should also be less important than in the past. Blockades once made sense, but starving a nuclear-armed state to induce its capitulation would be almost as foolhardy as invading it. Strategic buffer zones and territory that can host military forces near key enemies are also significantly devalued in a nuclear world, because one simply does not need to project conventional force against distant rivals or fear they will do the same.[51] "Nuclear weapons can easily be hurled across great distances," Van Evera writes. "This makes geographic assets less significant. Wide buffer room cannot impede nuclear delivery, and the possession of distant bases does little to make it easier."[52] Competition over territory beyond the homeland or the homeland of close allies is especially nonsensical. Since self-defense is much easier and conquest much harder in a nuclear world, nuclear-armed adversaries should "take a more relaxed attitude toward events in third areas, including the third world. . . . Whatever had been the strategic importance of the third world in a nonnuclear world, nuclear weapons have vastly reduced it."[53] In sum, according to this logic, nuclear states appear to have neither the offensive motivation to seize key bases, territory, or economic resources, nor the defensive motivation to stop others from doing so.[54]

The nuclear era does not resemble this predicted world. Much of the actual tension and conflict in the Cold War was about competition for control of territory. Western Europe was valued by the United States partly because of its economic potential, but also because of its location as a bulwark against Soviet expansion and its ability to host U.S. power-projection forces. Italy was crucial for projecting air and naval power into the Mediterranean. Turkey controlled the Dardanelles and bottled up the Soviet fleet in the Black Sea. Great Britain was a crucial ally because of its location as an offshore base from which the United States could fly bombers and build up forces in the event of a major war in Europe. Greenland and Iceland were also crucial for bottling up the Soviet navy in the Baltic Sea and keeping the North Atlantic sea lanes safe. Similarly, the Soviet Union valued its Eastern European allies partly as physical buffers between itself and the West.

Throughout the Cold War, the superpowers struggled for strategic terrain around the world. Both countries battled for influence in Egypt (Suez Canal) and Ethiopia (which sits astride the sea route to Suez and down East Africa). The United States built close ties with the Republic of South Africa and Liberia because those key locations for protecting shipping routes around Africa could have been essential for getting Middle East oil to the NATO allies if war closed the Suez Canal. The United States sought ties in the Persian Gulf region, first with Iran, and when that fizzled, by strengthening ties with Iran's enemies on the other side of the Gulf. The Soviets were playing the same game in Latin America, Southeast Asia, and the Middle East.[55]

The competition for strategic territory—and the resources it contains—continues to this day. It is not a coincidence that the Persian Gulf region has been the focal point of U.S. national security policy since the end of the Cold War. To be sure, terrorism drew the United States deeper into the Gulf region, as did proliferation concerns. But the U.S. focus on the Persian Gulf—in the wake of Iraq's seizure of Kuwaiti oil, or in response to Iran's threats to the Strait of Hormuz—was well established prior to both 9/11 and the focus on Iran's nuclear efforts. U.S. military plans in East Asia revolve around critical terrain. The U.S.-Japanese naval position in the Western Pacific is anchored by control over key islands (for example, in the Ryukyu Islands chain), which can be used to monitor Chinese naval movements in peace and war. The United States maintains naval dominance in the straits that control oil routes from the Middle East to East Asia (e.g., Malacca, Lombok, Makassar), much to China's consternation. Increasingly, the United States seeks to draw new allies into its orbit (Vietnam) and reinvigorate old military relationships (Philippines) to provide additional sites to locate U.S. military forces and sensors. China strongly objects, and has intimated that its neighbors would be unwise to ally with far-away powers. Russia, despite having a formidable nuclear arsenal, has behaved as if it cares deeply about strategic terrain: it vociferously opposed NATO expansion up to its border, and it launched two wars—against Georgia in 2008, in the strategically important Transcaucasia region, and against Ukraine in 2014, which resulted in the seizure and annexation of Crimea. Russia, the United States, and China are ramping up their competition for strategically valuable resources and transit routes in the Arctic. Nuclear weapons have not ended the competition for strategic terrain.

A WORLD TRANSFORMED? TALLYING THE EVIDENCE

Just as deterrence theory predicts, nuclear weapons seem to be excellent tools for preventing war. Based on the evidence since 1945, these weapons appear to strongly inhibit one of the most destructive human activities: war among the world's great powers. However, even on this score—the prevention of war—there are some reasons to be concerned. The instances of countries attacking nuclear-armed states over limited objectives suggest there is danger of escalation from conventional to nuclear conflict. The compelling logic of stalemate—that neither side can win—does not help states identify precisely how much they can harm a nuclear-armed adversary before triggering a nuclear attack, or which side will step back first from the brink during a limited, conventional conflict. To be clear, the case for the unique deterrent power of nuclear weapons is strong, but not as absolute as its advocates sometimes claim.

But the success of nuclear deterrence makes it all the more surprising that the nuclear age has been characterized by so much geopolitical competition. Relative-gains concerns, conventional and nuclear arms races, competition for allies, and rivalry for strategic terrain were defining features of the Cold War, and they continue to characterize international relations today. The basic contours of international politics in the nuclear era would be entirely familiar to nineteenth-century diplomats.

Leading scholars of nuclear deterrence recognized the empirical anomalies we highlight here. Waltz, Jervis, Brodie, Glaser, Van Evera, and other experts in nuclear deterrence were puzzled that the nuclear-armed superpowers appeared to be employing geopolitical strategies from the prenuclear age throughout the Cold War; those analysts criticized what they saw as excessively hawkish or competitive policies by the United States. But the behaviors they felt were unnecessary in the nuclear age defined the Cold War struggle and continue to define international politics today.

Herein lies the core puzzle: Why haven't nuclear weapons done more to mitigate international competition? Why haven't they done more to pacify relations among the major powers? Is it that despite over seventy years of experience, leaders still fail to comprehend the logic of the nuclear era? Or is there something wrong with our understanding of nuclear deterrence itself? We argue that the answers to these broader questions lies in the nature of nuclear stalemate. We explore the concept of stalemate, and its implication for geopolitics, in the sections below—and then in greater depth in subsequent chapters.

Solving the Puzzle: The Nature of Stalemate

At first glance, it seems straightforward to assume that a weapon that tends to create stalemate—the condition in which countries are unable to defeat each other—would greatly mitigate international competition.[56] But on closer examination, the ameliorating effect of nuclear weapons on international security competition depends on three assumptions about the nature of nuclear stalemate: (1) stalemate is easy to produce; (2) stalemate is nearly irreversible; and (3) stalemate effectively deters not just nuclear conflict but conventional war as well. If each is true, then acquiring nuclear weapons should solve a country's most fundamental security concerns and greatly reduce the incentives to compete. If any of those claims are wrong, the door to competition cracks open. And if all three of those claims about the nature of stalemate are wrong, then international politics in the nuclear era should resemble the world before these weapons were invented. We explain in the sections below why each of those assumptions is crucial to one's predictions about international politics in the nuclear age.

How much retaliatory capability must countries build to reliably deter nuclear attacks? Is it easy to establish nuclear stalemate? Will virtually any nuclear arsenal suffice? Or is the goal of creating a robust deterrent—one that will reliably deter nuclear attack in peacetime, during crises, and in the midst of conventional war—more demanding than simply building and deploying a few weapons? If so, how much more demanding?

According to one widely held view, stalemate is born as soon as countries acquire their first nuclear weapons. Small arsenals deter nearly as effectively as large ones because launching a nuclear strike against a country with *any* nuclear weapons would be foolhardy. In fact, according to this view, even vulnerable nuclear forces will create "enough" deterrence, because even the small probability of nuclear retaliation will dissuade any rational aggressor. Prominent deterrence theorists who extol the deterring power of "first-strike uncertainty" subscribe to this argument.[57] According to a competing view, a robust deterrent requires much greater capability—enough to confront potential attackers with near-certain retaliation. The logic here is that nuclear deterrence must never fail, even in the most trying circumstances. It must deter in dark times—during crises and war, when fear, fatigue, and desperation tend to cloud leaders' judgments—and in the face of extraordinarily ruthless enemies. After all, only risk-acceptant leaders start major wars, so nuclear arsenals must be postured to deter *them*.[58]

The implications of this debate for international competition are significant. If even small, possibly survivable arsenals are enough to deter, then nuclear weapons should dampen a wide range of competitive behaviors. In a world governed by the logic of minimum deterrence, after all, once a country acquires a few nuclear weapons it can relax. If even highly aggressive enemies will recoil from the mere possibility that an attack would trigger retaliation, then any nuclear-armed state will be fundamentally secure. No matter how much enemies improve their offensive capabilities, the possibility of retaliation will endure. In such a world, there is no need for arms racing, because the race is over once a country and its adversary possess small nuclear arsenals; it ends in a tie. There should be little concern about relative gains, because even if a country amasses greater economic capabilities, such capabilities cannot be turned into meaningful military advantage.

If, on the other hand, nuclear deterrence requires assured retaliation, then the nuclear age should see more enduring competition. The process of building a secure retaliatory force will often be drawn-out and fraught, as new nuclear states progress through the many steps that distinguish an initial nuclear capability from a truly survivable force and as their adversaries eye such steps warily. Creating a survivable deterrent force may also unleash arms-race dynamics as new nuclear powers build retaliatory capabilities (probably based on worst-case estimates of an enemy's disarming capabilities), while their adversaries enhance counterforce options (to delay or prevent the onset of stalemate). And a world in which deterrence requires that arsenals be truly secure is one in which preventive wars are a recurring danger, each time a new nuclear-armed state begins to climb the ladder to survivability.[59]

To be clear, even if robust deterrence requires assured-retaliation capabilities, nuclear-armed states can create a condition of stable nuclear stalemate. But if stalemate requires robust, survivable forces, nuclear-armed states should be expected to engage in arms races, pay attention to relative gains, and maintain interest in allies (to share costs or provide cover during their period of nuclear vulnerability).[60]

ESCAPING STALEMATE: CAN IT BE DONE?

A second critical question relates to the persistence of stalemate: Can countries escape from the condition of mutual assured destruction (MAD) once it has been established? One view is that the balance of power among nuclear-armed states moves in only one direction—toward stalemate. Once countries have deployed enough capability to reliably deter their adversaries, there are no reasonable steps that those adversaries can take to break out of stalemate.[61] But there is another possibility; survivability may be a two-way street. Perhaps investments in counterforce capabilities can pay off, and efforts to locate and destroy enemy nuclear forces can succeed. If so, arsenals that are safe from attack today may become vulnerable in the future.

This issue—whether stalemate is reversible—was the focus of intense debate during the Cold War, but never adequately settled. The conventional wisdom by the 1980s and 1990s was that there was no way to escape from the condition of MAD. Neither superpower was thought capable of launching a successful disarming strike. A minority of Cold War analysts disagreed, seeing promise in a range of emerging counterforce capabilities. They favored investing in advanced sensors that could locate Soviet nuclear targets during a war; accurate missiles and stealthy bombers to strike those targets; and missile defenses to protect the United States and its allies from any remnants of the Soviet arsenal. Yet, rigorous analyses of whether nuclear-armed adversaries could escape stalemate were rare, partly because of the polarized nature of Cold War foreign policy debates; partly because the superpower arsenals were so enormous that escaping stalemate was an extremely high bar; and partly because deterrence analysts did not know about many of the highly classified surveillance programs the United States was using to search for concealed Soviet nuclear forces.

The permanence or variability of stalemate is still a crucial question because the answer goes a long way toward understanding the effect of nuclear weapons on international politics. If stalemate is irreversible, then deploying a survivable nuclear arsenal should substantially mitigate a country's need to compete for security. After all, according to this view, such a country's arsenal will provide security today and into the future. Whether an adversary is gaining economic strength, gathering allies, or improving its weapons is therefore inconsequential. The fundamental security provided by nuclear weapons is enduring. Thus, countries that possess them can be calm in the face of growing adversary power, or eroding alliances, or the loss of strategically important territory.

If, on the other hand, the nuclear balance can meaningfully shift, then competition in the nuclear age will resemble prenuclear geopolitics. In such a world, there will be strong incentives for countries to arms race—to prevent adversaries from escaping stalemate and to pursue superiority for themselves. If stalemate is a two-way street, relative gains will still matter, because the rich and powerful will be most able to neutralize their adversaries' nuclear weapons. Alliances will still matter, as a means for pooling resources and projecting conventional and nuclear military power. And strategic territory will still matter, as a means to economic wealth and military dominance. If the nuclear balance of power between two states can shift in either direction—that is, toward stalemate or away from it—then most of the power-seeking behavior that has dominated international politics throughout history (such as containing rising powers, pooling resources with allies, impeding adversary alliances, and competing for strategic terrain) will continue to make sense.

DETERRENCE UNDER STALEMATE: HOW TO PREVENT CONVENTIONAL ATTACKS

For nuclear weapons to make countries feel safe enough to abandon the old geopolitical strategies, they must not merely deter nuclear war but also prevent major conventional attacks. But using nuclear threats to deter conventional war poses a conundrum: How can a victim of conventional attack credibly threaten to employ nuclear weapons if the attacker can respond in kind? That is, if escalating a conventional war will merely trigger a nuclear response, then rational nuclear-armed states would never do so.[62] Hence the question: once countries are locked in nuclear stalemate, how can they issue credible nuclear threats to deter conventional attacks? What nuclear capabilities would help them do so?

The subject of nuclear requirements for conventional deterrence was intensely debated during the Cold War, since the problem of "extended deterrence" was the central one facing the United States and its European allies. Once the Soviet Union developed a secure retaliatory arsenal, American leaders had to figure out how to use nuclear threats to deter a major Warsaw Pact invasion of NATO—a major challenge given that an all-out nuclear war would have destroyed the United States and its allies. If nuclear weapons made all-out nuclear war unthinkable, how could Europe be protected?

Some deterrence experts argued that this apparent conundrum was actually not difficult to solve. Whether or not the victim of a conventional attack would intentionally employ nuclear weapons to thwart an invasion is irrelevant for deterrence; the fact that escalation *might* occur—for example, through accident, misperception, or irrationality—is enough to deter.[63] Other experts disagreed, arguing that only credible threats reliably deter. In their view, countries that seek to use nuclear threats to deter conventional attacks must develop nuclear forces that provide options that would actually be usable in the event of a conflict. This view calls for creating sophisticated nuclear capabilities that provide flexibility for limited employment. Most important, an arsenal optimized for deterring conventional attacks must be highly survivable—not survivable only in peacetime, but still survivable after extended periods of conventional conflict have degraded nuclear forces, communications, and command and control.

The debate over the requirements of conventional deterrence is fundamental to understanding international politics in the nuclear age. If deterring conventional attacks with nuclear threats is fairly simple—that is, if virtually any nuclear arsenal will create enough fear to deter—then the nuclear age should be characterized by reduced arms racing, diminished alliances, and muted relative-gains concerns. After all, even small, simple arsenals would shield countries from conventional attack. But if deterring conventional war using nuclear threats requires usable nuclear options, then many of the competitive behaviors of the prenuclear age will remain rampant in the nuclear era as well. Nuclear-armed states that face major conventional threats (to themselves or key allies) will try to build large, diverse, and resilient nuclear forces—and their enemies will strive to develop counterforce capabilities to neutralize their opponent's wartime escalation strategy. The collective result will be the familiar dynamics of international politics: arms racing, relative-gains concerns, and the competition for allies and other sources of power and security.

The central puzzle of the nuclear age—the intensity of competition in an era in which victory seemed impossible—can be explained with a better understanding of the nature of nuclear stalemate. If it is easy for countries to create nuclear stalemate, if stalemate is essentially irreversible, and if it is simple for countries to deter major conventional attacks under nuclear stalemate, then one should expect nuclear weapons to truly revolutionize international politics. In such a world, there would be little point to security competition among nuclear-armed countries. On the other hand, if stalemate can be delayed or prevented altogether, if stalemate can be reversed, or if conventional deterrence among even nuclear-armed countries is difficult, then the empirical puzzle of the nuclear age is solved. In that case, adversaries should still be worried about relative gains because the balance of power matters; they should still value allies in order to pool resources; and they may need to arms race to achieve military superiority or prevent rivals from attaining it.

The next three chapters explain why power politics has endured in the nuclear age. Chapter 2 shows that the deployment of nuclear weapons does not automatically produce stalemate—in fact, it can trigger an intensely competitive process in which one state seeks to create stalemate and the other works hard to prevent it. Chapter 3 demonstrates that nuclear stalemate is reversible—that countries have worked hard to undermine the survivability of their adversaries' nuclear forces, have made great progress in doing so, and that technology is now making those efforts easier. Chapter 4 explains why even some countries in nuclear stalemate continue to face enormous deterrence challenges, and why the task of deterring conventional war unleashes its own competitive processes. In short, the rest of the book explains why security competition in international politics persists in the shadow of nuclear weapons.

Getting to Stalemate

How Much Is Enough?

Nuclear weapons are uniquely effective tools of deterrence because they tend to produce stalemate, the condition in which military victory is impossible. If nuclear-armed countries cannot be conquered, and are largely immune to any major military attacks, then they have little reason to worry about their security. The strategies that have defined international politics for centuries—for example, engaging in arms races, building alliances, and securing strategic territory—no longer seem relevant for countries locked in nuclear stalemate.

But behind this straightforward logic are important theoretical and empirical questions. For example, how much nuclear capability must countries build to create stalemate? Are even small and potentially vulnerable arsenals enough to reliably deter? That is, will the mere possibility of nuclear retaliation, with even a few nuclear weapons, be enough to paralyze potential attackers? Or are large and truly survivable forces required to deter enemies, including highly aggressive ones? In short, when it comes to building a nuclear arsenal for deterrence, how much is enough? The answers to these questions have important implications for international politics in the nuclear age.

If even small, potentially vulnerable arsenals are enough to create stalemate, then nuclear weapons should dampen a wide range of competitive behavior, just as many analysts expect. After all, in a world governed by the logic of "existential" or "minimum" deterrence, once a country acquires a few nuclear weapons it can relax—because even aggressive enemies will be deterred by the mere possibility of nuclear retaliation. In such a world there is no need for arms racing; once a country has a small nuclear arsenal, the race is over. There should also be little concern about relative gains (that is, shifts in the economic balance of power), because in a world of nuclear stalemate advantages in wealth cannot be easily translated into useful military advantage. The value of allies will be diminished, too, since pooling resources is unnecessary when countries have no need to fear attack.

On the other hand, if creating stalemate requires that nuclear-armed countries build truly survivable arsenals—that is, capable of confronting adversaries with "assured retaliation"—then the nuclear age will remain highly competitive. In this case, the process of establishing stalemate will be drawn-out and dangerous. New nuclear states will race to construct truly survivable arsenals; their adversaries will be tempted to enhance counterforce capabilities to delay the onset of stalemate, and those adversaries may be tempted to launch preventive disarming attacks. New nuclear states will seek alliances to share costs or provide protection during their period of nuclear vulnerability.[1] In most cases, nuclear armed countries will be able to build truly survivable arsenals if they invest time and resources, but the path to stalemate will be marked by arms racing, relative-gains concerns, and alliance competition.

Many studies conducted during the Cold War sought to answer the question, how much is enough? This chapter differs in two important ways. First, whereas most previous studies explored the effect of U.S. nuclear capabilities on Soviet behavior, we flip the analysis and track the impact of Soviet capabilities on U.S. behavior.[2] Our approach is advantageous because it was the Soviet Union that was playing catch-up for the first fifteen years of the nuclear age, fielding an existential deterrent in the early 1950s, a minimum deterrent in the late 1950s, and an assured retaliatory capability starting in the early 1960s. In order to determine how much is enough, one needs to track how the growth of the Soviet arsenal through those different phases affected U.S. behavior. That is the task we undertake here.

This chapter diverges from other studies in another way. Whereas many nuclear analyses look at the deterrent effects of nuclear weapons in peacetime, we are interested in how they deter aggressive actions in both peacetime and war. In peacetime, countries wish to deter adversaries from initiating conflict or pursuing aggressive foreign policies. In wartime, countries hope to constrain adversary military operations, by compelling the enemy to seek limited objectives and restricting the scope of adversary military strikes, for example. A nuclear arsenal that reduced the likelihood of conflict but also invited a devastating disarming strike if war occurred might not be enough to allow a nuclear power to feel secure, and thus might invite arms racing and other competitive behaviors. Therefore, the key question in this chapter is, how much nuclear capability is enough to satisfy both peacetime and wartime deterrent needs? Do small, simple arsenals meet those objectives? Or is a larger, more sophisticated arsenal required?

Our analysis leads to two principal findings. First, even a small and vulnerable Soviet nuclear arsenal likely bolstered peacetime deterrence during the first decade of the Cold War. Even when the Soviet nuclear force was highly vulnerable to a U.S. disarming strike during the 1950s, the United

States demonstrated notable restraint toward its rival. U.S. and Soviet leaders continued to frame their competition in Manichean terms—as a clash between pure good and evil—but the United States took pains to conduct its anti-Soviet policies in a manner designed to avoid war. This foreign policy approach had many causes, but the Soviet possession of nuclear weapons likely reinforced that cautious orientation.[3]

The second finding is crucial: the Soviet Union's initial deployment of a nuclear arsenal did not make it safe and secure. In fact, by fielding a vulnerable nuclear force, the Soviets energized U.S. efforts to build weapons and war plans to rapidly destroy the Soviet arsenal if war erupted. The small, vulnerable Soviet nuclear force was a double-edged sword: it benefited the Soviets in peacetime by making U.S. aggression less likely, but it vastly increased the damage the Soviets would suffer in the event of war. The United States remained committed to winning World War III through a massive nuclear disarming strike as soon as war erupted, at least until the Soviets developed a true assured retaliation force.

The findings in this chapter help explain the general puzzle of why international competition remains so intense in the nuclear age. A small, vulnerable nuclear force did not give the Soviet Union adequate protection, which explains why the Soviets continued to build up their nuclear capabilities. The United States valued its ability to win a nuclear war if conflict with the Soviets erupted, and therefore worked hard to retain its disarming capabilities as long as possible. The result was an intense arms race, concerns over relative gains, and competition for key allies and the use of their territory for staging bases for nuclear strikes. The first decades of the nuclear age saw intense competition because small nuclear forces were not enough to create real stalemate.

How Much Is Enough? Four Views

How much nuclear capability do states need to deter aggressive behavior during peacetime and limit enemy military operations during war? If even small and potentially vulnerable arsenals are enough to reliably deter, then the nuclear age should be characterized by greatly reduced security competition. In such a world, the presence of even a few nuclear weapons will thwart ambitions and assuage fears—two primary causes of conflict in anarchy. Countries could build modest nuclear forces and then relax. But if small and vulnerable arsenals do not make countries truly secure—because risk acceptant enemies will initiate conflicts or attempt disarming strikes during wars—then competition should remain intense in the nuclear age. If large and truly secure arsenals are required for robust deterrence, the development of nuclear weapons will trigger extended arms races and perhaps preventive wars.

Scholars have developed four major schools of thought about the requirements of deterrence. One view, that of *existential deterrence*, contends that fear of nuclear war is so great that the mere possibility of nuclear retaliation is enough to deter any act that could trigger escalation. The implication of this view is that a nuclear arsenal need not be large, survivable, or even easily deliverable to terrify and thus deter; its mere existence is enough. The *minimum deterrence* school argues that states must do more than join the nuclear club to establish robust deterrence, but not much more. Deterrence will be robust whenever retaliation in the wake of an attack is plausible, instead of merely possible. To create the plausibility of retaliation, a country needs to be capable of delivering nuclear weapons against an adversary. A small deliverable nuclear arsenal—even if it is not certain to survive a disarming strike—will still deter attack because the chance of retaliation will be sufficiently terrifying.

The *assured retaliation* school is rooted in a more pessimistic view about potential aggressors, and judges a deterrent capability against a higher bar than either of the preceding schools. This school views deterrence as robust only when the defender's ability to retaliate after suffering a disarming strike is nearly certain. The threat of retaliation need not be society ending, however; the prospect of absorbing "just a few" nuclear strikes will deter any aggressor. The fourth school, *assured destruction*, contends that truly robust deterrence requires that retaliation be both assured and massive.[4]

These four views lie along a continuum, without concrete boundaries between them. But each school is based upon a distinct understanding of the requirements of deterrence, and each posits a different level of nuclear capability required for a robust deterrent. We next examine each school's basic claims in greater detail, the causal logic behind those claims, and the kind of retaliatory posture indicative of each approach. Then the remainder of the chapter evaluates these views against the historical record from the Cold War.

EXISTENTIAL DETERRENCE

The first school of thought contends that the mere existence of nuclear weapons is enough to reliably deter attack. "Everything about the atomic bomb," Bernard Brodie wrote at the dawn of the nuclear age, "is overshadowed by the twin facts that it exists and its destructive power is fantastically great."[5] According to the existential deterrence view, details such as the relative size of a country's nuclear arsenal compared to that of its adversary or the vulnerability of a country's arsenal to attack are essentially irrelevant for generating deterrence. What matters instead is fear—the brooding shadow of destruction cast by the mere presence of these weapons. In this sense, deterrence is "a simple philosophical consequence of the existence of thermonuclear bombs."[6] Nuclear weapons "have only to exist and deterrence is the law of their existence."[7]

McGeorge Bundy, perhaps the most famous public figure associated with this school of thought, wrote: "The terrible and unavoidable uncertainties in any recourse to nuclear war create what could be called 'existential' deterrence, where the function of the adjective is to distinguish this phenomenon from anything based on strategic theories or declared policies."[8] Elsewhere, Bundy argued that even one chance in a hundred that a country will use nuclear weapons to retaliate is enough to deter an aggressor.[9] Bundy noted, "We must remember that at the upper levels of force the two greatest powers have been extraordinarily cautious with each other. This is not the result of estimates of each other's first- or second-strike counter-force capability, or a consequence of the possession or absence of escalation dominance. . . . They do not dare get close to war with each other because of their fear of what would happen if it turned nuclear, as it always might."[10]

The logic of the existential deterrence view rests on the potent combination of uncertainty, fear, and the sheer destructive power of nuclear weapons. As James Lebovic writes, "The existential deterrent acquires its power from the non-rational world of fear, psychological bias, and uncertainty and not from the rational world of deduction and mathematical precision."[11] Similarly, according to Hedley Bull, "A potential attacker is deterred when his leaders are in a certain state of mind. Their state of mind, even when advised that the opposing retaliatory forces can be eliminated with near certainty, is still likely to include feelings of uncertainty about weapons that have not been tried in battle. . . . The essential conditions of mutual deterrence are subjective or psychological, and these conditions may in principle be satisfied even in the absence of totally invulnerable retaliatory forces."[12]

An existential deterrent does not require much actual nuclear capability. Even a rudimentary arsenal will dissuade potential attackers, since a disarming strike must be virtually assured of success before a rational leader would undertake such a momentous gamble. Relative nuclear force levels matter little when it comes to creating a sliver of doubt about success—and generating fear. Sophisticated retaliatory delivery systems, robust command-and-control systems, and serious training for nuclear retaliatory operations are irrelevant. Simply joining the nuclear club should be sufficient, although analysts can differ on whether this entails just testing a nuclear device or actually building a few weapons. Some even argue that states with the technological know-how to readily build nuclear weapons (such as Japan today) could be considered to have an existential deterrent.[13]

In sum, existential deterrence holds that nuclear deterrence is easy to achieve. As soon as a country develops nuclear weapons, other states will be very unlikely to initiate major attacks, even if the new nuclear power has no clear ability to deliver its warheads. And if conventional war does occur between nuclear-armed states, even a rudimentary nuclear force will ensure that the adversaries will conduct military operations with great caution. As

Michael Howard aptly summarizes the existential deterrence view, "It is the prospect of nuclear war *as such*, not any calculation of the balance of probable losses or gains, that now deters statesmen from taking risks."[14]

The implications of existential deterrence theory for international politics are straightforward. If the existential deterrence view is correct, then the development of nuclear weapons should have eliminated most of the factors that have driven states throughout history to compete for security and power. For advocates of existential deterrence, the development of nuclear weapons and the creation of a robust deterrent are synonymous.

MINIMUM DETERRENCE

A second school of thought posits that deterrence will be robust whenever nuclear retaliation is *plausible*. Retaliation does not need to be assured in order to ward off a disarming attack. Instead, the mere chance of triggering a catastrophic retaliatory response will deter any rational potential aggressor. As Kenneth Waltz argued, "An adversary need only believe that some warheads *may* survive its attack and be visited on it. That belief is not hard to create."[15] For advocates of minimum deterrence, a sufficient nuclear retaliatory force is simple to build, cheap to maintain, easy to hide, and mostly unaffected by adversary nuclear force levels, deployment policies, and strategies.

The minimum deterrence view is built upon a simple and powerful logic. A rational person does not need to be *certain* that an attempted disarming strike will trigger apocalyptic retaliation to conclude that such a strike is a terrible idea—the mere chance of triggering a catastrophe will deter anyone rational.[16] Waltz explains, "Contemplating war when the use of nuclear weapons is possible focuses one's attention not on the probability of victory but on the possibility of annihilation. Because catastrophic outcomes of nuclear exchanges are easy to imagine, leaders of states will shrink in horror from initiating them. . . . Anyone—political leader or man in the street—can see that catastrophe lurks if events spiral out of control and nuclear warheads begin to fly."[17] The prospect of nuclear retaliation is sufficient to deter any rational attacker, but that prospect, according to the minimum deterrence view, must be realistic, not just hypothetical. William Kaufmann differentiates minimum from existential deterrence when he writes, "The enemy must be persuaded not only that the instrument exists but also that its power is operational."[18] As long as a country's deterrent force makes nuclear retaliation plausible, its adversaries will be extremely reluctant to initiate war—and highly restrained in their military operations if war occurs.

Avery Goldstein explains the logic of minimum deterrence in clear, rationalist terms. "The standard of first-strike uncertainty," he writes, "assumes that a potential attacker facing a nuclear-armed state will find almost any slippage from 100 percent certainty in successful preemption excruciatingly inhibiting." In other words, "nuclear-armed states do not need to convince a potential aggressor that retaliation is certain, or even likely, only that it is possible."[19] Even a small chance of retaliation will deter because of the catastrophic consequences that retaliation would bring.

Capabilities matter in the minimal deterrence view, but this school does not place much emphasis on the size of arsenals or the strategic interaction of capabilities among adversaries. A minimum deterrent force is more than a "bomb in the basement," but less than the large and diversified arsenals deployed by the superpowers in the Cold War. A sufficient retaliatory arsenal need not be large, since "even with numbers immensely disproportionate, a small force strongly inhibits the use of a large one,"[20] and it need not be guaranteed to survive an enemy first strike. What is crucial is the plausibility that a portion of the force might survive and retaliate.

The precise dividing line between an existential deterrence and minimum deterrence posture is somewhat arbitrary. We thus distinguish between the two views in a manner that holds true to their underlying logic, yet permits coding of arsenals and testing of their competing claims. In our conceptualization, the deployment of operational weapons—with sufficient range to reach a potential attacker's territory—is enough to move beyond *existential* and qualify as a *minimum* deterrence posture.[21]

If a minimum deterrence posture were enough to create robust deterrence, one would expect the nuclear age to be much less competitive than previous eras. If countries require only small, deliverable arsenals to deter their enemies, then moving from an initial nuclear test to a robust deterrent would be a fairly modest step. If leaders reason the way minimum deterrence theorists believe they do, then the nuclear age may see brief periods of intense competition—after new nuclear states test their initial devices and before they successfully deploy operational delivery systems. In those periods, their adversaries may contemplate preventive strikes. But those periods of anxiety will be short and competition will die down. After all, once a country has a deliverable force, its most essential security needs will be fulfilled. In a world characterized by minimum deterrence reasoning, gaining any kind of military advantage over an enemy with a deliverable nuclear arsenal provides no real strategic benefits.

ASSURED RETALIATION

The assured retaliation school concludes that deterrence is robust when retaliation is *assured*, not when it is merely possible or plausible. A state that aims to deploy a robust deterrent needs to ensure that some portion of the force would almost certainly survive an enemy first strike. The goal is to convince potential attackers that even a flawlessly executed disarming strike, carried out under ideal circumstances, would still fail—and result in the destruction of several of the attacker's cities.

Robert Jervis is one of the most prominent scholars of the assured retaliation school.[22] He and other analysts writing in the 1970s and 1980s made the case for the sufficiency of assured retaliation because official U.S. nuclear policy reflected, in their view, an erroneous belief that only a big and sophisticated arsenal could reliably deter the Soviet Union. The "illogic" of the superpower arms race, according to Jervis, stemmed from a failure to grasp that building more and better nuclear weapons did not matter for deterrence and security.[23] He wrote: "The vulnerability of population centers in both the United States and the Soviet Union that comes with mutual second-strike capability has transformed strategy. Because a military advantage no longer assures a decisive victory, old ways of thinking are no longer appropriate. The healthy fear of devastation, which cannot be exorcised short of the attainment of a first-strike capability, makes deterrence relatively easy."[24]

The assured retaliation school takes a more pessimistic view of international politics than either of the first two schools, noting that most major wars in history began with leaders taking huge risks. Thus, proponents of assured retaliation worry that the mere possibility of nuclear retaliation may not be enough to deter such risk-acceptant leaders. Furthermore, proponents of assured retaliation may worry that a minimum deterrent force can become less capable over time, since first-rate militaries work hard to identify enemy weaknesses. For example, adversaries spy on each other to learn about the deployments and capabilities of enemy weapon systems; they study enemy command-and-control systems; and they devise doctrines and technologies to exploit the weaknesses they discover. In a crisis, or during a conventional war, a clever war plan designed to destroy the enemy's "existential" or "minimum" nuclear force may be attractive to decision makers.[25] To ensure robust deterrence—that is, to deter war and compel military restraint if conflict erupts—states must field nuclear retaliatory forces that cannot be destroyed in any conceivable disarming strike, regardless of the malevolence and creativity of potential enemies. In Jervis's words, a reliable nuclear deterrent should ensure that "even an emotional, short-sighted, and dim-witted opponent [would] see that to start a war would be the worst alternative."[26] An assured retaliatory force is required to ensure that all leaders exercise restraint in times of calm or crisis, peace or war.[27]

There is no single recipe for creating an assured retaliation arsenal. The ingredients of a survivable nuclear force typically include some combination of the following: moderate (or large) force size; diverse delivery systems; survivable basing modes; redundant command and control systems; and well-trained personnel. The survivability of an arsenal—meaning its ability to absorb a ruthless disarming strike and still retaliate—is not determined by a single feature of the force, such as a numerical threshold or the use of a particular delivery system. Instead, the condition of assured retaliation is the result of both the attributes of an arsenal and the capabilities of potential attackers. Unlike existential deterrence and minimal deterrence, which are theories of deterrence that are based on what the deterring party can do (possess nuclear weapons in the former case, and deliver them in the latter), the assured retaliation mission, by definition, depends on a calculation of both the attacking force's capabilities and the defending force's resilience.

If the condition of assured retaliation is required to produce stalemate, then one can begin to understand why international politics remains highly competitive in the nuclear age. We should expect that a truly survivable nuclear arsenal may require substantial time to develop, but also that a force's survivability will be the result of a competitive process—the net result of a country's efforts to secure its arsenal and its enemy's ability to target it. The competitive nature of "survivability" implies that the development of nuclear weapons may invigorate competition rather than inhibit it; new nuclear states will struggle to develop survivable arsenals while their enemies press to maintain superiority and keep such arsenals vulnerable. In fact, if "assured retaliation" is a key threshold for stalemate, then arms racing, alliance competition, and relative gains concerns may not wither away even after secure forces are deployed, since each side will face incentives to gain (or regain) superiority and negate the other side's assurances.[28]

The assured retaliation school might be correct about the capability requirements for robust deterrence. If so, that may help shed light on why international politics has remained so competitive in the nuclear age, as countries race to establish an assured retaliatory capability for themselves and are tempted to compete to deny that security to their adversaries.

ASSURED DESTRUCTION

The final school holds that retaliation must be *assured and massive* in order for deterrence to be truly robust. Potential attackers need to face the near certainty of retaliation, and the consequences of that retaliation must be mind-bogglingly bad. Attackers are deterred when there is no prospect of meaningfully limiting the amount of damage a target country can inflict after an attacker launches a first strike. When the potential victim possesses a very large and invulnerable retaliatory capability, a nuclear attack would be tantamount to national suicide—and no remotely rational leader would invite that outcome.

The basic logic of assured destruction is that nuclear arsenals need to do more than deter typical leaders in normal circumstances. A robust nuclear posture needs to terrify and frustrate the goals of even highly risk-acceptant leaders during high-stakes crises. Major wars, after all, are never initiated by the faint of heart; they occur when leaders accept enormous risks in pursuit of their goals.[29] Neither World War I nor World War II would have occurred had leaders been afraid to risk huge numbers of military and civilian deaths to advance their geopolitical goals. To assured destruction advocates, robust deterrence requires convincing highly aggressive potential attackers that their actions will result in a much worse outcome than the loss of a few cities. Only the guaranteed and utter destruction of the attacker's population, industry, and leadership suffices against the most motivated foes. Designing a deterrent policy to deter any leader less threatening, determined, and formidable would be foolhardy.

The indicators of an assured destruction arsenal are similar to those of an assured retaliation force, but with more of everything. The best example of such a force can be found in either of the superpower arsenals in the latter half of the Cold War. The United States kept roughly two-thirds of its ballistic-missile submarine fleet at sea in normal peacetime conditions, as well as a quick-response nuclear bomber force ready to take off with little warning. Launch control officers were trained to fire silo-based missiles moments after receiving orders to do so. These redundant precautions were designed to ensure that even if the Soviet Union completely surprised the United States with a bolt-from-the-blue nuclear-disarming strike, U.S. forces would still be able to deliver vast numbers of high-yield thermonuclear weapons against the Soviet Union in retaliation.

If leaders reasoned the way that the assured destruction school predicts, then the nuclear age would be characterized by significant competition. Nuclear-armed countries would compete to build larger and more potent arsenals. Some countries would be tempted to strive for damage-limiting capabilities in the hope of escaping stalemate, while many others would justly fear such efforts by their adversaries and thus feel compelled to respond with steps to make their own arsenals more secure and more lethal. The large force requirements and dispersed basing needs of an assured destruction force may require allies around the world. If robust deterrence might require truly assured destruction capabilities, there is little reason to expect that a stable world of plentiful security would follow.

Each of the four schools described above can been used to identify the threshold of nuclear capability needed to deter a wide range of behavior, including limited conventional strikes against nuclear-armed states, major conventional invasions, bolt-from-the-blue surprise attacks, and nuclear-disarming strikes in the midst of war. In each of these circumstances, the existential and minimum deterrence schools claim that a little nuclear retaliatory capability goes a long way; even a small, vulnerable nuclear arsenal will generate great caution among enemies contemplating any of those types of attack. Scholars who identify assured retaliation or destruction as the key threshold, on the other hand, will expect the benefits of deterrence to grow substantially when a country deploys a truly survivable force.

There are reasons to be cautious about generalizing these concepts, however. Perhaps none of these schools of deterrence is correct across the board. For example, one posture might be sufficient to induce caution during peacetime, yet a higher level of capability may be necessary in darker times, such as during an intense crisis or during a conventional war. Relatedly, perhaps not all national leaders reason about nuclear weapons in the same way. For example, the policies of the Eisenhower administration in the 1950s might not be a good guide to the nuclear employment policies of other leaders around the world today.

We believe the analysis below reveals some general truths about deterrence, despite such concerns. Whatever historians may think about Eisenhower, to stick with the example, few would describe his administration as more aggressive, irrational, or insensitive to costs than those of the risk takers who initiated major wars throughout history. This is relevant because if an existential or minimum deterrent force is insufficient to deter a "normal" leader (like Eisenhower) in both peacetime and wartime, then one would expect such deterrent strategies to be inadequate for deterring highly aggressive foes.

Furthermore, unlike other areas of social science, where scholars seek to understand averages and trends (rather than extremes and outliers), the goal of nuclear deterrence is different. Nuclear arsenals are designed to deter not a median enemy but rather the most ruthless plausible adversary—and they must do so all the time, including in the darkest days of a crisis or war. Therefore, a deterrent posture that does *not* deter seemingly normal leaders is clearly inadequate.

The remainder of this chapter evaluates the four schools of deterrence in the canonical case—the Cold War superpower standoff. As the Soviet nuclear arsenal grew from an existential posture to a minimum deterrent force, and eventually to a true assured retaliation arsenal, how did the United States react? What level of Soviet nuclear capability, if any, made the United States accept stalemate? Which of those postures made the Soviet Union safe in peacetime and in war?

The Evolving Strategic Balance

The United States emerged from World War II as the world's most powerful country. In the years immediately following the conflict, the United States accounted for roughly half of total world economic output.[30] Unlike other great powers, the United States was neither heavily bombed nor occupied during the war; as a result, the country lost 0.32 percent of its population in the fighting, whereas Japan lost 4 percent, Germany 9 percent, and the Soviet Union 14 percent—a staggering forty-five times higher fatality rate than the United States suffered.[31] For every major combatant country except the United States, the war was a calamity.

Not only did the United States emerge from war with an intact industrial base and population, but Washington suddenly had access to a network of military facilities in friendly countries around the world. No longer was the United States geographically isolated; for the first time in history the United

States could project substantial military power across the oceans on a day-to-day basis, rather than for just short periods during wars. Overall, on the basis of the aggregate measures that scholars often use to assess power in international politics—for example, gross domestic product (GDP), population, alliances—the immediate post–World War II period seems like a time of triumph and supremacy for the United States.

It did not feel like supremacy at the time, however. The data on GDP and other abstract measures of power fail to capture the dilemmas that the United States faced as the Cold War began. For one thing, U.S. leaders feared that economic despair in Europe and Japan would allow local communist parties to gain political power and then usher their countries into the Soviet orbit. U.S. leaders viewed that possibility as a strategic disaster for the United States, as it would create a massive sphere of Soviet dominance across two of the world's most important industrial regions.[32]

The military situation was even more dire. Specifically, the imbalance in conventional military power in Europe in the late 1940s was staggering. In 1948 the U.S. Joint Chiefs of Staff (JCS) estimated that the Soviet Union had 135 army divisions in Europe, with 100 more divisions available from Soviet allies. Standing between the Soviet Red Army and all of Western Europe were just two U.S. divisions, and those divisions were not combat-ready because they were engaged in postwar occupation duties. Nor could the United States rush major reinforcements to Europe in a crisis; the United States had only ten other divisions worldwide.[33] America's principal military partner, the United Kingdom, had twelve divisions (including forces from the British Dominions), but they were scattered across the world and could not be deployed quickly to the European continent.[34] In retrospect, the JCS estimates probably overstated the size and readiness of Soviet forces in Europe, but the imbalance of conventional military power was so stark that it hardly mattered.

One crucial factor that mitigated the sense of vulnerability in the immediate postwar period was the U.S. monopoly on atomic bombs.[35] How did those weapons affect the balance of power, and how did the balance shift in ensuing years as the Soviet Union developed and deployed its own nuclear arsenal?

1945–1949: U.S. NUCLEAR MONOPOLY

The United States monopoly on atomic weapons lasted from August 1945 until August 1949. The arsenal grew from eleven bombs in 1946 to three hundred in 1950, but this period was no golden age of American supremacy. The main problem was that the U.S. Air Force initially had only a rudimentary capability to deliver these bombs against the Soviet Union. In the late 1940s, a U.S. atomic assault on the Soviet Union would have been a slow and uncertain operation. Few U.S. bombers could carry atomic bombs—approximately thirty-five such aircraft were available from 1946 to 1948—and they lacked the range to strike the Soviet Union directly from the United States, meaning that they would need to launch attacks from bases close to the Soviet periphery.[36] To make matters worse, U.S. fighter aircraft at the time had even shorter ranges, so they could not escort the bombers on their way to Soviet targets, even when flying from forward bases. Thus, a U.S. atomic attack on the Soviet Union in the late 1940s would have required its small fleet of bombers to fly unescorted through Soviet airspace to find and strike Soviet cities. If the U.S. atomic offensive were launched in response to a Soviet invasion of Western Europe—or during another acute crisis—the Soviet air defenses would have been on alert, reducing the odds that the heavily laden B-29s would ever make it to their targets.[37]

The lack of effective fighter escorts was only one of many major problems facing the U.S. bomber force in the era of nuclear monopoly, all of which meant that the air force was unable to launch a single coordinated strike to surprise or overwhelm Soviet air defenses. The United States stored all of its bombs unassembled; a thirty-nine-man crew needed two full days to assemble a single weapon. Since the United States had only four such crews in 1948, at best, it could prepare two atomic bombs per day.[38] Even then, an assembled bomb had only a forty-eight-hour shelf life before its battery died.[39] An atomic offensive would have unfolded slowly, using a few bombs and bombers at a time, giving the Soviet Union ample opportunity to organize its air defenses.

The slow pace of attack might not have been the worst problem facing the U.S. bomber force. War plans called for bombers to conduct operations at night in order to increase the odds of surviving against enemy air defenses, but for safety reasons, the bomber crews trained only in daylight. Furthermore, although U.S. aircrews relied on onboard radar to navigate in the dark, they lacked reliable maps of Soviet territory that would have offered them suitable geographic reference points for radar navigation. In some cases, U.S. bombers were assigned to strike Soviet cities whose locations were not precisely known because U.S. planners were relying on Russian tsarist-era maps. (The Soviet Union exacerbated U.S. intelligence problems by restricting the circulation of maps and introducing errors into them to complicate U.S. targeting.) Finally, although atomic bombs in this era had an estimated destructive radius of approximately 1 mile against a city, the history of U.S. bombing in World War II suggests that at least half of the weapons that American pilots released would fall more than a mile from the intended target.[40]

With all this taken together, the balance of power looked bleak for the United States and its allies in the late 1940s. Given the great conventional military imbalance, the shortcomings in U.S. atomic capabilities were glaring. If war erupted, small numbers of U.S. bombers would be sent unescorted to penetrate an alerted Soviet air defense system at night in search of Russian cities they had never flown over, using old and unreliable maps.[41] U.S. leaders were justifiably worried about the military balance during the age of their atomic monopoly.

The Soviet Union tested its first atomic bomb in 1949, and produced 150 atomic bombs over the next five years. But these weapons were not deliverable against the United States, and the Soviet arsenal was not particularly survivable in the face of a U.S. attack. While the Soviets scrambled to create a bare-bones nuclear deterrent, the United States vastly upgraded its offensive nuclear strike capabilities. The Soviet nuclear arsenal deployed during this period was an "existential" deterrent force.

Although Moscow tested a thermonuclear weapon in November 1955, paving the way for an arsenal filled with vastly more powerful fusion bombs, the country still had no bombers that could reach the United States on a round-trip mission.[42] Soviet bombers could target European cities, but unless they flew one-way suicide missions, they could not reach the U.S. homeland. The problem was as much about the lack of allies and geography as it was about aircraft technology. The only Soviet aircraft capable of delivering atomic bombs was the Tu-4 Bull, which was a copy of the U.S. B-29. But while the United States could launch its nuclear-armed B-29s from bases around the Soviet periphery (including airfields in the United Kingdom, Egypt, Turkey, Pakistan, Japan, and Guam), the Soviet Union had no allied bases close enough to the U.S. homeland that were suitable for the Tu-4. The Soviets sought to extend the bomber's range by experimenting with midair refueling and placing external fuel tanks on a few Tu-4s, but these efforts failed to give the plane sufficient range to strike targets in the United States and return to Soviet territory.[43]

While the Soviets struggled to develop a rudimentary capability to strike the United States, U.S. offensive nuclear capabilities soared.[44] From 1947 to 1955, the U.S. stockpile of strategic weapons doubled almost every year, from 32 to approximately 1,750. The lethality of U.S. weapons also grew exponentially. The United States tested a fusion bomb in 1952, and quickly began to integrate the new "hydrogen bombs" into the force.[45] The leap in destructiveness from the "simple" fission bombs of the 1940s to the hydrogen bombs of the early 1950s is staggering; for example, the bomb dropped on Nagasaki had an explosive yield of approximately 22 kilotons, whereas the first U.S. thermonuclear weapon had a yield of about 12 *megatons*—540 times the explosive yield of the Nagasaki bomb.[46]

Not only did the number and yield of U.S. bombs soar, but also the United States greatly expanded its strategic bomber force. The number of aircraft assigned to conduct nuclear strikes grew from roughly two hundred bombers in 1950 to over twelve hundred in 1955, including long-range bombers and medium-range aircraft that could attack Soviet targets from Europe.

By 1955, the nuclear balance was anything but balanced. Soviet bombers still could not reach the U.S. homeland, while the United States could deliver more than fifteen hundred atomic and thermonuclear weapons against a wide range of Soviet military, industrial, and leadership targets in a few days.[47]

To label the Soviet arsenal of 1950 to 1955 as "existential" does not mean it had zero chance of responding to a U.S. nuclear attack with retaliation against the U.S. homeland. Indeed, the core idea behind existential deterrence is that *some possibility* of retaliation exists as long as nuclear weapons exist. In the early 1950s, the Soviets could have tried to retaliate after a U.S. nuclear strike by cobbling together a one-way, suicide mission using any surviving bombers. Nevertheless, the Soviet armed forces had no units trained to carry out such an attack; their bomber crews had not planned or trained to conduct intercontinental missions. Their mission in war was to strike targets throughout Europe, not the U.S. homeland.

1956–1961: SOVIET MINIMUM DETERRENT

The Soviets finally progressed from an "existential" to a "minimum" deterrent force around 1956, when their first intercontinental bombers entered service. Their new, long-range bomber, the Tu-95 Bear, could fly round-trip missions to the United States—though they still needed to refuel at Arctic air bases along the northern edges of the Soviet Union before they headed over the pole.[48] In 1956 there were only twenty Tu-95 bombers in the Soviet inventory, but by 1961 the fleet had grown to 150 aircraft. Although the Soviet Union finally had the capability to strike the United States, its nuclear force remained vulnerable to a disarming attack—that is, it was still not yet a survivable deterrent force.[49]

A bomber force like the one the Soviets fielded could be deployed in a manner that would make it survivable, by developing sophisticated warning systems, creating a nimble command-and-control system, and keeping a portion of the force on alert. The Soviets took a step in that direction by deploying a radar network around their periphery to detect U.S. bombers and cue Soviet fighter planes to intercept them. The radars could also allow Soviet commanders to warn their bomber bases of an incoming U.S. strike. However, the Soviet efforts to enhance nuclear force survivability did not yet bear real fruit for several reasons. First, the United States extensively probed the Soviet periphery with bombers and reconnaissance aircraft to identify holes in the Soviet warning network—specifically, routes and altitudes that U.S. bombers could fly without being detected by Soviet radar. Evidence suggests that the United States found several holes and expected to slip through the Soviet radar screen without much difficulty.[50] More important, even if U.S. aircraft were observed by radar, the Soviets' new bombers were not prepared to disperse quickly to escape the attack; Soviet planes required six to eight hours of preparation before takeoff, and their nuclear warheads were not stored on the same air bases as the aircraft.[51] Finally, although the Soviets could have raised the readiness of their bombers during a crisis, and moved nuclear weapons to the bomber bases, there was yet another major Soviet vulnerability: the Arctic refueling bases required by Soviet bombers to reach U.S. cities were easy targets for a U.S. first strike. In fact, U.S. bombers would fly over those bases (and presumably bomb them) on their way over the pole to strike airfields and other targets further south in the Soviet Union. Moscow's new long-range bomber fleet was a step in the right direction for the Soviets, but the result was far from a survivable deterrent.

In 1958 to 1959, the Soviets took two additional steps that did not end their vulnerability immediately, but which laid the groundwork for a truly survivable deterrent force: they began to deploy nuclear-armed submarines and intercontinental ballistic missiles (ICBMs). Initially, the submarine force and the ICBMs were at least as vulnerable as the Soviet bombers. Early Soviet submarines were loud and hence relatively easy for the U.S. Navy to track. Furthermore, the early Soviet submarines had to come within approximately 75 miles of the U.S. coast to fire their missiles, and unlike modern ballistic missile submarines (SSBNs), they had to surface before firing. Most importantly, the early Soviet submarines spent most of their time in port and did not bring their nuclear warheads with them when they went on patrol;[52] the warheads were kept in weapons storage sites on land.[53]

Similarly, the first-generation Soviet ICBMs were highly vulnerable. The R-7 (SS-6 as designated by NATO) had to be fired from a fixed launchpad out in the open rather than from a hardened underground protective silo, as with a modern missile. Even worse from the Soviet perspective, the missile required twenty-four hours of preparation to launch.[54]

Although the Soviet nuclear arsenal was still highly vulnerable throughout the 1950s, the window for a successful U.S. strike was beginning to close. The Soviet submarine force, flawed as it was, continued to grow, from fifteen submarines in 1960 to forty by 1961.[55] Additionally, in 1961 the Soviets began sending submarines on deterrent patrols with their nuclear warheads onboard. At any given time in 1961 only a fraction of the forty Soviet submarines were at sea, and U.S. naval forces could probably destroy many of those, but the challenge of destroying all the Soviet nuclear weapons that could reach the United States was growing rapidly. Another problem for U.S. war planners was the gradual deployment of new Soviet ICBMs. By 1961 the Soviets were fielding newer missiles that were more reliable than the first generation and could be launched in a few hours or less.[56]

Of course, some of the Soviet gains in survivability were countered by growing U.S. offensive capabilities. By 1961, the United States had a robust triad: five hundred B-52 long-range bombers, five Polaris submarines, and fifty ICBMs.[57] U.S. target intelligence was improving as well. In August 1960, the United States acquired its first spy satellite photographs of the interior of the Soviet Union. But these improvements could not prevent U.S. nuclear superiority from slipping away. The Soviet arsenal was becoming too large and too diversified to completely destroy. A successful attack would require striking more than a few hundred Soviet airfields; now ICBM sites, submarine bases, and submarines at sea would all have to be located and destroyed. Moreover, these targets would need to be hit nearly simultaneously. By late 1961, the Soviet "minimum" deterrent was becoming an "assured retaliation" force.

1962–1964: SOVIET ASSURED RETALIATION

The Soviet Union's vulnerability to a U.S. disarming attack disappeared as the Soviet arsenal grew larger, more sophisticated, and more diverse. In 1958, a U.S. nuclear strike against Soviet strategic nuclear forces likely would have worked unless several things went wrong; by late 1961, it could have worked only if everything went right. And just a few years later, even that would have left the Soviet Union with nuclear retaliatory forces that could be delivered against the U.S. homeland. In short, the balance of power shifted from a condition of Soviet minimum deterrence to one of Soviet assured retaliation.

A simple numerical comparison of U.S. and Soviet strategic nuclear forces in 1962 makes it appear that the United States still enjoyed nuclear supremacy. The United States could have used as many as 2,000 nuclear weapons in a surprise attack against the Soviet Union, with most being delivered by B-52 bombers stationed in the United States.[58] The Soviets had 160 bombers, 38 ICBMs, and 48 nuclear-missile armed submarines. Attacking these forces would require destroying up to 140 major Soviet airfields, plus 10 to 25 ICBM launch sites and up to 30 submarine bases.[59] A U.S. first strike would have targeted other sites, too—including an enormous number of additional airfields—but the critical targets numbered only about 200.

But simply counting the number of U.S. warheads and Soviet targets does not give the full picture of the strategic balance at the time. Coordinating a nuclear attack on a diversified nuclear arsenal raised tremendous complications for U.S. war planners. One major problem was the expanded deployment of Soviet nuclear-armed submarines. By 1962, only a fraction of the Soviet fleet was at sea at any given time; however, with forty-eight boats in the force (each with three nuclear warheads), the probability that a few missiles would survive and be launched at U.S. cities had grown dramatically. American antisubmarine warfare (ASW) capabilities were good, but as the United States learned during the Cuban Missile Crisis, it could not always track Soviet submarines in the open ocean.[60]

A second problem for U.S. war planners stemmed from the deployment of newer Soviet ICBMs, which required less time to launch after warning of an attack. Incoming U.S. bombers might be detected as they approached Soviet airspace, about an hour or two before reaching Soviet missile sites.[61] The United States could target Soviet ICBMs with American missiles (ICBMs and SLBMs), but in 1962 U.S. ballistic missiles were relatively inaccurate and unreliable.[62] Even worse, a quick U.S. missile strike on Soviet ICBMs would arrive many hours before U.S. bombers reached some of their targets, giving the Soviets time to get their bombers in the air and submarines out to sea. A third approach would launch U.S. bombers first and delay the missile attack on Soviet ICBMs until American bombers approached Soviet air defense radars. However, this plan ran the risk that U.S. bombers would be detected early (for example, by human spotters near U.S. bomber bases), giving the Soviets hours to push submarines out to sea and launch their ICBMs in retaliation.[63] In sum, once the Soviets built a nontrivial number of ICBMs and submarines, coordinating an effective nuclear strike became much more complicated.

The odds of the United States executing a successful disarming strike against the Soviet Union had dropped substantially by 1962. There was no precise moment at which a U.S. first strike became impossible; instead, it melted away as Soviet capabilities grew. The age of mutual assured retaliation had arrived. Mutual assured destruction would soon follow.

1965–1990: MUTUAL ASSURED DESTRUCTION

Between 1964 and 1967, the Soviet ICBM force grew rapidly, to over eight hundred missiles. American planners contemplating a disarming first strike in 1967 thus faced the prospect of needing to locate and destroy more than one thousand Soviet long-range nuclear-delivery vehicles (including missiles, submarines, and bombers), which were equipped with more than fifteen hundred warheads. And U.S. planners would need to do so quickly, nearly simultaneously, and with complete strategic surprise. Such a first strike almost certainly would have resulted in dozens of surviving Soviet forces able to inflict massive nuclear retaliation on the United States. In short, at some point in the mid-1960s, the Soviet Union acquired an assured destruction capability, thus ushering in the condition of mutual assured destruction (MAD) that would endure through the end of the Cold War.

PERCEPTIONS OF THE SHIFTING STRATEGIC BALANCE

The strategic balance of power shifted with the gradual growth of Soviet nuclear capabilities. But how did the nuclear balance appear to U.S. leaders? Did they perceive these shifts correctly?[64]

Conventional wisdom about frequent misunderstandings during the Cold War—especially popular notions about a "bomber gap" and "missile gap" in the 1950s and early 1960s—might lead one to believe that U.S. leaders were in the dark about the balance of power, but they were not. At various points in the 1950s there were fears, which we now know to be baseless, about Soviet nuclear superiority. Yet these misperceptions were not about the contemporary balance of power, but about trends in the balance of power—that is, fears about the future. Ironically, even during periods of anxiety about a bomber and missile gap, U.S. leaders had accurate intelligence assessments of existing Soviet strategic nuclear forces.

Given the limits of early Cold War technology, U.S. government intelligence estimates of Soviet strategic nuclear forces were remarkably good.[65] U.S. and NATO officials received intelligence about the number of Soviet nuclear forces operational limitations and vulnerabilities. For example, as early as 1956, intelligence reports concluded that Soviet long-range bombers could strike targets in North America only if they were staged through Arctic refueling bases. This information meant that the United States and its allies could look for the movement of Soviet bombers to Arctic bases as a critical early warning signal of an impending Soviet attack, and it led U.S. commanders to target the handful of such bases with nuclear strikes as a means of neutralizing the backbone of the Soviet strategic nuclear force.[66]

Western intelligence also learned important facts about the operational limitations of Soviet submarines and ICBMs. Intelligence reports noted that the nuclear missiles on early Soviet submarines were short-range, so they could be fired at the United States only if the submarines came very close to the American coast. Intelligence also learned that Soviet submarines had to surface to fire their missiles, and that they spent most of their time in port.[67] Regarding ICBMs, intelligence correctly inferred that early Soviet ICBMs were so big that the launch sites had to be located on railroad lines, which helped U.S. planners identify likely locations of Soviet launchpads even before they were confirmed by satellite photos.[68] Excellent intelligence about the operational limitations of Soviet bombers, submarines, and ICBMs gave U.S. leaders an accurate picture of America's nuclear advantages.

American leaders correctly perceived their nuclear supremacy, and they also understood that it was slipping away.[69] During the last years of the Eisenhower administration, key foreign policy advisors—including National Security Advisor Robert Cutler and Secretary of State John Foster Dulles—focused intently on the question of how U.S. and NATO security strategy would need to change as the U.S. nuclear edge disappeared.[70] In May 1958 the National Security Council (NSC) debated how policy should change to account for nuclear parity, which Dulles expected would occur "in two or three years."[71] President Eisenhower understood the impending challenge, but he also recognized that the Soviets were not building nuclear weapons as quickly as some forecasts claimed, and he privately expressed confidence that if it ever came time to fight a nuclear war with the Soviet Union—to push America's "whole stack of chips into the pot," as he put it—the United

States could win with acceptable casualties.[72] In 1959, Eisenhower told then senator Lyndon Johnson, "If we were to release our nuclear stockpile on the Soviet Union, the main danger would arise not from retaliation but from fall-out in the earth's atmosphere."[73]

Even the Kennedy administration, which was skeptical about the wisdom of the previous administration's nuclear-centric war plans, understood that the United States still had viable nuclear employment options as late as 1961. During the 1961 Berlin Crisis, Kennedy's national security advisor, McGeorge Bundy, authorized a high-level group of senior civilian and military plan-ners to create plans for a specially tailored nuclear-disarming strike against Soviet long-range nuclear forces in case the crisis escalated. The group cre-ated an attack plan that they thought might work: it would probably destroy all Soviet intercontinental nuclear forces on the ground, though there was a danger that one or two bombers or submarines might get through, and hence that a few million Americans would be killed.[74] The report concluded with a mixture of optimism and uncertainty that captures the conflicted mindset of leaders facing the dusk of U.S. nuclear supremacy. According to Kaysen's report: "While a wide range of outcomes is possible," the United States has "a fair probability of achieving a substantial measure of success."[75] In other words, there was also a "fair probability" that the United States would *not* achieve substantial success and would, presumably, be hit by a Soviet retal-iatory strike. The window for a U.S. first strike may have still been open, but it seemed barely big enough to squeeze through.

U.S. political leaders and military planners understood that nuclear stale-mate lay just around the corner. A December 1960 study by the Pentagon's Weapon Systems Evaluation Group (WSEG) observed that nuclear suprem-acy would be long gone by the mid-1960s; by then, according to WSEG cal-culations, a U.S. disarming strike against the Soviet Union would still leave the Soviets with the capacity to retaliate and kill 70 to 80 percent of the U.S. population.[76] Another 1961 study explicitly questioned the feasibility of U.S. national security policy: "In a condition of nuclear stalemate we can no lon-ger rely on the assumption that if hostilities get above a relatively low thresh-old we will use nuclear weapons."[77] In sum, the United States still enjoyed strategic superiority in 1961—and its top political leaders knew it—but the margin of superiority was closing.

By mid-1962, senior U.S. leaders understood that nuclear superiority had essentially disappeared. The United States could no longer strike first at So-viet nuclear forces without suffering a substantial Soviet nuclear counterat-tack. Whereas in 1961 the chairman of the JCS had told President Kennedy that if war erupted the United States would "prevail," by September 1963 Kennedy was briefed that such an outcome was no longer plausible.[78] That same month, McGeorge Bundy prepared a memo for Kennedy on the results of a report by the NSC's Net Evaluation Subcommitee (NESC), which had modeled the consequences of nuclear war in the 1964 to 1968 time frame based on whether the United States or the Soviet Union struck first. In either scenario, according to Bundy, "the fundamental conclusion is that these wars are unacceptably destructive for both sides."[79] On September 12, 1963, Kennedy received a briefing on the nuclear balance of power. According to the minutes of the meeting, "the President asked whether, even if we attack the USSR first, the loss to the U.S. would be unacceptable to political leaders. General Johnson replied that it would be, i.e., even if we preempt, surviving Soviet capability is sufficient to produce an unacceptable loss in the U.S. The President asked whether then in fact we are in a period of nuclear stalemate. General Johnson replied that we are."[80]

The military was not alone in its skepticism about the United States' continued ability to conduct a successful disarming nuclear strike. Former secretary of defense Robert McNamara argued (in 1989) that "there was no reasonable chance that we could get away with a first strike unscathed [in 1962]. We simply didn't know where all the Soviet warheads were." According to McNamara, launching a nuclear war in 1962 "would have destroyed us as well as the Soviets," and "if we'd tried a first strike, the Soviets might have had 25 percent of their original three hundred [strategic nuclear warheads] left."[81] One should be highly skeptical about statements by former government officials offered decades after the pertinent events, but in this case McNamara's views about the military balance were documented in a private memo he wrote to Kennedy in 1962, just a few weeks after the Cuban Missile Crisis. McNamara wrote, "I am convinced that we would not be able to achieve tactical surprise, especially in the kinds of crisis circumstances in which a first-strike capability might be relevant. Thus, the Soviets would be able to launch some of their retaliatory forces before we had destroyed their bases."[82]

It appears that senior U.S. policymakers believed, at least by the fall of 1962, that the Soviet Union had an assured retaliatory capability. This does not mean that a preemptive strike against Soviet nuclear forces was impossible. As Marc Trachtenberg shows, as late as mid-1963, Kennedy believed he might have to attempt a disarming first strike if certain extreme circumstances arose, such as the imminent conquest of Europe by the Soviets.[83] But leaders appreciated that the odds of the United States executing a successful disarming strike against the Soviet Union had dropped substantially by 1962.

Tracking Changes in U.S. Strategic Posture

As discussed above, the first fifteen years of the Cold War witnessed several significant changes in the nuclear balance of power. But how did those changes affect U.S. behavior? In this section we track U.S. behavior—defined as "strategic posture"—along two key dimensions: peacetime foreign policy and war plans. The first dimension focuses on the relative level of caution or aggressiveness that the United States demonstrated in its strategic orientation toward the Soviet Union: What foreign policy goals did the United States pursue, and how much risk were U.S. leaders willing to take in pursuit of those goals in peacetime conditions and during crises? Specifically, what level of deployed Soviet nuclear capability was enough to significantly moderate U.S. behavior? Did the emergence of a Soviet existential or minimum deterrent arsenal induce much greater U.S. caution? Or did more cautious foreign policies emerge only after the Soviet Union deployed an assured retaliatory force?

The second dimension of strategic posture consists of U.S. plans for war against the Soviet Union. We track three details about those plans: the centrality of conventional versus nuclear operations; the timing of nuclear escalation (immediate or delayed); and the war aims. What level of nuclear capability did the Soviets have to build to compel the United States to restrain itself during war? Was a small, vulnerable Soviet deterrent frightening enough to force Washington to downgrade the role of nuclear forces in U.S. plans? Was it enough to encourage the United States to restrain its war aims during a conflict? Or did those changes only happen at higher levels of Soviet nuclear capability?

1945–1949: THE ERA OF NUCLEAR MONOPOLY

For more than four years the United States was the only country in the world armed with nuclear weapons. Since there was no Soviet nuclear arsenal to deter the United States, U.S. fears about war with the Soviet Union were based primarily on the expected costs of conventional conflict. This period of U.S. nuclear monopoly, therefore, offers a useful baseline for evaluating the effects of Soviet nuclear deployments in subsequent years. What was the U.S. foreign policy stance toward the Soviet Union during this period? Did the United States pursue ambitious objectives and adopt uncompromising positions during early Cold War crises? If war had erupted during the period of U.S. nuclear monopoly, how would the United States have fought?

U.S. foreign policy toward the Soviet Union during the era of U.S. nuclear monopoly was characterized by relative prudence and caution. To be sure, by 1947, just two years after the end of World War II, the former wartime allies were already engaged in serious geopolitical competition. Both the United States and Soviet Union sought to extend their influence across Europe, and thus limit the influence of their main rival. Tensions flared over the status of divided Germany (and divided Berlin). The United States was not meek during the early years of the Cold War—for example, Washington played hardball to ensure that the people of Western Europe elected anticommunist leaders—but the United States did not maximize its potential leverage from nuclear monopoly.

The generally restrained approach adopted by the United States in this period is reflected in its response to two policy challenges. In 1948 the Soviet Union and its East German partners blockaded the access routes that connected West Germany with West Berlin. Confronting the difficulties of supplying a city located inside hostile territory, and faced with a highly unfavorable conventional military balance, U.S. leaders could have reasonably acquiesced to Soviet pressure and abandoned its position in West Berlin. Alternatively, buoyed by their monopoly on nuclear weapons, U.S. leaders could have dispatched ground forces down the access routes toward Berlin, daring the Soviet Union to start a war. The United States instead chose a middle course in aiming to break the Berlin blockade with an airlift. This strategy was designed to avoid directly challenging Soviet or East German military forces, while placing the onus on Moscow to escalate the conflict.[84]

The United States also faced a decision in the late 1940s that would define the course of its foreign policy for decades. As its relationship with the Soviet Union deteriorated, U.S. leaders debated how to respond to increasing Soviet hostility. Some advocated a return to isolationism, to avoid being dragged into another costly European war. Others advocated "rollback": an effort to use political and military means to expel the Soviet Union from Eastern Europe. Instead, the United States adopted containment—a strategy for limiting the spread of Soviet influence without seeking to overthrow East European communist regimes.

Although one might have expected the period of U.S. nuclear monopoly to be marked by bold and aggressive American policies toward the Soviet Union, the United States opted for a relatively restrained approach for confronting the Soviet Union.

No such restraint was evident in U.S. war plans at the time. If a major conflict had erupted in Europe during the period of nuclear monopoly, the United States planned to employ its advantage in atomic weapons to defeat the Soviet Union and win the war. Three aspects of U.S. planning are notable. First, in terms of the conventional-nuclear balance of operations, atomic weapons played the central role in U.S. war plans. The details of those plans changed from year to year, but the overall military concept remained unchanged: U.S. conventional forces would be rapidly defeated or retreat from the continent; the United States would initiate an atomic bombing campaign against Soviet cities and industry, which would weaken the Red Army; after destroying Soviet industry, the United States would reconquer Europe.[85] The point is that during the period of nuclear monopoly, U.S. atomic bombs were not weapons of last resort; they were the primary means for wearing down Soviet power, allowing the United States to defeat the Soviet army.

Second, in terms of the timing of escalation, atomic attacks on Soviet cities would commence at the outset of a major war. The bombing campaign would unfold slowly, because the United States could assemble only two atomic weapons per day, and had few bombers that could deliver them. It would, therefore, take many weeks to attack all twenty Soviet cities that comprised the target set in 1948, or the seventy cities targeted in the 1949 plan. But the methodical pace of the strategic campaign—like the strategic bombing of Germany and Japan a few years earlier—merely reflected the time it would take to execute the plan.[86]

Third, in terms of war aims, throughout the 1940s the U.S. goal in any war against the Soviet Union was the same as it was during World War II: victory.[87] There was no concept in the plans for limited attacks or midwar negotiations; the goal was to destroy Russia's major cities and then—months later—mop up the remnants of the Red Army.[88]

In sum, throughout the 1940s, U.S. foreign policy and war plans seemed little changed by the atomic age. The foreign policy was designed to contain the Soviet Union without triggering war. U.S. war plans in particular were strikingly similar to U.S. strategies employed during World War II. Next we turn to the question of what, if anything, changed in the U.S. foreign policy approach and war plans after the Soviet Union tested its first atomic weapon in 1949.

1950–1961: EXISTENTIAL AND MINIMUM DETERRENCE

If the existential deterrence school is correct, 1949 should have been a watershed in U.S. foreign policy. The deployment of even a small nuclear arsenal should have made the United States extremely cautious in its dealings with the Soviet Union, to avoid any risk of war. Furthermore, if conventional war did occur, the mere possibility that one or more Soviet nuclear weapons would detonate in Western Europe or the United States should have injected great caution into U.S. war plans. Those plans should have reflected a high degree of military restraint, including steps to terminate the war on acceptable terms as soon as possible. If the minimum deterrence school is correct, on the other hand, each of those changes should have occurred in the mid-1950s, after the Soviet Union deployed its first long-range delivery systems. So, how did U.S. foreign policy change as the Soviets deployed an existential and then minimal deterrence arsenal? And how did U.S. war plans evolve?

The early 1950s were a period of enormous U.S. military advantage. If war had erupted between the superpowers, the Soviet military could have occupied all of continental Europe, and possibly dropped a few nuclear weapons on U.S. allies in Europe and Asia. Ultimately, however, the Soviet Union would have been utterly destroyed by a massive U.S. thermonuclear bombing campaign. Yet, as in the preceding age of U.S. nuclear monopoly, American leaders sought to merely contain communist expansion and avoid war with the Soviet Union, rather than attempting to roll back Soviet control of strategically important regions or provoking military conflict.

The U.S. goal of avoiding a costly war with the Soviet Union was a reasonable one. Given the enormous imbalance of nuclear power, however, it is surprising that the United States was willing to make political concessions and moderate its behavior in the face of Soviet provocations. Armed with far superior firepower, why didn't U.S. leaders adopt hard-line positions on virtually every point of dispute, and dare the Soviets to start a war that the United States would surely win?

Advocates of existential and minimum deterrence have a ready-made answer to this puzzle. From the U.S. perspective, even a small chance of war—and thus a small chance of triggering Soviet nuclear attack—was too great a risk to accept. Therefore, U.S. leaders opposed Soviet expansion but moderated their policies to minimize the risk of war.

Two occasions during the early 1950s lend credence to the existential and minimum deterrence view. First, U.S. nuclear restraint during the Korean War is difficult to explain without reference to deterrence logic. In late 1950, U.S.-led forces repelled a North Korean invasion of South Korea and pushed Pyongyang's retreating army all the way to the Chinese border. But China intervened, sending thousands of troops into North Korea and inflicting heavy losses on U.S. forces. In the following months, the United States suffered tens of thousands of casualties in brutal fighting against the Chinese army, with the conflict bogging down into a battle of attrition for two more years. Why did the United States accept such a crushing military defeat and stalemate? Why didn't Washington employ nuclear weapons against massed Chinese forces in North Korea, or against government or military targets in China? After all, China had no nuclear weapons, and its Soviet partner should have been too terrified by U.S. military advantage to either retaliate in kind or launch an invasion of Western Europe. With its enemies outgunned, why did the United States keep its most powerful weapon holstered?

More broadly, in 1953 the new Eisenhower administration conducted a review of U.S. strategy toward the Soviet Union. The basic options on the table were to stick with containment or adopt a more uncompromising stance of forcing leaders in Moscow to choose between accommodating the West and fighting it. The Eisenhower administration opted for the former—containment. Clearly the Eisenhower administration did not want to pay the costs of war, but why did it believe that a hard-line position would lead to violence? Why wasn't Eisenhower confident that superior U.S. military power would force the Soviets to choose peace?

The logic of existential and minimum deterrence may have played a role in U.S. restraint, although historians continue to debate the causes in both cases. For example, in terms of the nonuse of nuclear weapons in Korea, some scholars argue that normative constraints or reputational concerns were decisive;[89] others claim there were few meaningful targets in North Korea, or highlight concerns that ineffective nuclear use would undermine U.S. geopoliti-cal leverage.[90] Nevertheless, the military balance was far more favorable to the United States in the early 1950s than it had been in the late 1940s, so why were U.S. leaders reluctant to employ the coercive leverage that their military supe-riority should have provided, to force China to halt and deter Russia from intervening? It is at least plausible that the mere possibility of provoking a Soviet nuclear strike—the logic of existential and minimum deterrence—was sufficiently terrifying to moderate U.S. policies during this period.

Although the Soviet existential and minimum deterrent posture *may* have restrained U.S. foreign policy, it did nothing to moderate U.S. military plans. In fact, the growth of Soviet nuclear capabilities had the opposite effect. The United States continued to depend on nuclear threats to deter attacks on Europe, and to rely on nuclear war as the preferred means of fighting if major conflict erupted. U.S. war plans were not designed to prevent or delay esca-lation, but to conduct nuclear strikes against Soviet targets as quickly as possible. The plans did not limit the targets to be destroyed; they aimed to disarm the Soviet nuclear force, kill the Soviet leadership, and destroy Soviet urban-industrial centers. The goal of U.S. war plans in the 1950s was simple: decisive victory.

U.S. war plans remained as nuclear-centric as ever throughout the 1950s. What changed were the size of the planned U.S. attack and the prioritization of targets. Immediately after the first Soviet atomic test, a Pentagon study concluded that the coming deployment of Soviet nuclear weapons required the United States to shift its war plans; rather than focus on Soviet cities, U.S. operations would need to prioritize Soviet nuclear capabilities.[91]

The focus on counterforce targets required a vast increase in U.S. nuclear forces. Some analysts have derided the expansion of the U.S. nuclear arse-nal in the 1950s as the beginning of the era of "overkill," when the number of weapons far exceeded what was necessary to destroy every meaningful Soviet city. But destroying Soviet cities was no longer the main purpose of the arsenal. The goal was, first and foremost, to destroy Soviet nuclear forces. Back in 1949, before the Soviets had tested an atomic bomb, the U.S. war plan called for destroying seventy Soviet cities. In 1955, the plan still included attacks on cities—118 of them—but the focus of the attack had become the destruction of 645 airfields located across the Sino-Soviet bloc, plus Soviet air defense sites (whose destruction was necessary for U.S. bombers to reach their main targets).[92] Destroying those airfields was the key to victory, as it would prevent the Soviet Union from launching its own atomic raids against NATO cities and forces. Whereas the plans in the 1940s could afford to be methodical, the strikes in the 1950s had to hit the Soviets quickly, before Soviet bombers could begin their own operations. (By the late 1950s, the U.S. attack plan also required that Soviet ballistic missiles needed to be hit before they could launch.)[93]

The development of a Soviet existential deterrent—and the subsequent transition to a minimum deterrent force—therefore changed some aspects of U.S. war plans, such as increasing the speed and ferocity of a U.S. strike. But a key element remained constant: the objectives. The goal of U.S. war plans during the age of existential and minimum deterrence was neither coercion (to compel war termination) nor vengeance, but simply victory. The goal was to win World War III by destroying the Soviet Union's nuclear force, as well as the industry that could support Soviet conventional military operations.

Other scholars have highlighted, with good reason, the ways that U.S. war plans were shaped by internal organizational or bureaucratic politics (for example, a mission rivalry between the U.S. Air Force and Navy), or a military-industrial complex. But the strategic logic underpinning those plans was clarified as the age of minimum deterrence neared its end and the Soviet arsenal became more difficult to destroy. In 1961, the United States found itself embroiled in a crisis over Berlin. President Kennedy's national security advisor established a small group within the White House to evaluate U.S. nuclear plans and suggest ways to improve U.S. counterforce capabilities. The White House group, led by Carl Kaysen, proposed a smaller strike option comprised of only forty-one bombers, to maximize the odds of them slipping through holes in the Soviet radar network undetected. The downside of that strike plan, though, was that it would be too small to eliminate the medium- and short-range Soviet nuclear weapons that threatened Washington's European allies. When President Kennedy was briefed on the Kaysen group's report, he was apparently not shocked to learn that U.S. success in a nuclear war hinged on focusing U.S. strikes against the Soviet *long-range* nuclear forces (meaning, delaying attacks on the Soviet bombers that targeted European cities). Instead, Kennedy asked for a briefing the following day from General Thomas Power, the commander of the Strategic Air Command, to address the mechanics of the plan. Kennedy wrote to Power: "How would you plan an attack that would use a minimum-sized force against Soviet long range striking power only, and would attempt to achieve tactical surprise? How long would it take to develop such a plan?"[94]

U.S. strategic posture in the 1950s is often harshly criticized. Some analysts claim that it left the United States unable to deal with more limited acts of Soviet aggression because Washington would be unwilling to trigger a mutually catastrophic nuclear war to counter such aggression. Other critics claim that the rapid growth of the U.S. arsenal reflected an illogical desire for overkill because there were not nearly enough Russian cities to require such a vast U.S. nuclear force.

But those criticisms miss the mark. In the 1950s, the Truman and Eisenhower administrations were not planning to respond to an act of Soviet limited aggression—for example, against West Berlin—by triggering a *mutual* catastrophe. Rather, they planned to use U.S. nuclear forces to conduct a

massive disarming strike to eliminate Soviet nuclear forces during any significant conventional conflict in Europe. In other words, the large U.S. arsenal
would have been "overkill" had their mission been to destroy Soviet cities,
but they were deployed with an altogether different objective: to rapidly
destroy the Soviet nuclear arsenal at the outset of any major war. As long as
the United States felt it could destroy the Soviet arsenal (be it an existential
or minimum deterrent one) with a nuclear-disarming strike, it relied on
plans to do so.

1962 AND BEYOND: THE ERA OF ASSURED RETALIATION

If advocates of assured retaliation are correct that fielding a survivable
retaliatory force is the key threshold for creating stalemate, then the 1960s
should have seen significant changes in U.S. defense plans. The Soviet Union's
deployment of a secure retaliatory force should have created major problems
for the United States. After all, how could the United States defend Europe
if war erupted, given that a major nuclear strike against the Soviet Union no
longer made sense in light of that country's ability to retaliate? The United
States also faced a deterrence problem. If responding to a conventional
Soviet attack with a nuclear strike no longer made sense, how could Washington use its powerful nuclear arsenal to deter that attack in the first place?
And how could U.S. nuclear capabilities be used to assure NATO allies?

If the assured retaliation school is correct, then U.S. leaders would have
needed to grapple with these dilemmas in the early 1960s. The United States
should therefore have grown more cautious in its dealings with the Soviet
Union, and its strategy for deterring and waging war should have changed
as well.

The Soviet deployment of an assured retaliation capability did not cause
a notable decline in U.S. foreign policy assertiveness, mainly because U.S.
foreign policy already aimed at containing the Soviet Union without provoking war. The crisis that erupted just as the Soviets were deploying their
first survivable capabilities—the Cuban Missile Crisis—is indicative of both
of these threads in the U.S. approach. On one hand, the United States was
willing to confront the Soviet Union to contain the expansion of Soviet power.
On the other hand, the United States crafted its policies at each stage of the
confrontation to reduce the probability of war. At the start of the crisis, the
United States chose to blockade Cuba rather than launch air strikes. At
the end of the crisis, the United States chose to trade away its missiles in
Turkey rather than invade Cuba.

Throughout the Cold War, the United States sought to resist Soviet political and military gains, but do so in a manner designed to avoid direct military conflict. The development of an assured retaliation capability did not
compel the United States to abandon the former, but neither was it necessary

for the latter. The more relevant changes in U.S. strategic posture occurred in the realm of war plans.

U.S. leaders reacted to the changed strategic landscape in the 1960s as advocates of assured retaliation would anticipate. The United States realized that U.S. strategy could no longer rest on threats to start a general nuclear war, which would have been suicidal to execute and hence lacked credibility. U.S. leaders, therefore, sought other options for war and deterrence, such as stronger conventional defenses, limited nuclear options, and plans for gradual nuclear escalation. Post–Cold War historical accounts have shown that the actual changes in U.S. war plans occurred slowly, and each concept for implementing limited nuclear options raised new problems for the United States and its allies.[95] Nevertheless, the United States did adjust its war plans in response to the emergence of a Soviet assured retaliatory capability, even though U.S. planners never fully "solved" the challenges posed by the Soviets' growing arsenal. In short, the growth of the Soviet nuclear arsenal finally forced the United States to abandon its prompt and massive nuclear war–winning plan; in that crucial respect the Soviet force had finally produced real peacetime and wartime security benefits for Moscow.

Previous historical interpretations of the "flexible response" turn in U.S. war plans in the 1960s are consistent with the assured retaliation school of deterrence, but those accounts are not accurate. According to the old interpretation, because the United States could no longer win a nuclear war, its threats to respond to a Soviet invasion of Western Europe with massive retaliation lacked credibility; therefore, the United States and NATO developed a flexible response strategy. Flexible response had two related components. First, NATO would strengthen its conventional forces so they would be powerful enough to thwart minor Soviet incursions. This would mean that only a full-scale Warsaw Pact invasion could overwhelm NATO's conventional forces. Faced with a full-scale invasion, however, NATO's threats to escalate to the nuclear level would be more credible—especially if the United States and its allies had options for escalation that might not trigger a full-scale nuclear war. The second component of flexible response was the development of "limited" or "graduated" nuclear options. Rather than force a president to choose between surrender and suicide, flexible response allegedly offered U.S. and NATO leaders a menu of choices for nuclear escalation, to coerce the Soviet Union to halt the war before all sides had plunged into the abyss.

Evidence from the 1950s and 1960s reveals that U.S. leaders from both the Eisenhower and Kennedy administrations diagnosed the problem they faced exactly as the assured retaliation school would expect. Even before the Soviet Union had deployed a survivable arsenal, senior officials in the Eisenhower administration anticipated the coming problem.[96] For example, during a May 1958 NSC meeting, Eisenhower's national security advisor Robert Cutler declared that the United States needed to reevaluate its overarching national security strategy, given the impending situation in which nuclear forces, "capable of delivering massive nuclear devastation (regardless of which side strikes first) increasingly deters each side from initiating, or taking actions which directly risk general nuclear war."[97] Cutler argued that the coming era of "nuclear parity and mutual deterrence" would require a "flexible and selective capability . . . to deter or suppress limited military aggression." Secretary of State John Foster Dulles agreed that the United States would need to develop options that would not rely on the threat of "wholesale obliteration," and suggested that tactical nuclear weapons might contribute to NATO's defense without triggering Soviet retaliation.[98] Dulles had written an earlier memo describing the looming situation, in which he said it would be "suicide" to engage in a nuclear exchange with the Soviet Union and advocated increased spending on conventional forces and the development of limited nuclear options, which he referred to as "graduated retaliation-coercion."[99] In a conversation later that year, Dulles told Eisenhower that the existing U.S. strategy was "rapidly outliving its usefulness and we need to apply ourselves urgently to finding an alternative strategic concept."[100]

But diagnosing the problem and solving it were entirely different matters. Throughout the Kennedy and Johnson administrations, senior U.S. leaders urged the Pentagon to produce limited war options, but were frustrated by the slow progress. In fact, when the Nixon administration took office in 1969, the president and his national security advisor Henry Kissinger were horrified at the lack of flexibility in U.S. war plans, and the enormous scale of even the smallest option.[101] Although recent histories attribute the Pentagon's resistance to changing the war plans to organizational inertia and interservice rivalries, there is another persuasive explanation. We now know that the Pentagon was working hard to escape stalemate (that is, to render the Soviet arsenal a minimal, rather than assured, deterrent force once again), by tracking Soviet submarines, by exploiting weaknesses in Soviet command and control (C2), and by enhancing U.S. offensive strike capabilities. Pentagon planners understood that executing limited war options might forestall the possibility that subsequent strikes could disarm the Soviet arsenal—since limited attacks would bring the Soviet arsenal up to full alert, as well as task some delivery systems critical for a disarming strike to those limited operations—and thus they did not want such options to be available.[102] Regardless of the explanation for the Pentagon's reluctance to overhaul U.S. strategic war plans, the changes were indeed slow.

Newer historical accounts provide a necessary corrective to the previous interpretation of strategic plans in the 1960s, but they should not obscure the fact that real changes did occur, and U.S. options did grow. The war plan that was briefed to Nixon and Kissinger in 1969—SIOP-4, which had been the plan since 1966—was less flexible than Nixon or Kissinger wanted, but it provided them with significantly more options than the plans from the era of U.S. superiority. SIOP-4 divided targets in the Soviet Union into three categories: Soviet nuclear forces and command-and-control (Alpha), nonnu-clear military forces (Bravo), and urban-industrial targets (Charlie). The war plan offered flexibility in at least four respects: it allowed the president to choose virtually any combination of Alpha, Bravo, and Charlie target sets, and exclude the others; it permitted country-specific "withholds," meaning that nuclear targets outside the Soviet Union could be spared; it allowed for capital city withholds (Moscow and Beijing), so that Soviet and Chinese leaders would survive and be available for war termination discussions; and it included "at least ninety 'sub-variations' of target withholds."[103] U.S. lead-ers still wanted more and better options, and even the smallest attack in the war plan (an Alpha-only disarming strike) was a massive operation. The plan did not offer the sort of limited options called for in a flexible response doctrine.[104] But the changes reflected progress in that direction.

Equally important, the United States and its allies possessed a second set of nuclear capabilities—NATO's regional nuclear forces—that appear to have given U.S. and allied leaders much more flexibility. By the mid-1960s, the NATO commander (a U.S. general) had control of more than one hundred nuclear weapons to be delivered by aircraft and ground forces under his command. Furthermore, NATO had by then created a range of nuclear plans for using those weapons that look very much like what "flexible response" advocates would have desired. There were nuclear plans for scenarios involv-ing small-scale Soviet attacks, which called on NATO to use very few nuclear weapons (specifically, five) in demonstration strikes to coerce the Soviets to halt operations.[105] There were also bigger nuclear options for scenarios in which the Warsaw Pact launched a major invasion of Western Europe, in-volving NATO nuclear strikes against Soviet theater nuclear forces, Soviet tactical nuclear forces, Warsaw Pact conventional forces, and logistical sites in Eastern Europe that would be essential to the Warsaw Pact conventional operations.[106]

To be clear, these NATO nuclear plans had their own limitations, which is why every U.S. administration sought better limited war options. The great-est limitation was that several NATO members—including Britain, France, and West Germany—disagreed among themselves and with the United States about how, when, and whether these limited nuclear options would be ex-ecuted.[107] But the (understandable) reluctance to execute limited nuclear war plans does not obviate the fact that the plans and capabilities were created, and thus NATO possessed real limited-war options it could have executed in a crisis or war.[108]

To take a step back, the assured retaliation school predicts that the con-cepts for defending Europe would *not* change in 1950 when the Soviet Union deployed its initial, rudimentary arsenal, nor in 1956 when the Soviets first developed the capability to strike the United States. If the assured retalia-tion school is correct, then the United States would have retained its war-winning plans throughout the 1950s, undeterred by the Soviet existential and then minimum deterrence postures. Rather, according to the assured retaliation view, U.S. plans for defending Europe—and waging war if it occurred—would be thrown into disarray when the Soviets deployed a truly survivable nuclear capability. That is exactly what happened.

The inability of U.S. leaders to truly "solve" the problem posed by an enemy that possessed an assured retaliation force is not surprising. Getting to stalemate is, indeed, a very useful security strategy. But what this chapter reveals is that the process of getting into stalemate can be long and dangerous. It was long and dangerous for the Soviet Union: their effort to create an assured retaliation force triggered a major arms race in the 1950s and 1960s. Furthermore, establishing stalemate did not end the competition. U.S. war planners worked throughout the Cold War to reestablish superiority (with a level of success that the historical literature has not yet fully absorbed). And even in the condition of stalemate, competition continued, as the United States and its allies developed nuclear capabilities to mitigate the problem that stalemate caused: how to deter or fight an enemy that possessed superior conventional forces and a secure retaliatory arsenal.

Perhaps Plans Are Just Plans?

Skeptics may wonder whether we can draw reliable conclusions about deterrence by looking at changes in war plans. After all, peacetime plans are often discarded the moment war begins. Political leaders rarely focus on the details of military matters unless war seems likely, and once they do, they often demand significant changes to those plans. Furthermore, military planners frequently present multiple plans and options to leaders. In short, according to this criticism, the existence of one war plan in some dusty archive may not reveal anything meaningful about actual leaders' prewar preferences or the option they would select if conflict erupted.[109] The Kennedy administration's efforts to revise U.S. war plans in the midst of the Berlin Crisis of 1961, discussed above, is but one example of plans being revised on the cusp of war.[110]

There are at least three reasons to believe that the changes and continuities in U.S. strategic posture from the 1950s to the 1960s shed light on how the United States would have waged World War III. First, unlike many war plans, the U.S. strategic posture received considerable and sustained attention from senior political officials. In NSC meetings and other settings, the Eisenhower and Kennedy administrations repeatedly debated U.S. plans for defending Europe, including the wisdom of relying on a nuclear-centric strategy. The "principals" themselves, rather than military planners, were ultimately the ones to resolve these debates over U.S. strategic posture.

Second, although leaders facing the outbreak of war are often able to choose from a range of contingency plans, in the 1950s the United States did not have a range of options—it had one plan.[111] The plan steadily evolved during this period, as U.S. Strategic Air Command (SAC) acquired more weapons and bombers to deliver them, and as the number of targets in the Soviet Union ballooned. Indeed, the predelegation of nuclear use authority to military leaders in both the Eisenhower and Kennedy administrations meant that in certain circumstances the SAC commander may have had the ability to use nuclear weapons on his own initiative.[112] Until the mid-1960s, the U.S. president did not have a list of attack options from which he could choose if the Soviets crossed the inner German border; instead, he had only one option.[113]

Third, although there are many examples in history of political leaders modifying peacetime plans as war approaches, one should recognize the limits of those modifications. It is possible to adjust a plan before implementing it—for example, by strengthening the attack in one sector and weakening the effort in another. But adjusting the location of a ground offensive, or adding additional ships to a naval task force, is different from radically changing plans at the last minute about how one is going to fight. The argument that we should not attribute too much significance to what were "just plans" in the 1950s suggests that during a major crisis, U.S. leaders might have fundamentally revised the U.S. military's core concepts for fighting the Soviet Union. Such critics posit that the peacetime plan—a massive strategic nuclear offensive—might have been overturned in favor of a conventional defense of Western Europe with only limited nuclear operations. But it is very difficult to see how U.S. leaders could conjure up such a replacement plan in the midst of a crisis. A change of that magnitude would require entirely different concepts of military operations, as well as a different mix of forces.

One example described above, of the rushed efforts by the White House to create alternative military options during the 1961 Berlin Crisis, illustrates both the validity and limitation of this critique. As the Kennedy administration realized that the crisis over Berlin could lead to war, they reviewed U.S. war plans and were unsatisfied with the only option they had—a single massive nuclear strike on the entire Sino-Soviet bloc. But the White House effort to create an alternative war plan did not come up with a radically different way of fighting the Soviets, such as with a conventional-only defense of Europe. Instead, they created a modified strategic nuclear offensive. The biggest change was a reduction in size of the initial U.S. nuclear strike force in order to help slip bombers through holes in the Soviet radar network, thereby increasing the odds of destroying all long-range Soviet nuclear-delivery systems on the ground. The operational concept (rapid nuclear disarming strike) and goal (victory, by destroying the Soviet arsenal) remained the same.

Leaders can adjust plans during crises, but they are limited in what they can do by the available forces, military doctrine and training, and the need for political and military coordination with allies. The United States faced such constraints in the 1950s, and thus was committed to only one option for defending Europe: launching a strategic nuclear offensive against the Soviet Union. Alternative plans and options were seriously considered only as the Soviet ability to respond with nuclear weapons grew to the point where retaliation was virtually assured.

The development and growth of the Soviet arsenal in the 1950s did not have the impact on U.S. strategic posture that either the existential or minimum deterrence schools would expect. The Soviet Union's initial deployment of nuclear weapons did not make it much safer and more secure. Instead, al-though the shifting nuclear balance may have led U.S. leaders to back away from covert actions aimed at subverting the Soviet system, it energized U.S. efforts to build weapons and war plans to rapidly destroy the vulnerable Soviet arsenal if war erupted.[114] American leaders only began to moderate U.S. strategic posture in the early 1960s, when the Soviets began to field a true assured retaliation capability, by seeking ways to avoid triggering a mutual nuclear holocaust at the outset of any war.

Two additional observations about the Cold War case are noteworthy, not least because they reinforce the findings in subsequent chapters. First, the development of a Soviet assured retaliation capability did not end the super-power nuclear arms race or competition more generally. Instead, the onset of nuclear stalemate in the 1960s led U.S. leaders to search for ways to rees-tablish nuclear superiority. Just as the United States spent the 1950s strug-gling to delay the onset of nuclear stalemate, U.S. leaders spent the rest of the Cold War trying to escape nuclear stalemate and return to the prior era of strategic superiority. For example, U.S. efforts to track, target, and destroy Soviet nuclear weapons and delivery systems, as well as to monitor and jam Soviet strategic command and control, reflected this mission. Although the details of these efforts are only slowly emerging, and those contemporary nuclear plans remain highly classified, there is substantial evidence that the United States has consistently responded to adversary nuclear develop-ments by enhancing its own counterforce capabilities in case war occurs. This reinforces the conclusion that vulnerable arsenals may bolster deter-rence in peacetime but prove dangerous in wartime. And it provides evi-dence for the argument—which is the focus of the next chapter—that even when a country establishes an assured retaliation capability, its geopolitical challenges continue because its enemies may seek to reverse the condition of stalemate.

The second important observation to flow from the Cold War history is that despite the onset of stalemate sometime in the 1960s, the United States and its NATO allies remained committed to deliberate nuclear escalation as a strategy to fight and deter a Soviet conventional attack. Even when facing the massive, survivable, and redundant nuclear capabilities that the Soviets deployed in the later decades of the Cold War, a pillar of NATO defense plans was to launch tactical and theater nuclear strikes in order to deter or coerce the Soviets to halt any invasion. The challenge of deterring conventional war with nuclear weapons under conditions of nuclear stalemate is the theme of chapter 4.

The analysis in this chapter sheds substantial light on the overarching question of this book: Why have international relations remained so competitive during the nuclear age? One answer—the subject of this chapter—is that at least during the Cold War, deploying a small, vulnerable force was not "enough" to give the Soviet Union the security they needed. A small and vulnerable nuclear force did not give the Soviet Union adequate protection from attack, which explains why the Soviets continued to strive to establish more robust capabilities. Moreover, U.S. behavior—especially the massive arms buildup in the 1950s—makes sense once one understands how highly the United States valued its ability to win a nuclear war if conflict with the Soviets erupted. The result was an intense arms race, concerns over relative gains, and competition for key allies (and the use of their territory for staging nuclear strikes).

This chapter offers one window into power politics in the nuclear age. Although nuclear weapons provide an excellent deterrent against attack, there are good reasons for new nuclear-armed states to be dissatisfied with a small and vulnerable arsenal. Such a force might induce caution during peacetime, but it might also invite attack during a crisis or war. New nuclear powers are therefore wise to build up their nuclear forces and develop truly survivable arsenals. The other side of the coin is that rivals of new nuclear states may prefer to retain war-winning options in case conflict occurs, and hence those rivals have an interest in deploying counterforce capabilities to delay the onset of assured retaliation. The understandable result of this dynamic is arms racing, balance-of-power competition, and continued hostility.

As Thomas Schelling once warned, "a fine deterrent can make a superb target."[115] The Soviet Union's initial deployments of nuclear weapons in the 1950s likely bolstered deterrence by reinforcing the desire of U.S. leaders to avoid war, but the bigger effect was to vastly increase the number of targets in Soviet territory that would have been hit by U.S. nuclear forces had World War III erupted. It was not until the early 1960s that the Soviet arsenal ceased being primarily a target and started becoming a robust deterrent. The evidence from the Cold War indicates that arsenals that lack robust, capable, and survivable delivery systems do not constitute a solid foundation for nuclear deterrence, much less offer reasons to expect a transformed, more pacific state of international politics.

Escaping Stalemate

The New Era of Counterforce

The previous chapter suggests that countries need to build robust nuclear arsenals to create stalemate with their adversaries. Since nuclear stalemate is based on the threat of retaliation, an arsenal must be able to survive an enemy first strike and still inflict unacceptable damage on the attacker. Building such an assured retaliatory force is a major challenge; as the Cold War case demonstrates, the road to stalemate can be long, dangerous, and highly competitive.

Once nuclear-armed countries establish secure second-strike forces, are those countries truly safe? Can they stop arms racing and abandon all the other kinds of costly competitive behaviors that have defined international relations? Or are there incentives that compel them to compete even after they have built survivable arsenals? To restate the central puzzle of the nuclear age, why has intense geopolitical competition continued even under conditions of stalemate?

This chapter advances a second explanation for the puzzle: stalemate is reversible. For countries to relax and abandon the geopolitical strategies of the prenuclear age—that is, to stop worrying about shifts in the balance of power, engaging in arms races, and competing for alliance partners and strategic territory—nuclear-armed countries would need to be confident that the condition of stalemate is irreversible. In reality, however, countries can escape from stalemate. Therefore, even well-armed nuclear countries continue to engage in military competition. They compete to prevent adversaries from developing effective disarming strike capabilities, and in some cases they compete to build first strike capabilities themselves.

The reversibility of stalemate explains much of the competition in the last decades of the Cold War—as well as an increase in great power competition today. During the Cold War, the Soviet development of a survivable retaliatory force in the 1960s did not end or even dampen the nuclear arms race; instead, it triggered decades of intense U.S. efforts to track and target Soviet nuclear forces, to give the United States a war-winning option if deterrence failed. Those highly-classified U.S. efforts were more effective than most analysts have appreciated, and they explain much of the U.S. and Soviet arms racing behavior until the end of the Cold War. Today new technologies are increasing the vulnerability of nuclear forces around the world—unleashing renewed competition among the major nuclear powers.

In short, nuclear weapons are the best tools of deterrence ever created, but they do not negate the incentives for countries to engage in intense geopolitical competition. The fear that adversaries might acquire disarming strike capabilities—and the opportunity to acquire those counterforce capabilities for themselves—helps explain why international competition is alive and well in the nuclear age.

This chapter focuses on the efforts of nuclear-armed countries to exploit new technologies to escape from stalemate. To explore the links between technology and stalemate, we first describe the main strategies that planners employ to ensure arsenal survivability. Next, we explore one of the major technological trends eroding survivability today—the great leap in weapons accuracy—and illustrate how improved accuracy creates new possibilities for disarming strikes. We then focus on another major current trend—dramatic improvements in remote sensing—and explain how the resulting increase in transparency threatens concealed and mobile nuclear forces. We conclude with a summary of our findings and their implications for geopolitics in the nuclear age.

Nuclear Survivability in Theory and Practice

Analysts often take the survivability of nuclear retaliatory forces for granted, perhaps with good reason. Successful "counterforce" attacks (those aimed at destroying enemy nuclear forces) appear impossible once countries deploy large and dispersed arsenals, since nuclear weapons are easy to hide and protect.[1] Some analysts argue that even moderate numbers of deployed weapons are inherently survivable.[2] According to the arguments, survivability is a one-way street: once an arsenal becomes survivable, it never goes back.

What if this confidence in the survivability of nuclear arsenals is misplaced? What if survivability is reversible? If arsenal survivability depends on the uncertain course of technological change and the efforts of adversaries to develop new technologies, states will feel compelled to arms race to ensure that their deterrent forces remain survivable in the face of adversary advances. They will worry about relative gains, because a rich and powerful adversary will have more resources to invest in technology and military forces. They will value allies, which help contribute resources and valuable territory. Moreover, states may be enticed to develop their own counterforce capabilities in order to disarm their adversaries or limit the damage those adversaries can inflict in case of war.

In short, if nuclear stalemate can be broken, one should expect countries to act as they always have when faced with military threats. They will try to exploit new technologies and strategies for destroying adversary capabilities. They will eye each other's economic power and military capabilities warily; strive for superiority over their adversaries in conventional and nuclear armaments; aim to control strategically relevant territory; seek to build and maintain alliances; and prepare for war. If survivability and stalemate are reversible, then the central puzzle of the nuclear era—continued geopolitical competition—is no longer a puzzle.

We argue not only that stalemate is reversible in principal, but also that changes in technology—rooted in the computer revolution—are making all countries' arsenals more vulnerable than they were in the past. The fear of suffering devastating retaliation will still do much to deter counterforce attacks, but countries will increasingly worry that their adversaries are trying to escape stalemate, and they will feel pressure to do the same. Deterrence will weaken as arsenals become more vulnerable. In extreme circumstances— for example, if an adversary threatens escalation (or begins to escalate) during a conventional war—the temptation to launch a disarming strike may be powerful.[3] In stark contrast to the expectations of the nuclear peace, security competition not only has endured but also will intensify as enhanced counterforce capabilities proliferate.

Military planners have employed three basic approaches to protect their countries' nuclear forces from attack: hardening, concealment, and redundancy. "Hardening" refers to the deployment of nuclear forces (such as delivery systems, warheads, and command sites) in reinforced structures that are difficult to destroy. For example, planners deploy missiles in reinforced silos designed to resist blast, heat, ground shock, and the other effects of nuclear detonations; place aircraft in hardened shelters; create protective sites for patrolling mobile missile launchers; and bury command-and-control sites, as well as the secure means used to communicate launch orders.

Nuclear planners also rely heavily on concealment, by which we mean efforts to prevent adversaries from identifying or locating one's forces (such as through the use of camouflage, decoys, and especially mobility). Concealment is the foundation of survivability for mobile delivery systems, such as ballistic missile submarines (SSBNs) or mobile missile launchers (known as transporter erector launchers, or TELs), both of which hide in vast deployment areas. Aircraft are harder to hide because they require airfields for takeoff and landing, but they too can employ concealment by dispersing to alternate airfields or remaining airborne during alerts. Even the most difficult facilities to hide, hardened missile silos and command bunkers, can be concealed using camouflage and decoys.

Finally, redundancy is used to bolster every aspect of the nuclear mission, especially force survivability. Most nuclear-armed states use multiple types of delivery systems and warheads to complicate enemy strike plans and protect against warhead design flaws. They spread their forces and warheads across multiple bases. Moreover, the most powerful nuclear-weapon states employ redundant communication networks, command-and-control arrangements, and early warning systems.

No single strategy of survivability is ideal because each entails important trade-offs. Hardening is attractive, but it comes at the price of concealment—for example, it is difficult to hide the major construction entailed in building a nuclear silo. Also, hardened sites are not mobile; once discovered, they remain so.[4] Similarly, concealment comes at the price of hardening. If mobile forces are discovered, they tend to be easy to destroy. Concealment has another significant drawback: it is a "fail deadly" strategy, meaning that if an adversary develops a way to locate one's forces, one's arsenal might go from highly survivable to completely vulnerable almost overnight. Even worse, one might not know that the nuclear balance has shifted in such a calamitous manner.[5] Some countries have adopted operating doctrines that attempt to capitalize on the advantages of both hardening and concealment; for example, China today appears to be planning to distribute its mobile missiles in a nuclear crisis from its peacetime garrisons to remote protective sites.[6] Such approaches capture the benefits of both strategies, but they also pay the costs. For example, China's strategy leaves its forces vulnerable if an attacker has identified its dispersal sites or detects mobile missiles in transit.[7]

Major technological trends are directly undermining these strategies of survivability. Leaps in weapons accuracy threaten nuclear forces that rely on hardening, while an unfolding revolution in remote sensing threatens nuclear forces that depend on concealment. (Another major change since the end of the Cold War, far smaller nuclear arsenals among potential adversaries, weakens the third strategy of survivability, redundancy.)[8] The consequences of pinpoint accuracy and new sensing technologies are numerous, synergistic, and in some cases nonintuitive. Taken together, these developments are making the task of securing nuclear arsenals against attack much more challenging. Developing survivable forces is not impossible, but a new age of vulnerability has begun.

To be clear, nuclear arsenals around the world are not becoming equally vulnerable to attack. Countries that have considerable resources can buck these trends and keep their forces survivable, albeit with considerable cost and effort. Other countries, however—especially those facing wealthy, technologically advanced adversaries—will find it increasingly difficult to secure their arsenals, as guidance systems, sensors, data processing, communication, artificial intelligence, and a host of other products of the computer revolution continue to improve.[9]

One might think that only weak countries need to worry about an adversary "escaping stalemate"; surely, powerful countries have the resources to thwart any adversary's efforts to attain nuclear superiority. But history is not reassuring. In the Cold War, once the Soviet Union had built robust nuclear retaliatory forces, many observers assumed that stalemate could not be undermined and that U.S. leaders would recognize and respect the "objective" reality that mutual assured destruction was a permanent fact. Instead, American officials constantly sought counterforce weapons and technologies to gain a disarming first-strike or significant damage-limitation capability—such as more accurate missiles, missiles with multiple independently targetable reentry vehicles (MIRV), sensors for hunting mobile missiles at sea and on land, and a variety of weapons and innovations designed to undermine Soviet command-and-control and early warning systems.[10] By the end of the Cold War, Soviet leaders had little faith in their own retaliatory capabilities.[11] In the post–Cold War world, both Russia and China—America's two biggest nuclear competitors—have had good reason, at times, to fear for the survivability of their arsenals.[12]

Counterforce in the Age of Accuracy

For most of the nuclear age, neither bombers nor ballistic missiles could deliver weapons accurately enough to reliably destroy hardened targets. Too many variables affected the impact point of a bomb—such as the aircraft's speed and altitude; the air defense environment; and atmospheric conditions including wind, temperature, and humidity—for even highly skilled crews to deliver bombs precisely.[13] Long-range ballistic missiles were even less accurate. Although their initial deployment conjured fears of "bolt-from-the-blue" disarming strikes, throughout the 1970s long-range missiles were not accurate enough to destroy fields of hardened silos.[14]

Technological improvements chipped away at the sources of inaccuracy, however. Leaps in navigation and guidance, including advanced inertial sensors with stellar updates, improved the ability of missiles to precisely determine their positions in flight and guide themselves, as needed, back onto course. Other breakthroughs allowed mobile delivery systems, such as submarines and mobile land-based launchers, to accurately determine their own positions prior to launch, greatly improving their accuracy.[15] As a result of these innovations, new missiles emerged in the mid-1980s with far better accuracy than their predecessors, rendering hardened targets vulnerable as never before. For bombers, onboard computers now continuously measure the variables that previously confounded bombardiers. Data on aircraft speed and location are uploaded from the aircraft into the computers of bombs and cruise missiles, which in turn automatically plot a flight path from the release location to the target. The weapons adjust their trajectory as they fly to remain on course.[16] As a result, bombs and missiles can achieve levels of accuracy unimaginable at the start of the nuclear age.

The leap in munitions accuracy has been showcased repeatedly during conventional wars; videos of missiles and bombs guiding themselves directly to designated targets now appear mundane. Although the effects of the accuracy revolution on nuclear-delivery systems are equally dramatic, they have received far less attention, despite huge implications for the survivability of hardened targets.

IMPROVED MISSILE ACCURACY

Figure 3.1 illustrates one consequence of the accuracy revolution, as applied to nuclear forces, by comparing the effectiveness of U.S. ballistic missiles in 1985 to those in the current U.S. arsenal.[17] We use formulas that have been employed by nuclear analysts for decades to estimate the effectiveness of missile strikes against a typical hardened silo.[18] The figure distinguishes three potential outcomes of a missile strike: hit, miss, and fail. "Hit" means that the warhead detonates within the lethal radius (LR) of the aimpoint, thus destroying the target. "Miss" means that the warhead detonates outside the LR, leaving the target undamaged. "Fail" means that some element of the attacking missile system malfunctioned, leaving the target undamaged.

Figure 3.1 shows that the accuracy improvements of the past three decades have led to substantial leaps in counterforce capabilities. In 1985 a U.S. intercontinental ballistic missile (ICBM) had only about a 54 percent chance of destroying a missile silo hardened to withstand 3,000 pounds per square inch (psi) overpressure. In 2019 that figure exceeds 74 percent. The improvement in submarine-launched weapons is starker: from 9 percent to 80 percent (using the larger-yield W88 warhead). Figure 3.1 also suggests, however, that despite vast improvements in missile accuracy, the weapons still are not effective enough to be employed individually against hardened targets. Even modern ballistic missiles are expected to miss or fail 20 to 30 percent of the time. The simple solution to that problem, striking each target multiple times, has never been a feasible option because of the problem of fratricide—that is, the danger that incoming weapons might destroy or deflect each other.[19] The accuracy revolution, however, also offers a solution to the fratricide problem, opening the door to assigning multiple warheads against a single target, and thus paving the way to disarming counterforce strikes.

THE FADING PROBLEM OF FRATRICIDE

One type of fratricide occurs when the prompt effects of nuclear detonations—radiation, heat, and overpressure—destroy or deflect nearby warheads. To protect those warheads, targeters must separate the incoming weapons by at least three to five seconds.[20] A second source of fratricide

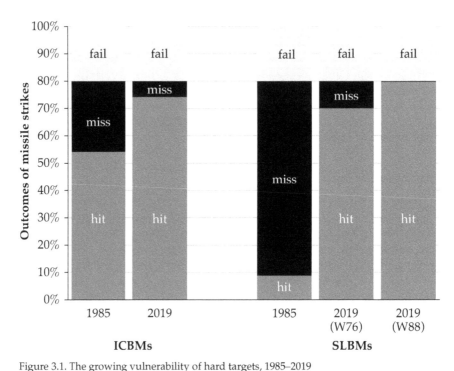

Figure 3.1. The growing vulnerability of hard targets, 1985–2019

Note: The calculations assume targets hardened to withstand 3,000 pounds per square inch (psi). Data for 1985 are based on the most capable U.S. land-based intercontinental ballistic missile (ICBM) and submarine-launched ballistic missile (SLBM) at the time: the Minuteman III ICBM armed with a W78 warhead and the Trident I C-4 SLBM armed with a W76 warhead. The 2019 ICBM data are based on the same Minuteman III/W78, with an improved guidance system. The 2019 SLBM data show both contemporary configurations of the Trident II D-5 missile: one version armed with the W76 and the other with higher-yield W88 warheads.

is harder to overcome. Destroying hard targets typically requires low-altitude detonations (so-called groundbursts), which vaporize material on the ground. When the debris begins to cool, six to eight seconds after the detonation, it solidifies and forms a dust cloud that envelops the target. Even small dust particles can be lethal to incoming warheads speeding through the cloud to the target. Particles in the debris cloud take approximately twenty minutes to settle back to ground.[21]

For decades, these two sources of fratricide, acting together, posed a major problem for nuclear planners.[22] Multiple warheads could be aimed at a single target if they were separated by at least three to five seconds (to avoid interfering with each other); yet, all inbound warheads had to arrive within six to eight seconds of the first (before the dust cloud formed). As a result, assigning more than two weapons to each target would produce only marginal gains; if the first one resulted in a miss, the target would likely be shielded when the third or fourth warhead arrived.[23]

Improvements in accuracy, however, have greatly mitigated the problem of fratricide. As figure 3.1 shows, the number of misses—the main culprit of fratricide—is falling. To be clear, some weapons will still fail; that is, they will be prevented from destroying their targets because of malfunctioning missile boosters, faulty guidance systems, or defective warheads. Those kinds of failures, however, do not generally cause fratricide, because the warheads do not detonate near the target. Only those that miss—that is, those that travel to the target area and detonate outside the LR—will create a dust cloud that shields the target from other incoming weapons. In short, leaps in accuracy are essentially reducing the set of three outcomes (hit, fail, or miss) to just two: hit or fail. The "miss" category, the key cause of fratricide, has virtually disappeared.[24]

THE CUMULATIVE CONSEQUENCES FOR COUNTERFORCE

The end of fratricide is just one development that has helped negate hardening and increased the vulnerability of nuclear arsenals. The computer revolution has led to other improvements that, taken together, significantly increase counterforce capabilities.

First, improved accuracy has transformed the role of ballistic missile submarines, turning these instruments of retaliation against population centers into potent counterforce weapons. Recall (from figure 3.1 above) that a 1985 submarine-launched ballistic missile (SLBM) had only a 9 percent chance of destroying a hardened target. This meant that although ballistic missile submarines could destroy "soft" targets (e.g., cities), they could not destroy the hardened sites that would be a key focus of a disarming attack. Increased SLBM accuracy has added hundreds of SLBM warheads to the counterforce arsenal; it has also unlocked other advantages that submarines possess over land-based missiles. For example, submarines have flexibility in firing location, allowing them to strike targets that are out of range of ICBMs or that are deployed in locations that ICBMs cannot hit.[25] Submarines also permit strikes from close range, reducing an adversary's response time. And because submarines can fire from unpredictable locations, SLBM launches are more difficult to detect than ICBM attacks, further reducing adversary response time before impact.

Second, upgraded fuses are making ballistic missiles even more capable than figure 3.1 reports. The new "burst-height compensating" fusing system, now deployed on all U.S. SLBM reentry vehicles, uses an altimeter to measure the difference between the actual and expected trajectory of the reentry vehicle, and then compensate for inaccuracies by adjusting the warhead's height of burst. Specifically, if the altimeter reveals that the warhead is off track and will detonate "short" of the target, the fusing system lowers the height of burst, allowing the weapon to travel farther (hence, closer to the aimpoint) before detonation. Alternatively, if the reentry vehicle is going to detonate beyond the target, the height of burst is automatically adjusted upward to allow the weapon to detonate before it travels too far. Without this technology, as figure 3.1 shows, the lower-yield W76 warheads are much less effective against hardened targets than their higher-yield cousins, the W88s. The improved fuse cuts the effectiveness gap roughly in half, making the hundreds of W76s in the U.S. arsenal potent counterforce weapons for the first time. The consequences of the fuse upgrades are, therefore, profound, essentially tripling the size of the U.S. submarine-based arsenal against hard targets.[26] More broadly, the technology at the core of compensating fuses is available to any state capable of building modern multistage ballistic missiles.[27]

A third key improvement, rapid missile reprogramming, increases the effectiveness of ballistic missiles by reducing the consequence of malfunctions. As figure 3.1 illustrates, when accuracy increases, missile reliability becomes the main hurdle to attacks on hardened targets. For decades, analysts have recognized a solution to this problem: if missile failures can be detected, the targets assigned to the malfunctioning missiles can be rapidly reassigned to other missiles held in reserve.[28] The capability to rapidly retarget missiles was installed at U.S. ICBM launch control centers in the 1990s and on U.S. submarines in the early 2000s, and both systems have since been upgraded.[29] We do not know if the United States has adopted war plans that fully exploit rapid reprogramming to minimize the effects of missile failures.[30] Nevertheless, such a targeting approach is within the technical capabilities of the United States and other major nuclear powers and may already be incorporated into war plans.[31]

Table 3.1 illustrates the consequences of these improvements against two hypothetical target sets: one hundred moderately hard mobile missile shelters and two hundred hardened missile silos.[32] Row 1 shows the approximate counterforce capabilities of a 1985-era U.S. Minuteman III ICBM strike; a two-on-one attack would have been expected to leave eight mobile missile shelters intact. A strike against two hundred hardened silos would fare worse, with forty-two targets expected to survive.

The remaining rows in table 3.1 highlight the implications of the changes that have occurred from 1985 to 2019. Row 2 illustrates the impact of improved Minuteman III guidance, which reportedly reduced circular error probable (CEP) from 183 to 120 meters. Row 3 employs the most capable missile and warhead combination in the current U.S. arsenal: the Trident II armed with a high-yield W88 warhead. As the results in both rows show, upgraded missiles perform better than their predecessor, but not well enough to conduct effective disarming strikes against large target sets.

Rows 4 to 7 demonstrate how the various improvements in missile technology have combined to create transformative counterforce capabilities. In row 4, we use a more realistic figure for missile system reliability. Although 80 percent missile reliability is traditionally used as a baseline, much evidence

Table 3.1. The demise of hard target survivability

	Description	Weapon	Weapon characteristics			Attack	100 mobile missile shelters		200 hardened missile silos	
			Yield (kt)	CEP (m)	Reliability		p(K)	Survives	p(K)	Survives
1	Baseline 1985	Minuteman W78	335	183	0.8	2:1	0.92	8	0.79	42
2	Baseline 2019	Minuteman W78	335	120	0.8	2:1	0.96	4	0.93	13
3		Trident II W88	455	90	0.8	2:1	0.96	4	0.96	8
4	Realistic reliability	Trident II W88	455	90	0.9	2:1	0.99	1	0.99	2
5	Reprogramming					2:1R	0.99+	0	0.99+	0
6	Many on 1					3:1	0.99+	0	0.99+	0
7	Compensating fuse	Trident II W76	100	90	0.9	2:1R	0.99+	0	0.99	1

Note: Results are displayed for 100 mobile missile shelters hardened to withstand up to 1,000 pounds per square inch (psi) or 200 missile silos hardened to 3,000 psi. Yield is in kilotons and circular error probable (CEP) is in meters. The category "Attack" indicates the number of warheads assigned to each target; "R" (for reprogramming) means that the attacker uses reserve missiles to replace boost phase malfunctions. The columns titled "p(K)" list the probability that each individual target is destroyed, and "Survives" is the expected number of targets surviving the attack. The designation of "0.99+" under p(K) indicates 99.9 percent or greater chance of destroying each individual target. Lightly shaded cells indicate successful disarming attacks; darker cells indicate very successful strikes. Note that a single surviving mobile missile shelter does not necessarily imply that a mobile missile survived, whereas a surviving silo suggests a surviving missile.

suggests that the actual reliability of modern missiles exceeds 90 percent.[33] Row 4 shows attack outcomes for a Trident II/W88 with 90 percent reliability. Row 5 shows the consequences if the United States can reprogram its missiles to replace boost-phase failures. As row 5 reveals, a two-on-one attack with reprogramming would be expected to destroy every hardened shelter or silo. Row 6 omits reprogramming, but it demonstrates the impact of the decline in fratricide by adding a third warhead to each target, resulting again in the destruction of either target set.

Row 7 illustrates the impact of compensating fuses. This row, unlike the others, employs the lower-yield warhead on the Trident II missiles (the W76). With the compensating fuse, a two-on-one attack using W76s would be expected to destroy all the mobile missile shelters and all but one of the hardened silos. (An attack that mixed W88s and W76s could destroy the entire hardened silo force.)

The results in table 3.1 are simply the output of a model. In the real world, the effectiveness of any strike would depend on many factors not modeled here, including the skill of the attacking forces, the accuracy of target intelligence, the ability of the targeted country to detect an inbound strike and "launch on warning," and other factors that depend on the political and strategic context. As a result, these calculations tell us less about the precise vulnerability of a given arsenal at a given time—though one can reach arresting conclusions based on the evidence—and more about trends in how technology is undermining survivability.[34]

One crucial consequence of the accuracy revolution is not captured in the above results. Yet, its impact on the vulnerability of nuclear arsenals may be just as profound. The accuracy revolution has rendered low-casualty counterforce attacks plausible for the first time.

THE DAWN OF LOW-CASUALTY COUNTERFORCE

In nuclear deterrence theory, the primary factor preventing nuclear attack is the attacker's fear of retaliation. In reality, however, additional sources of inhibition exist, including the terrible civilian consequences of an attempted counterforce strike. If a leader contemplating a disarming strike knows that such an attack will inflict massive casualties on the enemy, that leader will also understand that the failure to disarm the enemy will provoke a massive punitive response, foreclosing the possibility of a limited nuclear exchange. Furthermore, if a disarming strike would cause enormous civilian casualties in the target country, but also possibly in allied and neutral neighboring countries, leaders who value human life or the fate of allies would contemplate such an attack in only the direst circumstances. The link between civilian casualties and nuclear inhibition explains why many arms control advocates oppose the development of less destructive nuclear weapons; they worry that such weapons are more "usable."[35]

Counterforce was tantamount to mass casualties throughout the nuclear age, but the accuracy revolution is severing that link. In the past, the main impediment to low-casualty nuclear counterforce strikes has been radioactive fallout. Targeters would have had to rely on groundbursts to maximize destructive effects against hardened facilities such as silos and storage sites. Detonations close to the ground have a major drawback, however: debris is sucked up into the fireball, where it mixes with radioactive material, spreading radiation wherever it settles. Although the other effects of nuclear detonations (e.g., blast and fire) can have large-scale consequences for civilians, in many circumstances those effects can be minimized.[36] If a strike produces fallout, however, the consequences are potentially vast and difficult to predict.[37]

In theory, it has always been possible to employ nuclear weapons without creating much fallout. If weapons are detonated at high altitude (above the "fallout threshold"), very little debris from the ground will be drawn up into the fireball, greatly reducing fallout.[38] In practice, however, this targeting strategy has never been feasible against hardened sites. The problem is that any high-yield weapon that detonates low enough to destroy a hardened target will also be low enough to create fallout. Low-yield weapons could do the job and remain above the fallout threshold, but that has always been impractical because low-yield weapons would need to be delivered with great precision to destroy hardened sites, which was previously impossible.[39]

Figure 3.2 illustrates why high-yield strikes against hard targets inevitably create fallout, and it highlights the potential low-yield solution to the fallout problem. The vertical axis reflects weapon yield, and the horizontal axis depicts the hardness of potential targets—with the approximate values for mobile missile shelters and missile silos indicated. The solid black line shows the maximum yield of a weapon that can generate enough overpressure to destroy a target from above the fallout threshold. For example, figure 3.2 shows that for a 3,000 psi target, the highest-yield weapon that can destroy it while remaining above the fallout threshold is 0.35 kilotons. A larger-yield weapon will necessarily cause fallout if it destroys the target. A low-fallout strike against a 1,000 psi mobile missile shelter would require a weapon with 50 kilotons yield, or less. In short, low-fatality nuclear counterforce is possible, but it requires low-yield weapons, and hence very accurate delivery.

The accuracy of nuclear-delivery systems is now to the point that low-casualty disarming strikes are possible. For example, a 0.3 kiloton bomb would require a CEP of 10 to 15 meters to be highly effective against hard targets;[40] that level of accuracy is likely within the reach of the new guided B61-12, which is slated to replace all nuclear gravity bombs in the U.S. arsenal.[41] Similarly, a 5-kiloton missile warhead, which may approximate the yield of the fission primary on many existing ballistic missiles, could destroy a hardened target if its CEP was approximately 50 meters.[42] That level of

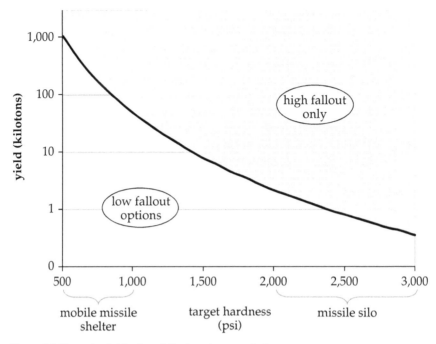

Figure 3.2. The potential for low-fallout nuclear counterforce

Note: "Target hardness" (the horizontal axis) is measured in pounds per square inch (psi), with a typical range of psi for hardened mobile missile shelters and missile silos noted. "Yield" (the vertical axis) is measured in kilotons and plotted on a logarithmic scale. The curve depicts the maximum weapon yield that can destroy a given target from above the fallout threshold. Any weapon yield/target hardness combination above the line that is effective enough to destroy the target will necessarily result in fallout. Points below the line indicate that weapons can be detonated at an altitude that will destroy the target yet produce little or no fallout.

accuracy was implausible for most of the Cold War, yet it is within reach of many countries today.[43]

By detonating weapons above the fallout threshold, targeters can greatly reduce fallout relative to groundbursts. But how significant are these reductions? How many fewer deaths would be caused in comparison with ground-burst strikes?

To compare the fallout and potential fatalities from high-yield and low-yield counterforce operations, we used unclassified U.S. Defense Department software called Hazard Prediction and Assessment Capability (HPAC).[44] We modeled two different counterforce strikes, one using a "traditional" high-yield approach and one employing low-yield airbursts, against five hardened targets in North Korea (e.g., nuclear storage sites or hardened mobile missile shelters). Because there is no available unclassified information about the location of North Korea's nuclear storage sites, we modeled strikes against notional locations around the nation's periphery.

The results of the two strikes, illustrated in figure 3.3, are starkly different. The traditional approach (on the left side) would likely destroy the targets, but at a terrible price: millions of fatalities across the Korean Peninsula. The low-yield option, by contrast, would produce vastly fewer deaths. As long as the targets were located outside North Korean cities, the number of Korean fatalities from a low-yield strike would be comparable to the human losses from conventional operations. In fact, the fallout contours that are visible in figure 3.3 for the low-yield scenario correspond to annual radiation levels deemed acceptable by the U.S. Occupational Safety and Health Administration.

The precise results of the HPAC simulation should be treated with skepticism, as wind speed and direction change constantly, altering fallout patterns. The amount of fallout generated in the low-yield scenario is so low, however, that the results of figure 3.3 are robust regardless of which way the wind blows; few people located away from the actual targets would be killed. The point of figure 3.3 is not to predict the outcome of a counterforce strike on North Korea but to reveal the relationship between accuracy and fallout. When accuracy was poor, the only approach to nuclear counterforce was high-yield strikes, which would create catastrophic results such as the

High-yield option: 10 W88 warheads	Low-yield option: 20 B61 bombs

Results:
- All five targets destroyed
- **2-3 million dead** (in North / South Korea)

Results:
- All five targets destroyed
- **Fewer than 100 dead** (at target sites)

Figure 3.3. Low-fallout counterforce option against North Korea

Note: The figure illustrates the potential fallout consequences of two alternative counterforce strikes against five notional North Korean hardened nuclear sites. In both strike options each target is destroyed with greater than 95 percent probability. The high-yield attack employs 10 W-88 warheads (455-kiloton yield), with two warheads against each target. Because high-yield weapons cannot destroy hardened sites from above the fallout threshold, the W-88s are ground bursts. The low-yield attack uses 20 B-61 bombs (0.3-kiloton yield), set to detonate at an altitude that maximizes effectiveness while minimizing fallout. The fallout patterns and casualty figures were generated using unclassified U.S. Defense Department software, called Hazard Prediction and Assessment Capability.

one depicted above. The accuracy revolution has changed the calculus, however; low-fatality nuclear strikes are now possible.[45]

The accuracy revolution is ongoing. As accuracy continues to improve, the effectiveness of conventional attacks on hard targets will continue to increase. Today, low-yield nuclear weapons can destroy targets that once required very large-yield detonations. In the future, many of those targets will be vulnerable to conventional attacks.

In sum, from the start of the nuclear age to the present, force planners have relied on hardening as a key strategy for ensuring the survivability of their arsenals. That strategy made sense, and until recently it ensured that disarming strikes would not only fail but also kill millions of civilians in the process. Technology never stands still, however, and the technical foundations of deterrence, particularly for the strategy of hardening, have been greatly undermined by leaps in accuracy.

Counterforce in the Age of Transparency

While advances in accuracy are negating hardening as a strategy for protecting nuclear forces, improvements in remote sensing are undermining the other main approach: concealment. Finding concealed forces, particularly mobile ones, remains a major challenge. Trends in technology, however, are eroding the security that mobility once provided. In the ongoing competition between "hiders" and "seekers" waged by ballistic missile submarines, mobile land-based missiles, and the forces that seek to track them, the hider's job is growing more difficult than ever before.

Five trends are ushering in an age of unprecedented transparency.[46] First, sensor platforms have become more diverse. The mainstays of Cold War technical intelligence—satellites, submarines, and piloted aircraft—continue to play a vital role, and they are being supplemented by new platforms. For example, remotely piloted aircraft and underwater drones now gather intelligence during peacetime and war. Autonomous sensors, hidden on the ground or tethered to the seabed, monitor adversary facilities, forces, and operations. Additionally, the past two decades have witnessed the development of a new "virtual" sensing platform: cyberspying.[47]

Second, sensors are collecting a widening array of signals for analysis using a growing list of techniques. Early Cold War strategic intelligence relied heavily on photoreconnaissance, underwater acoustics, and the collection of adversary communications, all of which remain important. Now, modern sensors gather data from across the entire electromagnetic spectrum; they employ seismic and acoustic sensors in tandem; and they emit radar at various frequencies depending on their purpose—for example, to maximize resolution or to penetrate foliage. Modern remote sensing exploits an increasing number of analytic techniques, including spectroscopy to identify the vapors leaking from faraway facilities, interferometry to discover underground structures, and signals-processing techniques (such as those underpinning synthetic aperture radars) that allow radars to perform better than their antenna size would seem to permit.[48]

Third, remote-sensing platforms increasingly provide persistent observation. At the beginning of the Cold War, strategic intelligence was hobbled by sensors that collected snapshots rather than streams of data. Spy planes sprinted past targets, and satellites passed overhead and then disappeared over the horizon. Over time those sensors were supplemented with platforms that remained in place and soaked up data, such as signals-intelligence antennas, undersea hydrophones, and geostationary satellites. The trend toward persistence is continuing. Today, remotely piloted vehicles can loiter near enemy targets and autonomous sensors can monitor critical road junctures for months or years. Persistent observation is essential if the goal is not merely to count enemy weapons but also to track their movement.

The fourth factor in the ongoing remote sensing revolution is the steady improvement in sensor resolution. In every field that employs remote-sensing technology, including medicine, geology, and astronomy, improved sensors and advanced data processing are permitting more accurate measures and fainter signals to be discerned from background noise. The leap in satellite image resolution is but one example. The first U.S. reconnaissance satellite (Corona) could detect objects as small as 25 feet wide; today, commercial satellites (e.g., DigitalGlobe's WorldView-3 and WorldView-4) can collect images with 1-foot resolution and U.S. spy satellites are reportedly capable of resolutions of less than 4 inches.[49] Advances in resolution are not merely transforming optical remote-sensing systems; they are extending what can be seen by infrared sensors, advanced radars, interferometers and spectrographs, and many other sensors.

The fifth key trend is the huge increase in data transmission speed. During the first decades of the Cold War, it took days or longer to transmit information from sensors to analysts. At least a full day passed before the photographs snapped by U-2 aircraft were developed and analyzed. Early satellites were slower: the satellite had to finish its roll of film and then eject the canister, which would be caught midair and flown to a facility for development and analysis; all told, it might take weeks before images collected at the beginning of a satellite mission arrived at an analyst's desk. Today, by contrast, intelligence gathered by aircraft, satellites, and drones can be transmitted in nearly real time. The data can be transmitted to intelligence analysts, to political leaders, and in some cases directly to military commanders conducting operations.

None of these technological trends alone is transformative. Taken together, however, they are creating a degree of transparency that was unimaginable even two decades ago. These new remote-sensing technologies are not proliferating around the world evenly; the United States, for example, seems to have exploited new sensing technologies more intensively than other countries. Many countries are developing expertise in advanced sensing, however. The sensing revolution is a global phenomenon with implications for the survivability of all countries' nuclear arsenals.

Remote-sensing technologies have improved greatly, but the crucial question is whether these advances have meaningfully increased the vulnerability of the two most elusive types of nuclear-delivery systems: SSBNs and mobile land-based missiles. If the ability to track submarines at sea or mobile missiles on patrol remains out of reach, then the counterforce improvements we identify are less significant, at least for now. In fact, SSBNs have never been as invulnerable as analysts typically assume, and advances in remote sensing appear to be reducing the survivability of both submarines and mobile missiles.

REMOTE SENSING AND TRACKING SUBMARINES

During the Cold War, the competition between submariners and antisubmarine warfare operators was shrouded in secrecy, but that history is finally being revealed. We now know that the United States was able to locate and even track Soviet SSBNs during extended periods of the Cold War.[50]

The core of U.S. ASW efforts against the Soviet Union consisted of a series of breakthroughs in passive sonar and signals processing, as well as doctrine and tactics to exploit those advances. Starting in the 1950s, the United States deployed an expanding network of underwater hydrophones designed to identify and locate adversary submarines. Data from the hydrophones were transmitted across undersea cables to onshore computing facilities, where powerful computers discerned the faint sounds of submarines from ocean noise. Potential targets were then passed along to aircraft and attack submarines (SSNs) for further location and tracking. U.S. capabilities to track Soviet submarines leapt forward in the late 1960s and 1970s as the United States deployed new attack submarines that were equipped with powerful sonars in their bows, towed sonar arrays, and improved on-ship computing power, giving U.S. SSNs an unprecedented combination of acoustic-gathering and data-processing capabilities.[51]

The competition between Soviet SSBNs and the pack of U.S. submarines, aircraft, and surface ships hunting them varied throughout the Cold War. There were periods in which U.S. forces were winning, trailing every Soviet SSBN on patrol, from port to sea and back. Later, after discovering their vulnerability, the Russians pulled their forces into protected "bastions" near Soviet territory to counter the U.S. ASW strategy. The United States did not give up, and worked until the end of the Cold War (and beyond) to regain undersea superiority.

The duration of U.S. Cold War ASW superiority cannot be accurately assessed today because of enduring classification constraints. But for periods of the superpower competition, U.S. naval leaders believed they had the ASW problem well in hand. As the former commander of the U.S. Pacific Fleet in the mid-1980s remarked, the United States was able to "identify by hull number the identity of Soviet subs . . . and know exactly where they were. In port or at sea. If they were at sea, N3 [director for operations] had an SSN [on them]."[52]

There are three key lessons to draw from the Cold War ASW competition. First, previous advances in remote sensing greatly increased the vulnerability of deployed submarines.[53] Second, escaping vulnerability was no easy task. In the late 1960s, the Soviet Union learned that its submarines were vulnerable. But despite Moscow's significant economic and technological resources, it took the Soviet navy more than a decade to develop good countermeasures against the evolving U.S. ASW capabilities.[54]

Third, and most broadly, the Cold War ASW competition demonstrates that the deployment of ballistic missile submarines neither ended the Cold War nuclear competition nor negated hopes on either side of attaining military superiority. The United States led the undersea competition for a time because of its superior technology and tactics; the Soviet Union developed countermeasures because it discovered its vulnerabilities and innovated. This back-and-forth struggle between hiders and seekers looks more like a traditional struggle for naval superiority than the common depiction of invulnerable submarines.

Today's technological advances in remote sensing, data processing, and communication are occurring at a rapid pace, and their ultimate impact on the submarine competition is too uncertain to predict with confidence (especially given the tight controls over information on contemporary ASW capabilities). Yet, there are good reasons to suspect that the dramatic leaps in remote sensing are increasing the transparency of the seas and undermining the ability of submarines to remain concealed. Some of the promising new antisubmarine technologies include improved acoustic sensors (including low-frequency active sonars and new networks of seabed passive sonars); nonacoustic techniques (using lasers, magnetometers, and satellites); sophisticated "big data" analysis (which exploits leaps in processor speed to sift vast quantities of sensor data); and a variety of unmanned and autonomous underwater vehicles (including those designed to find and shadow adversary submarines for weeks or months).[55]

The point is not that submarines are now easy to locate or that the challenges of ASW have been solved. Locating technologically sophisticated, well-operated submarines in vast ocean sanctuaries remains a substantial challenge. Rather, the key point is that even the nuclear-delivery system sometimes touted as the most survivable has been vulnerable in the past and appears to be increasingly vulnerable today, as ASW efforts and capabilities rapidly improve.

What about mobile land-based missiles? Are breakthroughs in sensing technology increasing their vulnerability as well?

We illustrate the impact of two advanced surveillance systems, radar satellites and remotely piloted aircraft, on the survivability of mobile land-based nuclear missiles. The effectiveness of sensing systems depends on the characteristics of the target country—for example, its size, location, topography, and defenses. As such, their impact is difficult to quantify in the abstract. Instead, we explore the potential contributions of two advanced sensor systems in a hypothetical case: a U.S.-led operation to destroy a small arsenal of North Korean nuclear-tipped mobile missiles.[56] We assume that North Korea's TELs are postured like most other countries' mobile missiles—they remain in hardened shelters during peacetime, with plans to disperse a portion of the force during a conflict.[57]

U.S. and allied strategic intelligence would have at least three critical roles in support of a military operation against North Korean TELs. The first, a peacetime mission called *intelligence preparation of the battlefield* (IPB), involves locating North Korea's nuclear and missile facilities, identifying the patrol routes utilized by its missile forces, learning its organizational routines, and mapping its command and communication network. The other two roles are principally wartime missions. *Detection* refers to sensing possible targets; it typically involves sensors that can monitor large areas but have inadequate resolution for positive identification or targeting. *Identification* is the next step; once a possible target is detected, other platforms (often with higher-resolution sensors) are cued to identify and precisely locate the target.[58]

A core element of U.S. surveillance capabilities is the constellation of satellites that use synthetic aperture radar (SAR) to image targets on the ground. Satellites provide a unique capability to peer deep into adversary territory, and they are especially useful for missions that require frequent observations of critical facilities. Whereas manned aircraft and unmanned aerial vehicles (UAVs) are often restricted from adversary airspace, satellites routinely overfly adversary territory. Moreover, unlike satellites with optical or infrared sensors, radar satellites can image targets at night and through cloudy weather.

Until recently, the type of radar employed on most satellites—SAR—could not image moving targets, which limited the effectiveness of space-based sensors for hunting mobile missiles.[59] But over the past two decades, engineers have developed data-processing techniques that enable SAR systems to detect moving targets and determine their speed and direction of travel.[60] Although the precise capabilities of intelligence satellites are classified, civilian radar satellites can scan approximately 150-kilometer-wide swaths along the ground as they pass overhead, with sufficient resolution to detect truck-sized moving vehicles.[61] New techniques are being developed that may soon double or triple the width of the swath that can be scanned on each pass.[62]

SAR-equipped satellites, now able to find mobile targets, have the potential to transform counter-TEL operations. If U.S. intelligence satellites can detect moving vehicles within a 150-kilometer-wide swath along the ground—a conservative assumption, given that a civilian satellite launched nearly a decade ago can do so—then centering the radar on a mobile missile garrison would put all the roads within two hours' drive time of that facility within the radar's swath width.[63] A single satellite can generate up to twelve 150-by-150-kilometer swaths in a single pass over North Korea, enough to image all the country's roads more than once—and key sections multiple times—before passing over the horizon.[64]

Although SAR satellites have become powerful tools for hunting TELs, they have important limitations. Surveillance satellites provide only intermittent coverage of key areas, passing overhead and then descending over the horizon. Thus, even if a constellation of satellites could image the entire road network in North Korea every hour, North Korean TELs might be able to disperse without being observed, by seeking shelter whenever a satellite approaches. Furthermore, if many of North Korea's critical facilities are located in its mountainous regions, topography may block the satellite's line of sight, which would allow targets within the swath to be hidden from the radar. The potential effectiveness of radar satellites for hunting mobile missiles, therefore, depends on two key factors: the time interval between satellite passes and the percentage of road network that is observable in a given pass.[65]

To assess the effectiveness of SAR satellites for hunting North Korean mobile missiles, we conducted an analysis with three key steps. First, we created a digital map of North Korea's roads. Second, we used geospatial analysis software to determine the visible portion of those roads as a function of a satellite's position. Third, we calculated the frequency with which satellites pass within an orbital band that provides high levels of visibility of the road network.[66]

Our analysis of satellite orbits and North Korean topography reveals that satellites passing through an orbital band that stretches as far as a 1,500-kilometer lateral distance from the Korean Peninsula can view, on average, 90 percent of North Korean roads. A typical radar satellite (which operates in low earth orbit) will pass through such a band—what we call a "usable pass"—roughly 2.5 times per day. The total number of usable passes per day thus depends on the number of SAR satellites in orbit that are available for hunting mobile missiles. The number of available satellites, in turn, depends on the willingness of the United States and its close allies to share sensitive satellite imagery, the technical preparations that have been undertaken to facilitate that sharing, and the precise technical capabilities of the satellites. Table 3.2 shows the implications of different assumptions about those

Table 3.2. Synthetic aperture radar (SAR) satellites and frequency of usable passes

	Number of SAR satellites	Available satellites	Usable passes per day	Minutes between usable passes
United States	6	6	15	91
Other NATO	9	15	37	34
Japan	3	18	44	27
Israel	2	20	50	24

Note: The column "Number of SAR satellites" counts major military and intelligence SAR satellites operated by the United States and key allies. The other columns are cumulative and show how satellite coverage grows when one adds the assets of various U.S. partners. "Usable passes per day" indicates the daily satellite over flights that pass through an orbital band that offers, on average, 90 percent coverage of North Korean roads.

uncertainties. If the United States and key allies create the political and technical arrangements to share satellite data during wartime, North Korean TEL commanders would have little time between passes—specifically, as few as twenty-four minutes.[67]

Twenty-four minutes between satellite passes could provide enough time for TELs or other vehicles to move quickly from shelter to shelter, but that strategy requires precise information on satellite orbits, and the short time interval between passes leaves little margin for error for vehicles racing for cover. Moreover, the challenge for TEL operators is more serious than the data suggest. The analysis here focuses on the twenty military and intelligence SAR satellites, not the half dozen or more U.S. and allied civilian platforms that might be pressed into service in wartime.[68] Nor does the analysis count the optical and infrared satellites that supplement SAR coverage. Finally, the number and capability of radar satellites available to the United States is growing.[69] As that number increases, the window for mobile missiles to scoot away without being observed will narrow further.

SAR satellites do not solve the problem of locating mobile targets. For one thing, Russia and China are improving their ASAT capabilities, partly in response to U.S. capabilities.[70] Furthermore, adversaries will seek to place missile garrisons and conduct deterrent patrols in locations that are difficult to observe.[71] Those choices, however, force adversaries into ever-narrower zones, which then become the focus of other surveillance tools—for example, stealthy penetrating UAVs and unattended ground sensors.

In terms of the three key sensing missions (IPB, detection, and identification), SAR-equipped satellites offer a high level of capability for the IPB mission, because they can repeatedly image stationary or moving targets in peacetime. They also contribute a high level of capability to detection, by offering frequent wide-area coverage of North Korean roads. Finally, SAR satellites offer fairly good capability for the identification mission; they can produce high-resolution images of stationary TELs and enough resolution of moving vehicles to determine that a target is "truck-sized."[72]

A second set of sensing capabilities lies in a fleet of aircraft, including manned and remotely piloted vehicles, that use powerful radars to scan adversary territory. These aircraft carry SARs, and many are equipped with ground moving target indicator (GMTI) radars, allowing them to create high-resolution images of stationary targets or track a large number of moving vehicles. Most surveillance aircraft must operate from "standoff" distances to reduce their vulnerability to air defenses. Some drones, however, are stealthy and can penetrate adversary airspace. Below we illustrate the capabilities of standoff SAR/GMTI platforms and penetrating UAVs in the context of a U.S. and allied operation against North Korean mobile missiles.

The United States uses several types of aircraft for standoff radar-reconnaissance missions; we base our model on one of them, the remotely piloted RQ-4 Global Hawk. We explore the potential effectiveness of radar surveillance from four continuous orbits 80 kilometers outside North Korean territory.[73] ArcGIS software allows us to identify orbital locations that maximize coverage of North Korean roads, as well as to calculate the visible percentage of the road network from those locations.[74] Figure 3.4 shows the results.

Figure 3.4 reveals that even against a small country such as North Korea, standoff airborne radars cannot, by themselves, provide complete coverage of key roads and regions. Four orbits can observe 54 percent of North Korea's roads; the remainder is out of sensor range or shielded by mountainous terrain. These results also suggest, however, that standoff UAVs could play a crucial role in a sensing operation; that is, the ability to continuously monitor roughly half of North Korea's road network during a conflict would compel North Korea to constrain its mobile missile operations to the north-central region of the peninsula.

In addition to standoff UAVs, the United States has developed drones for so-called penetrating operations.[75] These UAVs reduce their visibility to enemy radar by utilizing stealth technologies and a combination of passive sensors and "low-probability of intercept" (LPI) radars to observe targets on the ground.[76]

Even sophisticated, stealthy UAVs are vulnerable to air defenses. To some extent their vulnerability depends on technical issues, including the state of competition between radar engineers and designers of stealth technology. The vulnerability of penetrating drones, however, depends greatly on their mission. Of the two critical wartime missions, detection is likely more dangerous than identification. The detection mission—continuously monitoring a large area to detect possible targets—would require a drone to remain within the line of sight of a large portion of adversary territory. The mission would, therefore, require the drone to fly at high altitude (to maximize line of sight) and possibly use active sensors (to maximize the drone's sensor range). The

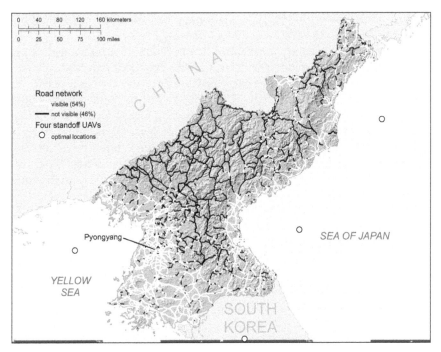

Figure 3.4. Coverage of North Korea with standoff unmanned aerial vehicles (UAVs)

Note: The white circles depict potential orbital locations for four UAVs; the locations were selected to maximize surveillance of North Korea's road network. The orbits are located 80 kilometers from North Korea's territory at an altitude of 60,000 feet, which reflect plausible operations for RQ-4 Global Hawks. White road segments are observable from at least one of the locations. The image was created using ArcGIS and road data from OpenStreetMap and DIVA-GIS.

identification mission, on the other hand, would allow penetrating drones to protect themselves better—to operate at lower altitude so that terrain would shield them from enemy sensors, and fly (when cued by detection systems) to investigate a possible TEL. Only then would the penetrating UAV employ LPI or passive sensors to examine the potential target.

We used ArcGIS to explore the potential capability of penetrating drones in the identification mission by determining the percentage of the North Korean road network that would be visible using four UAV orbits. Because the penetrating UAVs would need to rapidly identify the vehicles detected by other sensors, we restricted the UAVs to five minutes of flight time to maneuver into position to observe the suspected TEL.[77] Furthermore, because LPI radars and passive sensors have shorter ranges than the powerful radars on standoff platforms, we limit the sensor range to 50 kilometers.[78]

Our analysis reveals that four penetrating drones, operating as we describe above, can identify targets along 84 percent of North Korea's roads.[79] As figure 3.5 shows, penetrating and standoff systems would be particu-

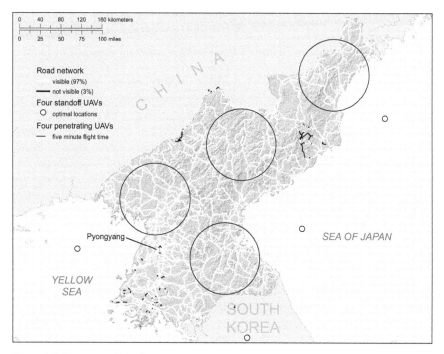

Figure 3.5. Coverage of North Korea with standoff and penetrating unmanned aerial vehicles

Note: The white circles depict potential orbital locations for four UAVs operating 80 kilometers outside North Korea's territory. The black circles depict the area over North Korea that four penetrating UAVs can overfly within five minutes of flight time starting from the center of each circle. Road segments are coded as visible (white) if they are observable from either a standoff or penetrating UAV. The image was created using ArcGIS and road data from OpenStreetMap and DIVA-GIS.

larly effective in combination, increasing the road network coverage to 97 percent. Assuming that penetrating UAVs can be cued by other reconnaissance systems such as satellites, unattended ground sensors, or (near the coast) standoff drones, North Korean TEL operators would have great difficulty moving safely along the country's road network without being detected. If U.S. and South Korean intelligence had identified mobile missile garrisons and operating areas before the conflict, the regions surrounding those zones might be fully covered by only one or two drone orbits.[80]

Each of the sensing systems explored here has important limitations. For example, radar satellites provide wide-area coverage, but do so intermittently and at only moderate resolution. Standoff drones provide persistent coverage, but only near the coast. Penetrating drones can provide persistent coverage inland (at the cost of increased risk to the aircraft) or intermittent inland coverage at lower risk. In many cases, however, the capabilities of one system can offset the limits of another. Moreover, this analysis merely scratches the surface in terms of new sensing platforms (e.g., unattended ground and seabed systems), signals (e.g., high-resolution spectroscopy), and approaches (e.g., cyber intrusions), many of which would be employed together for the same mission.

Old assumptions about the survivability of mobile forces need to be revised in light of new sensing technologies and capabilities. Concealment is not impossible, of course. An adversary's mobile delivery systems can remain secure if its air defenses can keep UAVs at bay, its navy can keep enemy ASW forces from its coastal waters, and antisatellite technology can blind satellites. But in this new era of transparency, whether concealed forces are survivable or not depends on the state of competition between opposing intelligence and military organizations. Survivability through concealment can no longer be assumed.

What about Countermeasures?

Countries will surely address the growing vulnerability of their nuclear arsenals by trying to develop countermeasures to thwart advanced sensor and strike systems. They will seek to deploy radar jammers, antisatellite weapons, and decoys. They will try to adapt mobile missile doctrines to reduce vulnerability, by timing movements to elude satellites and minimizing communications to thwart signals-intelligence efforts, for example. The new era of counterforce will not be static; it will be characterized by vigorous efforts to develop countermeasures, as well as equally vigorous efforts to overcome them.

Yet, there are good reasons to expect that the net result of these efforts will leave nuclear-delivery systems more vulnerable than they have been in the recent past. First, hunters are poised to do well in the back-and-forth battle of countermeasures. Counterforce is the domain of the powerful; those that are seeking to track enemy nuclear forces typically have greater resources than their rivals.[81] Additionally, the countries that are leaders in sensing technology have an advantage in the race to build (and thwart) countermeasures. As Brendan Green and Austin Long observe about the Cold War ASW competition, U.S. superiority in passive acoustics helped the United States quiet its own SSBNs, which in turn allowed it to practice and hone its tracking capabilities.[82] Expertise in sensors and countermeasures go hand in hand. Perhaps most importantly, many countermeasures reduce one vulnerability at the cost of exacerbating others. For example, limiting communications between mobile missiles or submarines and their command authorities reduces vulnerability to signals intercepts, but it increases vulnerability to attacks designed to sever (or simulate) their command and control.[83] Avoiding coastal roads neutralizes offshore sensors, but it channels forces into a smaller zone, easing the search problem. Even the simplest countermeasures, such as increasing security near sensitive facilities to prevent the emplacement of unattended ground sensors or improving air defenses around key sites to thwart UAVs, may cue hunters to the presence of high-value sites.

Second, the potential targets of disarming strikes cannot respond to just a single counterforce technology; they must respond to a daunting list of them. The revolutions in accuracy and sensing have had multiple, synergistic effects in bolstering counterforce. The task for hiders is not simply to thwart a single platform, such as SAR satellites, but rather to develop countermeasures to the entire array of (known) capabilities deployed by the hunters. For example, North Korea may find ways to interfere with U.S. radar satellites, but that still leaves missiles vulnerable to detection by optical satellites, UAVs, unattended ground sensors, and a variety of tagging, tracking, and locating capabilities.

Third, some vulnerabilities are difficult to fix. In the late 1960s, the Soviet Union learned that its SSBNs were being tracked by the United States, but it took more than a decade to counter this U.S. capability. Consider the challenge faced by China today in building a survivable ballistic missile submarine force. China deployed its first submarines in the 1960s, but more than half a century later Chinese submarines are still so noisy that experts predict it will be decades before Beijing can field survivable submarines.[84]

Finally, although the impact of emerging technologies on nuclear command, control, and communications (NC3) and early warning (EW) systems is difficult to predict, there are good reasons to expect that this will be an area of growing vulnerability for countries facing sophisticated adversaries. Nuclear retaliation, after all, depends on surviving NC3 capabilities (and in some cases, effective EW), not just the survival of warheads and delivery systems. During the Cold War, the Soviet Union was notably deficient in some aspects of NC3, increasing Soviet vulnerability to electronic warfare, stealthy aircraft and cruise missiles, and electromagnetic pulse (EMP) effects.[85] Today, all nuclear-armed countries need to be concerned that advances in quantum computing, artificial intelligence, and cyber could undermine the ability to detect a nuclear first strike or order and deliver a retaliatory response.

The battle between countermeasures and corresponding attempts to defeat them is under way, and its outcome will likely depend on the strategic context. Rich countries with advanced research and development infrastructure are developing technology and doctrine to protect their nuclear forces in the face of improvements in weapons accuracy and remote sensing. Weaker countries with modest resources, however, will be hard-pressed to develop effective countermeasures to the full spectrum of emerging means of counterforce.

For most of the nuclear age, there were many impediments to effective counterforce. Weapons were too inaccurate to reliably destroy hardened targets; fratricide prevented many-on-one targeting; the number of targets to strike was huge; target intelligence was poor; conventional weapons were of limited use; and any attempt at disarming an adversary would be expected to kill vast numbers of people. Today, in stark contrast, highly accurate weapons aim at shrinking enemy target sets. The fratricide problem has been swept away. Conventional weapons can destroy most types of counterforce targets, and low-fatality nuclear strikes can be employed against others. Target intelligence, especially against mobile targets, remains the biggest obstacle to effective counterforce, but the technological changes under way in that domain are revolutionary. Of the two key strategies that countries have employed since the start of the nuclear age to keep their arsenals safe, hardening has been negated, and concealment is under great duress.

These developments help explain the enduring puzzle of the nuclear age. Nuclear weapons seem like the ultimate instruments of deterrence, protecting those who possess them from invasion and other major attacks. Yet, if nuclear weapons solve countries' most fundamental security problems, why do nuclear-armed countries continue to perceive serious threats from abroad and engage in intense security competition? Why have the great powers of the nuclear era behaved in many ways like their predecessors from previous centuries, by building alliances, engaging in arms races, competing for relative gains, and seeking to control strategic territory—none of which should matter much if nuclear weapons guarantee the nation's security?

One might blame this persistent discrepancy between nuclear theory and practice on misguided leadership, bureaucratic or other decision-making pathologies, or dysfunctional domestic politics. The new era of counterforce suggests, however, that leaders have been correct to perceive that stalemate can be broken, and that the nuclear balance can vary dramatically across cases. If today's secure arsenal can become tomorrow's first-strike target, then there is little reason to expect the geopolitical competition between countries to end with the deployment of seemingly secure nuclear weapons.

The policy implications of the new era of counterforce are also important. First, if nuclear forces are becoming increasingly vulnerable to counterforce, then states need to improve their retaliatory arsenals just to maintain the same level of deterrence. Given that nuclear-delivery systems are expensive and must last for decades, the challenge for force planners is extraordinary: deploy weapon systems that will remain survivable for multiple generations, even as technology improves at an ever-increasing pace.

Second, the growing threat to nuclear arsenals (from nuclear strikes, conventional attacks, missile defenses, ASW, and cyber operations) raises major questions about the wisdom of cutting the size of nuclear arsenals. In the past, many arms control advocates believed that arms cuts reduced the incentives for disarming strikes; whether that assumption was right or wrong at the time, it is increasingly dubious as a recipe for deterrence stability today.

Finally, leaps in accuracy and remote sensing should reopen debates in the United States about the wisdom of pursuing effective counterforce systems.

Fielding those capabilities—nuclear, conventional, and other—may prove invaluable, enhancing deterrence during conventional wars and, if deterrence fails, allowing the United States to defend itself and its allies.[86] Enhancing counterforce capabilities, however, may trigger arms races and other dynamics that exacerbate political and military conditions.[87] In the past, technological conditions bolstered those who favored restraint; disarming strikes seemed impossible, so enhancing counterforce would likely trigger arms racing without much strategic benefit. Today, technological trends appear to validate the advocates of counterforce. Remote sensing, conventional strike capabilities, ASW, and cyberattack techniques will continue to improve and increasingly threaten strategic forces whether or not the United States seeks to maximize its counterforce capabilities. In this new era of counterforce, technological arms racing seems inevitable, so exercising restraint may limit options without yielding much benefit.

Nuclear deterrence can be robust, but nothing about it has ever been automatic or everlasting. U.S. leaders sought the capabilities to escape stalemate in the Cold War competition with the Soviet Union, and the United States remains in the vanguard of countries pursuing counterforce today. Stalemate might endure among some nuclear countries, and technology could someday reestablish the ease of deploying survivable arsenals. Today, however, survivability is eroding, and it will continue to do so in the foreseeable future. Weapons will grow even more accurate. Sensors will improve. The new era of counterforce will likely yield benefits to those countries that best adapt to the new landscape, and costs to those that fall behind. This familiar competitive dynamic explains why power politics endure in the nuclear age.

Deterrence under Stalemate

Conventional War and Nuclear Escalation

The central puzzle of the nuclear age is the persistence of intense international security competition. If nuclear weapons offer the ultimate protection against existential military threats, why do nuclear-armed countries continue to behave as if they face grave dangers abroad? Why do they arms race, build alliances, maneuver to control strategic territory, and fear changes in the balance of power? In short, why does geopolitical competition remain so intense under the shadow of nuclear stalemate?

The two previous chapters help explain this puzzle. Chapter 2 demonstrates that creating nuclear stalemate—from a first atomic test to achieving a robust survivable arsenal—can be a lengthy and competitive process. Chapter 3 shows how the reversibility of nuclear stalemate means that countries have good reason to compete even after they have deployed a secure deterrent force—not only to keep their own arsenal secure, but also in some cases to undermine the survivability of an adversary's deterrent force. Whereas the previous chapters discussed the challenges of *creating* and *sustaining* nuclear stalemate, this chapter focuses on a particular deterrence challenge *under* the condition of stalemate: how to use nuclear threats to deter conventional attacks.

Focusing on the ability of nuclear weapons to deter conventional attacks makes sense for two fundamental reasons. First, if nuclear weapons are the excellent tools of deterrence that their advocates claim—and are largely responsible for the past seventy-five years of peace among the major powers—then these weapons must deter conventional as well as nuclear attacks. After all, if they only deterred the latter, then nuclear weapons would merely cancel each other out and leave international politics as prone to war as before the weapons were invented. Second, if nuclear threats cannot be relied on to deter conventional attacks, then countries would need to generate other capabilities to do that job—presumably conventional forces. They would therefore need allies, value strategic territory, and fear shifts in the global balance of power. In short, the mission of deterring major conventional attacks is a fundamental problem of the nuclear age, and it bears directly on the question of why competition endures in the nuclear era.

But why is deterring major conventional attacks difficult? One might expect that any arsenal fearsome enough to deter a nuclear attack would be more than sufficient to deter limited attacks, such as conventional strikes on one's territory or against valued allies.[1] In fact, countries that use nuclear threats to deter conventional attacks face a conundrum known as the "stability-instability paradox." In short, if initiating nuclear war (under the condition of stalemate) is virtually tantamount to suicide, no country would do so in response to limited aggression. But if nuclear escalation is therefore not in the cards as a response to a limited conventional attack, then deterrent threats based on escalation will not be credible. Stated differently, the paradox is that the more stable that deterrence is at the level of strategic nuclear war, the less stable it will be at the level of limited conventional war. Deterring conventional aggression under the shadow of nuclear stalemate is anything but straightforward.[2]

Most nuclear analysts acknowledge the logic underlying the stability-instability paradox, but they debate its real-world consequences. Some analysts argue that the paradox exaggerates the difficulty of deterring conventional attacks. In their view, the mere possibility of escalation, perhaps bolstered by modest actions intended to manipulate (that is, increase) the level of risk in the mind of the attacker, will be enough to deter any major conventional attack. If these analysts are correct, nuclear-armed countries do not need to do much to deter conventional attacks beyond maintaining survivable retaliatory forces.

Other analysts take a more pessimistic view that hews more closely to the logic of the stability-instability paradox. They warn that countries seeking to deter conventional attacks must do much more than merely rely on their strategic nuclear arsenals. In particular, such countries need to deploy large, flexible, and resilient nuclear arsenals to provide credible escalation options during a war. Potential attackers would not want to be stalemated by credible threats to escalate, of course, so they would likely pursue capabilities of their own to neutralize a country's nuclear escalatory arsenal. The net result would be traditional military competition, with most of the dynamics familiar from the prenuclear world: arms racing, relative-gains concerns, and the competition for alliances, strategic territory, and other sources of power and security.

Scholars on both sides of this disagreement about the perniciousness of the stability-instability paradox acknowledge that NATO's Cold War nuclear plans resembled the recommendations of the pessimists. NATO deployed large numbers of tactical and theater nuclear forces in Europe in search of usable nuclear options in the case of conventional war, to better deter that war in the first place. To the pessimists, NATO's development of tactical nuclear options reflected the wisdom of their analysis; clearly, NATO's leaders had conducted careful analysis and realized the pessimists were correct. To the optimists, NATO's search for flexible nuclear options was unnecessary, dangerous, and reflected some failure of rational decision processes—either a lack of understanding by leaders of the nature of nuclear deterrence, or perhaps the influence of parochial military services or the military-industrial complex.

It is impossible to directly test whether the optimists or pessimists were right—that is, whether conventional deterrence was meaningfully bolstered by NATO's tactical and theater nuclear forces in Europe.[3] Nor can we easily determine whether Pakistan's adoption of a similar doctrine today deters conventional attack from India better than Pakistan's strategic nuclear arsenal could accomplish by itself, or whether Russia's nonstrategic forces give Moscow's nuclear deterrent additional credibility. But we can do two things. First, we can interrogate the logic that animates the pessimists' position. In particular, does the creation of nuclear options actually create a logical path for escalation during a conventional war? Second, we can identify which nuclear-armed countries have adopted this flexible, coercive nuclear doctrine. Is it a random subset of nuclear-armed states, as explanations rooted in misperception or organizational politics would suggest? Or does the pattern in nuclear doctrines across countries (and time) closely match the strategic logic advanced by the pessimists? If it is the latter, then the claim that these doctrines are rooted in misunderstanding is undermined.

In this chapter we make two key arguments. First, we show that a strategy of deliberate nuclear escalation in a conventional conflict can be rational—despite nuclear stalemate—if the side that wishes to escalate has flexible, limited nuclear options. Second, we show that nuclear-armed countries seeking to deter major conventional attacks with nuclear threats act *as if* substantial nuclear capabilities are required to make that mission credible. Both the nuclear-armed states that faced major conventional threats during the Cold War and those that do today are the same ones that seek to develop sophisticated and flexible nuclear arsenals, just as the pessimistic view suggests they should. Those countries that do not face major conventional threats decline to develop such nuclear options—again, as the pessimistic view implies. What this suggests is that leaders believe that they need flexible nuclear options to deter conventional attacks under the condition of stalemate. This constitutes another major cause of arms racing and competition during the nuclear era.

In the remainder of this chapter, we describe the conundrum of trying to deter conventional war with nuclear threats and how scholars differ over the implications and relevance of the stability-instability paradox. We then explain the strategic logic of coercive nuclear escalation, as well as describe the characteristics of nuclear arsenals designed to support that mission. Finally, we analyze which countries around the world have adopted nuclear postures tailored for coercive nuclear escalation, and whether such policies appear to be driven by a coherent strategic calculus.

Nuclear Threats and Conventional Deterrence: Alternative Views

How nuclear weapons can be used to deter conventional attack has been the subject of intense debate for decades. In the Cold War, the question preoccupied American decision makers well before the Soviet Union acquired a survivable nuclear retaliatory arsenal, as the Red Army posed a major conventional threat to NATO allies in Western Europe. But the onset of nuclear stalemate was particularly troubling for the credibility of a strategy based on nuclear threats, and U.S. leaders would remain focused on the problem until the end of the Cold War.

Among scholars grappling with the issue, Glenn Snyder was the first to clearly articulate the stability-instability paradox, and he and others posed a host of related vexing questions about the rationality of threatening nuclear retaliation for conventional attacks. In a world in which a conventional attacker does not have nuclear weapons, a nuclear-armed defender can credibly threaten nuclear escalation without much difficulty. While such an approach might constitute strategic overkill, or a violation of just war ethics (on the grounds of proportionality), it is a doctrine that should terrify any potential attacker.

The logic of conventional deterrence via nuclear retaliation is far more complicated in a world where both sides have secure nuclear retaliatory arsenals. For one thing, the defender now needs to consider the possibility that the attacker will retaliate with its own nuclear weapons. Such a mutually catastrophic exchange could greatly exceed the costs of suffering a conventional defeat—and hence lack credibility. Threats to use nuclear weapons to defend allies from conventional attack appear even more irrational and incredible. Moreover, nuclear stalemate might actually make a country more likely to initiate a conventional war if it is highly confident that its attacks will not trigger nuclear escalation. In such a case, the nuclear shield allows one to strike with the conventional sword. The strongest version of the stability-instability paradox sees conventional war as more likely because the potential attacker no longer needs to fear the worst possible consequence of a failed attack—surrender and conquest. According to the argument, nuclear weapons take those existential threats off the table.

The heart of Snyder's paradox is that nuclear stability could lead to conventional instability. Therein lies the strategic conundrum. How can a country make credible the threat of nuclear escalation in order to deter conventional attacks? While most analysts acknowledge the logic of the stability-instability paradox, not everyone agrees about the severity of the problem in the real world or its consequences for international behavior.

Below we discuss four principal views: two that are more optimistic, and two that are more pessimistic.

OPTIMISTIC VIEWS: EXISTENTIAL DETERRENCE AND MANIPULATION OF RISK

Some experts argue that the difficulty of deterring conventional attacks under nuclear stalemate is overstated. Two versions of this optimistic view are relevant.

According to the first view, the mere possibility of catastrophic escalation is sufficient to produce conventional deterrence. The fear that a conventional conflict could escalate to nuclear war—through a series of steps that cannot be foreseen and may not be intended—is enough to deter.[4] No potential benefit of launching a conventional attack could be worth the potential costs of fighting a nuclear war. Even if an attacker chooses limited conventional objectives so as not to trigger retaliation, it can never rule out the possibility of catastrophic escalation stemming from misperception, miscalculation, unauthorized use, or some other unintentional cause or irrational decision. The inherent risk of nuclear escalation in a conventional war, not the existence of any particular nuclear strategy or posture, is the key to deterring such a conflict.

For these reasons, analysts such as Kenneth Waltz largely dismissed the stability-instability paradox in the Cold War, claiming that the Soviets would never attack Western Europe because they understood that doing so could lead to full-scale nuclear war. As he wrote, "Anyone—political leader or man in the street—can see that catastrophe lurks if events spiral out of control and nuclear warheads begin to fly."[5] Whether or not the victim of a conventional attack would actually decide to use nuclear weapons to thwart an invasion is almost irrelevant. Instead, the fear that escalation might occur—through the usual fog and friction of war—is enough to deter.

In sum, according to this view, it is irrelevant whether a country that relies on nuclear weapons to deter conventional attack would have an interest in carrying out those threats during a war.[6] Simply the risk that a war could get out of control and result in nuclear escalation is enough to deter conventional attacks. Countries that have worked hard to develop usable nuclear escalatory options—for example, by deploying tactical delivery systems and planning for battlefield employment—are wasting their effort because conventional deterrence is all but assured by nuclear stalemate.

A second optimistic view acknowledges that conventional deterrence with nuclear weapons may not be as automatic as proponents of the first view claim, but holds that countries can take simple steps during crises to increase the risk of escalation, thereby coercing potential attackers to back down. This "manipulation of risk" strategy, as Thomas Schelling famously termed it, involves taking actions to deliberately raise the danger that things might get out of control and escalate to nuclear war.[7] The point of manipulating danger, Robert Jervis argues, is to generate unbearable risk in the minds of potential attackers, not to change the actual military balance in the conventional or nuclear realm.[8]

A strategy of manipulating the danger of nuclear escalation, according to proponents, requires only limited actions or military preparations. Under conditions of nuclear stalemate, the actual military balance—the way that nuclear forces would interact with each other or with enemy conventional forces on the battlefield—is irrelevant. The only thing that matters is for the potential attacker to comprehend the risk of stumbling over the nuclear brink, and this level of understanding is easy to teach.

To show they are willing to run risks, nuclear-armed defenders need not rely on large nuclear arsenals, sophisticated delivery systems, diverse kinds of warheads, complicated employment doctrines, resilient command-and-control systems, or even credible retaliatory options. Instead, some limited nuclear use options are sufficient, and these options can probably be found among strategic nuclear forces, obviating the need for specialized tactical or theater weapons for this mission. Under nuclear stalemate, any country struggling to develop a rational escalation strategy and the specific nuclear capabilities that would render such a strategy credible is wasting time, effort, and resources. What they need is what they already have: the secure possession of nuclear weapons.

Proponents of both of these optimistic views have long recognized the major disjuncture between their expectations and the actual policies of many countries.[9] Most poignantly, advocates such as Waltz and Jervis were vociferous critics of the U.S. and NATO nuclear escalation posture in Western Europe during the Cold War, since that posture sought to deter a Soviet conventional attack by developing a range of usable nuclear options, combining nuclear and conventional operations to prevail in battle at various stages of escalation. Today, as we show below, other nuclear-armed countries facing significant conventional threats engage in similar efforts to develop nuclear options to deter or, if deterrence fails, to halt a conventional attack. For example, Pakistan clearly fits the bill in regard to the threat from India, as does Russia in regard to what it perceives as a threat from NATO. According to the optimistic views presented here, such policies are hard to explain in rational terms. They appear to be flawed policies, which do not reflect the realities of the nuclear age.

Several other empirical anomalies raise questions about one or both of the optimistic views of conventional deterrence in the shadow of nuclear retaliation. Whereas the first view holds that the mere possession of nuclear weapons is sufficient to induce paralyzing fear among those contemplating conventional attack, on several occasions in history, leaders confronted those fears and decided to strike anyway. Some of the resulting conflicts were minor and inherently limited; the battlefield costs were low, and the geographic separation between the battlefield and the nuclear-armed defender's center of power meant that the fighting in those wars was unlikely to threaten the truly vital interests of the defender.[10] But when China intervened in the Korean War in 1950, it launched a major ground offensive that killed thousands of American soldiers in the initial battles. Subsequent fighting over the next two years resulted in more than thirty thousand U.S. fatalities. In 1991, during the Persian Gulf War, Iraq launched over forty conventional ballistic missiles against Israeli cities, yet somehow it was confident that the destruction inflicted (which it could not have accurately predicted) would not trigger a nuclear response.[11] In the case that should give conventional deterrence optimists the greatest pause, Syria and Egypt launched a major two-front attack on nuclear-armed Israel in 1973. Had Israel's defenses collapsed—and they almost did—Egypt and Syria would have faced the real prospect of nuclear escalation by a desperate Israel. Yet those countries' leaders apparently assessed the risks and decided that the probability of Israeli escalation was low enough to give a green light to the attack—which is at odds with the paralyzing, existential fear hypothesized by some scholars.

What this list suggests is that when considering launching conventional attacks on nuclear-armed adversaries, leaders apparently do not shrink back from the mere possibility of escalation, as the optimistic views claim. Instead, leaders seem to weigh the likelihood of adversary escalation when they contemplate launching conventional attacks—which implies that increasing that likelihood of escalation, for example by creating usable nuclear options, should bolster deterrence.[12]

PESSIMISTIC VIEWS: COERCIVE ESCALATION AND ESCALATION DOMINANCE

Other analysts are more pessimistic about the ease with which countries can deter limited attacks using nuclear threats. In their view, countries that threaten escalation to deter conventional attacks must develop flexible and resilient nuclear forces that could be used if war occurs. Only credible nuclear threats can reliably deter, and only usable options are credible. Again, it is helpful to delineate two of these views.

The first view agrees with optimists who contend that nuclear-armed countries can manipulate risk in order to deter limited attacks, but argues that this entails greater effort and attention to military capabilities than the optimists allow.[13] An attacker's fear that escalation might occur is not good enough for deterrence. Instead, to deter conventional aggression, potential aggressors should be confronted by real nuclear forces designed to carry out the escalation mission. This requires nuclear forces that are suitable for wartime employment, as well as concrete preparations and plans that make the use of such forces feasible.[14]

Advocates of this view suggest that nuclear-armed countries facing serious conventional threats should develop the capability to conduct coercive escalation campaigns to force a committed opponent to halt any conventional attacks. This strategy calls for building flexible and limited nuclear use options, and especially nuclear capabilities that would be survivable through extended periods of conventional conflict during which the adversary might substantially degrade delivery systems, command sites, and communications links. Potential defenders following this strategy will desire a diverse array of nuclear weapons (including those with lower yields and greater accuracy); greater targeting flexibility (for instance, to avoid attacker population centers); contingency plans (to adapt to rapidly changing circumstances); and improved command, control, and communications links (to be able to execute an escalation strategy in the midst of conventional war or after a limited nuclear response to escalation). In short, according to this view, countries seeking to deter conventional attack with the threat of nuclear use will face strong incentives to make their nuclear doctrines and postures suitable for coercive escalation.

The second pessimistic view, escalation dominance, goes further in arguing that conventional deterrence requires the capabilities to win at every stage of nuclear conflict. A core belief of this strategy is that military victory is possible, even in nuclear wars. Credible threats to escalate need to be based on actual capabilities to prevail in tactical nuclear combat, theater-level nuclear war, or in an all-out nuclear conflagration. This strategy, originally formulated by Herman Kahn, entails the ability to match or outmatch the potential attacker in strictly military terms at every possible rung of the escalation ladder. Only this ability, proponents argue, renders nuclear options truly "usable" and thus credible. In short, a potential attacker needs to understand clearly that it cannot win or will be defeated under any military contingency.[15]

Each of the four views described above call for a different level of nuclear capability to deter conventional war. The two optimistic views suggest that not much capability is needed beyond what countries likely have as part of a secure retaliatory arsenal. The two pessimistic views suggest the need for much greater capabilities. Which of those views prevailed in various nuclear-armed states? Is there a pattern that shows which nuclear-armed states adopted the more optimistic approach to deterring conventional attacks and which adopted the more pessimistic strategies?

To allow us to search for such a pattern, we first ask three key questions: How can a deliberate nuclear escalation strategy be rational? Under what circumstances are countries most likely to adopt such a strategy? And how precisely might a country employ nuclear weapons to coerce a nuclear-armed adversary to halt a conventional war?

The Logic of Coercive Escalation

The basic rationale behind a strategy of coercive nuclear escalation rests on the looming costs of defeat and the possibility of salvaging a more acceptable outcome. Defeat in conventional war is often a catastrophic outcome for leaders; they frequently lose their power, sometimes their freedom, and occasionally their lives. Faced with these terrible risks, leaders have rational incentives to take escalatory steps that might avert the coming disaster, even if there is only a small chance that escalation will produce a better result. Nuclear escalation may seem cold-blooded, but it is neither irrational nor far-fetched.

Throughout history, many nuclear-armed countries have faced a critical dilemma: how to keep enemies that possess overwhelming conventional military power at bay? Even conventional defeat, after all, can be disastrous. In some cases, battlefield losses result in conquest and occupation. If the adversary is particularly brutal, defeat may bring worse, including dislocation of conquered peoples or even genocide. But even when conquest is not on the table, military defeat is often disastrous for political leaders.

Leaders' desire to survive and retain power provides the simplest rationale for escalation. One study found that the leaders of countries who lost wars were nearly four times as likely to be punished—exiled, jailed, or killed—as those who managed to achieve a "draw."[16] Consider the consequences suffered by leaders who recently lost to the United States, a rather benign conquering power. Panamanian dictator Manuel Noriega was imprisoned for the rest of his life after the U.S. invasion of his country in 1989. Similarly, Slobodan Milošević, the president of Serbia and Yugoslavia during the 1999 U.S.-led NATO bombing campaign of his country, died in his prison cell in The Hague while standing trial for war crimes, and the Bosnian Serb leaders Radovan Karadžić and Ratko Mladić are still in detention pending their own war crimes trials. Saddam Hussein, the Iraqi leader when the United States invaded and occupied his country in 2003, was toppled, captured, and incarcerated in humiliating fashion; his sons and grandson were killed; and then he was executed by hanging in front of jeering enemies. In 2011, the Libyan leader Muammar Qaddafi spent his final days hiding from U.S.-supported rebels before being captured, beaten, reportedly sodomized, and then killed. Dozens of Qaddafi loyalists, including one of his sons, were also rounded up and executed. Avoiding military defeat is often the difference between a life of power and privilege and a grim future of debasement and death.

Even when wars do not raise the prospect of conquest, the nature of modern warfare often puts leaders at risk. Modern military operations often involve intense campaigns against command-and-control facilities, leadership sites, and communications hubs. These targets are destroyed to maximize military effectiveness, but doing so poses a direct threat to regime security—

to the leaders themselves, their key political allies, and their families.[17] In short, leaders who witness their militaries being destroyed, see their security services being savaged, and experience bombs raining down on their command bunkers will feel great pressure to halt a war as soon as possible.

In a wide range of other circumstances, leaders may face incentives to escalate a conventional war. If leaders perceive enormous stakes in a conflict, they may consider coercive escalation to avoid the loss for their country, or avoid the political consequences for themselves (in the form of a popular uprising or military coup). For example, a war between the United States and China over Taiwan would not appear to trigger worrying escalatory dynamics; presumably, leaders in Beijing do not fear "conquest," and the United States would likely restrain itself from launching strikes against China's leadership. But the loss of highly valued territory (Taiwan) would be a terrible blow to China's vital national interests, according to Chinese government declarations. If a conventional war led to the independence of Taiwan, or a very one-sided military defeat for China, the party leaders might feel they must "even the score" to avoid a nationalistic uprising against the party leadership in the wake of a humiliating defeat.[18]

All of these logics for escalation are worth highlighting because doing so reveals how many real-world scenarios could produce serious escalatory pressures. The problem is not limited to a single case where the adversary regime is likely to perceive any military campaign as a total war (i.e., North Korea) but rather could apply across the full range of plausible conflicts involving the United States (including with China, Russia, and someday perhaps Iran) or any other conventionally superior state facing a nuclear-armed adversary.

Coercive nuclear escalation during a conventional war would constitute an enormous gamble—a long shot at producing a cease-fire. But escalation can be a rational choice even if it offers only a small chance of success. Leaders on the verge of conventional defeat may rationally accept enormous risks to generate a cease-fire if the outcome of *not* escalating is sufficiently terrible. In fact, even if escalation *worsens* the expected consequences for the leaders on the losing side, they may still rationally choose this strategy if it increases the variance in the distribution of potential outcomes.[19]

Gambling for resurrection strategies are common in many domains of life. In American football, a team facing near-certain defeat will throw a long pass down the field at the end of the game—a "Hail Mary" play. Even though the play has little chance of succeeding, it creates some possibility of success, no matter how slim. Investment fund managers have been known to engage in increasingly desperate gambles with very low probability of success to try to recoup prior losses. This behavior (quite literally "throwing good money after bad") recurs despite company policies that prohibit it, laws that criminalize it, and regulators who use oversight to try to prevent it. In the realm of geopolitics, Japan's attack on Pearl Harbor is illustrative of the gamble. Japan was being strangled by U.S. economic sanctions; specifically, it was denied needed oil reserves by Washington's oil embargo. Japan's leaders understood that a surprise attack on a country with ten times the GDP would likely end badly, but they believed that the path they were on would inevitably lead to defeat.[20] So they gambled, taking a leap to create the *possibility* of success, even though they anticipated—correctly—that escalating the dispute with the United States would worsen their odds of success.

In short, losing wars often has horrendous consequences for both leaders and defeated societies. In the early decades of the Cold War, Western Europeans were understandably terrified by the notion of being conquered by the Soviet Union, losing their democratic institutions, and living under a murderous Stalinist tyranny. Today, many Israelis believe that a military defeat at the hands of their neighbors would usher in another tragic era in Jewish history, including another round of genocide. Even when defeat in war is unlikely to lead to mass societal suffering, enemy leaders (including not only the supreme leader, but also ruling party officials, military officers, and members of the domestic security services) rightly fear the consequences. Facing those outcomes, it is rational for leaders to gamble with escalation.

Strategies of Coercive Escalation

The escalatory strategies that nuclear-armed states might adopt to coerce an end to a conflict differ based on how early nuclear weapons are employed, and the steepness of the escalatory path. We use the term *coercive nuclear escalation* (or CNE) to cover a wide range of potential actions. At the low end of the escalatory ladder, employment could be merely issuing threats or visibly alerting forces. Climbing a few rungs, employment could include nuclear demonstrations—such as wartime weapons tests, or detonations over international waters. At the high end of the ladder, employment can mean strikes on military or civilian targets.[21] The effects of these actions will vary, but each involves employing nuclear weapons coercively.[22]

CNE does not account for the precise structure of any specific conflict, or every conceivable approach to coercive escalation. Crises and wars can unfold in countless ways. In some cases crises last for months and conventional wars are brief. In other cases war erupts without any prolonged crisis beforehand. But the basic CNE model allows us to explore the logic of coercive escalation and the operational requirements of such a strategy.

There are two principal force requirement implications for a coercive nuclear escalation strategy. First, all things being equal, the more survivable a nuclear arsenal is the better suited it is for CNE. The initial step of any CNE strategy is logical to the extent that the coercer can impose future pain if its terms are not met. If a country with a vulnerable arsenal were to attempt

CNE, the adversary has another option besides being coerced—it could respond with a counterforce strike to prevent any future escalatory use.

In fact, a nuclear arsenal designed for CNE would ideally offer more than peacetime survivability; it would possess *resilient survivability*.[23] For CNE to work, a country must be able to escalate in some fashion, absorb whatever its enraged enemy might do in return, and still be able to inflict more pain. If a country's CNE strategy is based on plans to employ nuclear weapons several times if necessary, the hurdles for survivability are even higher: the CNE force may need to absorb several rounds of conventional, nuclear, and other attacks and still be able to inflict more pain.

The challenge of resilient survivability is even greater than this brief description suggests. Modern conventional operations would likely degrade enemy control of nuclear forces, whether or not that is the intention.[24] And the act of employing nuclear forces, especially in a gradual fashion, may itself increase the arsenal's vulnerability. Firing some weapons would reduce the size of the remaining stockpile, which is relevant if a country has a small arsenal. Furthermore, the activities associated with nuclear employment may reveal valuable information to those who seek to locate and destroy the force. For example, alerting or firing nuclear forces could divulge information about the communication systems that connect political leadership, senior nuclear commanders, and delivery systems; firing procedures; command arrangements (and how to disrupt them); and other signatures that attackers could use to improve target intelligence. In short, the CNE mission compels countries to build larger arsenals, more diverse forces, and redundant command-and-control systems.

The second implication is about the ideal size and diversity of a nuclear arsenal for the CNE mission. In short, more is better. If pressed to do so, nuclear planners could devise a bare-bones CNE strategy with a single warhead. In that case, the initial act of nuclear employment would need to be merely a threat to fire the weapon (rather than a demonstration), presumably aimed at a target selected to maximize enemy pain.[25] But a large arsenal would permit planners to devise a coercive campaign with several rungs in the escalatory ladder. Having those rungs would allow a country to demonstrate its will and ability to use nuclear weapons without initially taking actions that would so enrage its opponents as to foreclose bargaining. Furthermore, a large arsenal would facilitate CNE by contributing to resilient survivability, deterring the target of coercion from responding to coercion with a disarming strike. Finally, diversity of nuclear systems would allow a coercer to modulate the amount of pain it inflicts on its enemies. For example, short-range accurate systems could be employed to target battlefield military targets, whereas longer-range delivery systems with larger-yield warheads would be ideal for holding targets deep in the enemy homeland at risk.

A country building a CNE posture may start small; even a few weapons on simple delivery systems can create a crude yet terrifying threat of escalation. But planners building a robust CNE posture would rationally desire a much larger force with enough weapons and a survivable command system to permit it to (1) ride out phases of conventional operations; (2) survive enemy conventional or nuclear counterforce strikes; and (3) confront the enemy with a nearly inevitable progression of nuclear attacks should the conventional war continue. Viewed in this fashion, it is no wonder that NATO developed a large arsenal of battlefield and theater nuclear weapons during the Cold War; it is not surprising that the Pakistani nuclear arsenal continues to grow; or that North Korea continues to test and build more nuclear weapons.

In sum, our discussion of the logic of coercive nuclear escalation makes three key points. First, intentional nuclear escalation can be a rational strategy during a conventional war. Second, the logic of a CNE strategy depends on the nuclear force posture of the country seeking to escalate in a coercive manner. Arsenal size, flexibility, and resilient survivability are key elements of a CNE posture. Finally, this discussion reveals that counterforce capabilities and force survivability (which are opposite sides of the same coin) drive many CNE dynamics; it explains the back-and-forth competition that occurred throughout the Cold War and that endures today. Countries that fear they will lose vital conventional wars have strong incentives to build nuclear escalation capabilities, and adversaries that expect such countries to employ CNE strategies have incentives to build much greater counterforce capabilities. Not surprisingly, the result is an arms buildup like the one between NATO and the Warsaw Pact during the Cold War, and the one underway in South Asia today.

Evidence of Escalatory Doctrines

The set of optimistic views discussed at the outset of this chapter hold that countries do not need much nuclear capability to deter adversaries from launching conventional attacks. A survivable nuclear retaliatory force is likely enough to create an unacceptable risk for any attacker, and it is unnecessary to strive to make nuclear weapons more "usable" for the purpose of deterring conventional war. Optimistic proponents recognize that some countries have exceeded this level of deterrence capability and effort—for example, as in U.S. nuclear policy during the Cold War, when the U.S. strategy for defending Western Europe from Soviet attack called for great redundancy, resilient survivability, flexibility, and usable options for its nuclear forces. But they contend that this excessive pursuit of survivability and usability is misguided. Such behavior is nonstrategic, and better explained by the cognitive limitations of leaders, electoral politics, bureaucratic or organizational competition, or other domestic pathologies.

We advance an alternative claim: the behavior we have seen reflects real-world incentives for strategic competition. The behavior that optimists view as anomalous instead reflects the desire of conventionally weaker states to have survivable and usable nuclear options in order to deter their relatively stronger adversaries. Deterrence is enhanced by making the threat of nuclear use more credible and by creating conventional denial capabilities on the battlefield. Moreover, the push to create more survivable and usable nuclear forces could conceivably help mitigate the consequences of war if deterrence fails. If our explanation is correct, then countries that require a CNE posture will build far more capable arsenals than optimists expect. And stronger countries that face these CNE postures will strive for counterforce to undermine or counteract those postures. The result reinforces the kind of strategic competition that we continue to see in the nuclear age.

Which view is correct? How can we judge? Do leaders actually think and prepare for escalation in this manner? Do nuclear-armed states that feel sufficiently threatened by conventionally superior foes develop defense plans around the concept of CNE? In other words, do countries seem prepared to follow a CNE strategy and make their forces survivable and usable?

To address these questions, we identify the conditions under which states would be most likely to adopt operational doctrines of coercive nuclear escalation. Second, we sort nuclear-armed countries according to those conditions. Finally, we determine whether those states that, according to our argument, should have adopted coercive nuclear postures have actually done so.

Two factors should have a powerful effect on whether nuclear-armed states develop coercive nuclear postures. *First, countries should be more likely to view nuclear weapons in this manner if they are conventionally inferior to their adversaries.* Nuclear escalation should be more appealing to conventionally weaker powers than stronger ones. *Second, these postures should be more attractive to states for which the consequences of conventional military defeat are dire.* When the United States loses conventional wars—for example, in Vietnam, or arguably in Afghanistan and Iraq—it may damage presidential approval, but the republic does not fall, and U.S. leaders are not hanged on the gallows. For other countries and their leaders, defeat often brings terrible consequences. Even countries that do not fear military conquest might worry that a humiliating conventional defeat might trigger uprisings or coups, and the overthrow of the existing regime. Leaders of nuclear-armed states who fear that conventional military defeat could lead to terrible consequences for themselves or their country should be more likely to develop coercive nuclear postures than those who do not share this fear.

Figure 4.1 identifies strategically relevant country dyads along these two dimensions. The two dimensions we describe are, in reality, continuous variables: the expected likelihood of defeat in a conventional war could take any value between 0 and 1, and the negative consequences of defeat could range from nothing to total annihilation. But to facilitate coding—and avoid giving

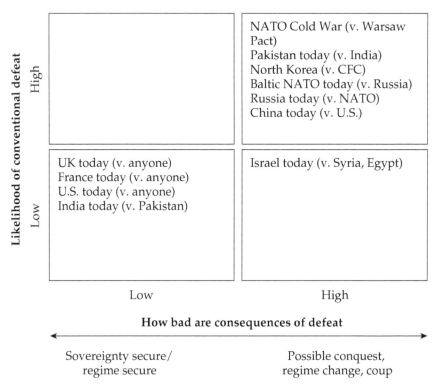

Figure 4.1. Countries expected to adopt coercive escalatory doctrines

the impression of greater precision than is possible using these variables—we treat each of the dimensions as if it were binary, thus resulting in four categories. If our argument about coercive nuclear escalation is correct, then the countries represented in the dyads in the upper-right corner—that is, those nuclear-armed states that expect to suffer conventional defeats over issues of grave importance—should be most likely to adopt coercive nuclear postures. Those in the bottom left corner should be least likely.

A country's nuclear posture defines the role that nuclear weapons are designed to play in the country's security strategy; it is what an adversary plans to do with nuclear weapons in the event of conflict. As such, as Vipin Narang writes, "Nuclear posture is best thought of as a state's operational, rather than declaratory, nuclear doctrine."[26] We identify and use two major indicators to code the nuclear postures of countries as being indicative of a coercive nuclear escalation posture.

First, such a posture would be marked by the deployment of nuclear forces and command systems that strive to be *resiliently survivable*. As described above, this refers to ensuring survivability not just in peacetime but also throughout a crisis, the various phases of conventional war, and against adversary counterforce strikes. Signifiers of resilient survivability would include concerted efforts at improving concealment, making delivery systems more mobile, and protecting command and control.

Second, a CNE posture is also identifiable by the deployment of nuclear forces and command systems designed to maximize wartime *flexibility* of nuclear employment. Here the signifiers include efforts to deploy tactical nuclear weapons (for example, short-range and variable-yield systems) for battlefield use, as well as the kinds of command-and-control arrangements that would facilitate such operations.

Country Cases

There is strong correlation between the strategic causal variables we identify and the nuclear postures we predict should follow. The most telling cases are those where a country's posture has changed over time—and done so precisely as expected according to changes in strategic context. Figure 4.2 reproduces the previous figure, but indicates (in bold) which countries appear

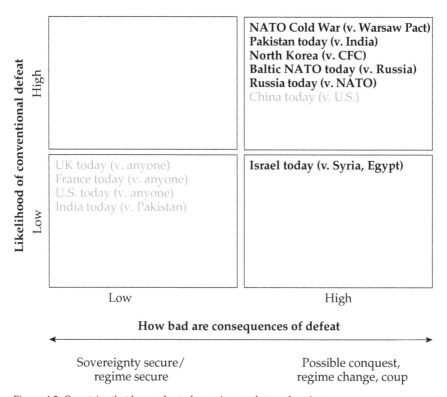

Figure 4.2. Countries that have adopted coercive escalatory doctrines

to have adopted coercive escalatory nuclear doctrines and have sought to deploy nuclear forces capable of executing that doctrine. Figure 4.2 also highlights (in gray) the countries that do not appear to have nuclear postures designed primarily for coercive nuclear escalation.[27]

Overall, figure 4.2 suggests that the nuclear-weapon states that worry most about calamitous military defeat tend to develop coercive nuclear postures to give them the capability to stalemate their most threatening adversaries. Consider further several cases. First, and perhaps most strongly supportive of our explanation, are the cases in which nuclear posture shifted as predicted along with a change in strategic context (theUnited States/NATO and Soviet Union/Russia during and after the Cold War); next, a contemporary case that offers a clear correlation between strategic context and nuclear posture (Pakistan); and lastly those cases that provide mixed, ambiguous, or contrary evidence (North Korea, Israel, and China).

Figure 4.2 suggests that there is a strong correlation between the level of conventional threat that a country faces and its likelihood of adopting a CNE posture. But perhaps we have miscoded their nuclear posture in the figure, or perhaps the correlation is spurious. We examine briefly the nuclear doctrines of several nuclear powers to strengthen our confidence in our initial coding and look for evidence that specifically links the choice of posture to the conventional military balance.

UNITED STATES/NATO

Aggregate measures of relative power suggest U.S. global dominance at the dawn of the nuclear age, but this masks the fact that the United States and its NATO allies faced two major problems. First, the Soviet Union and its Warsaw Pact allies enjoyed conventional superiority throughout most of the Cold War.[28] Second, by the early 1960s, the U.S. ability to win a major war through a massive nuclear-disarming strike was disappearing. As shown in chapter 2, by the mid-1960s the United States and its NATO allies were locked in a condition of nuclear stalemate at the strategic nuclear level, and were militarily inferior at the conventional level. What did they do? What sort of nuclear posture did they adopt?

Not only were the prospects for defending NATO territory with conventional forces dim, but also the likely consequences of a NATO conventional defeat were terrible for the allied states. Given the Soviet record of occupation, control, and annexation of Eastern European governments and territory, as well as the inroads communist ideology had made in Western European countries such as France and Italy, it is reasonable to assume that a war fought exclusively at the conventional level would have resulted in the destruction of NATO, conquest of most of Europe, and regime change across the board. U.S. leaders contemplating a Soviet attack were forced to envision conceding all of Eurasia, from the English Channel to the Sea of Japan.

Although the strategic picture would subsequently improve, at no time did U.S. or allied leaders see the consequences of conventional defeat in Europe as anything short of the end of independent democratic governance on the Continent.

With both the likelihood and consequences of NATO conventional defeat being high, we would expect the United States to deter and defend the alliance with a strategy of coercive nuclear escalation once the Soviets were able to establish stalemate at the strategic nuclear level. In fact, this was the nuclear posture that the United States and its NATO allies adopted in the mid-1960s. The fundamental goal of the posture was to deter a Soviet conventional attack through the credible threat to escalate to nuclear war and, if deterrence failed, then to deliberately use nuclear weapons to coerce the Soviets to halt its invasion.

Specifically, the United States and NATO sought to build a nuclear deterrent force that would be usable—meaning that it strove for both resilient survivability and flexibility. Most obviously, the United States and NATO deployed a wide variety and large number of tactical nuclear weapons, and developed theater-level nuclear war plans for their use, in order to offset NATO's perceived disadvantage in conventional forces. (At its peak around 1971, there were approximately 7,300 NATO nuclear weapons deployed in Europe.) NATO also went to great lengths to link nuclear and conventional military operations and allow for the quick release, dispersal, and delegation of launch authority. Every facet of the U.S.-NATO nuclear posture appeared designed to bolster the feasibility of using nuclear weapons in combat. The force (and the ability to command it) needed to survive any Soviet preemptive attacks, and it needed to be resiliently survivable—that is, protected from degradation or elimination in the initial phases of a conventional conflict through any postescalation retaliatory counterforce strikes. Although few American officials were convinced that these plans were completely coherent or that anyone could confidently predict what would happen if the plans were put into operation, these preparations were not merely symbolic gestures. U.S. and allied forces trained and exercised to carry out nuclear escalation if the Red Army attack ever came.[29] Even when NATO officially adopted the doctrine of "flexible response" in the late 1960s, which sought to reduce reliance on nuclear use by strengthening conventional forces, nuclear weapons employment was still viewed as the key to coercing a halt to a Soviet invasion if deterrence failed.

With the collapse of the Soviet Union and end of the Cold War, the conventional balance shifted decisively in NATO's favor. As we would expect, the United States and its NATO allies subsequently abandoned their plans to employ nuclear weapons coercively at the outset of any conflict, and they revised NATO's nuclear posture accordingly. For example, today roughly 150 tactical nuclear weapons (B-61 bombs) are stored at NATO bases in Europe.

Tellingly, the only members of NATO who still strongly favor retaining NATO's forward-deployed tactical nuclear weapons in Europe are those that face a real military threat from Russia and have good reason to fear a disastrous military defeat if NATO fails to muster enough conventional defense in time. The Baltic states of NATO, in particular, worry about the credibility of NATO's nuclear umbrella, especially compared to other allied countries whose territory is far from the Russian border. Thus, our expectations about strategic context as a cause of nuclear posture are validated not only by NATO's shifting nuclear posture during and after the Cold War but also by the divergent views in the alliance that remain today.

In sum, during the Cold War, when NATO felt unable to defend itself adequately from a major conventional attack, it adopted a coercive nuclear escalation posture. When the Cold War ended and the balance of power shifted—moving most NATO countries from the upper-right to the lower-left quadrants in figures 4.1 and 4.2—so did the views of many alliance members about NATO's nuclear doctrine, and even about the legitimacy of the weapons they recently had relied on themselves.[30]

RUSSIA

Meanwhile, Russia shifted in the opposite direction. When the Soviet Union was conventionally stronger (during the Cold War) it had favored, and encouraged the United States and NATO to agree to, a policy of "no first use" of nuclear weapons. Soviet doctrine claimed that limited nuclear war was not a viable concept and that nuclear escalation could not be controlled.[31] However, after the conventional military balance shifted sharply against Russia, it adopted a posture that emphasizes the use of tactical nuclear weapons to counter NATO's conventional superiority. Russia's nuclear strategy today aims to deter or terminate a conventional war, which it would otherwise likely lose, based on the threat of limited nuclear first use against military targets

Since the collapse of the Soviet Union, and especially after NATO's campaign in Kosovo in 1999, Russia has been acutely aware of its conventional military inferiority. This unfavorable balance is particularly worrisome for Russia because even a limited conflict with NATO would jeopardize vital national interests, including perhaps the survival of the regime. (Russia's posture is best understood as a response to the NATO threat, but China's growing capability in the Far East also plays an important role.) Its solution has been to adopt a doctrine of nuclear "de-escalation"—the use of limited nuclear strikes in a conventional war in order to compel a cease-fire and return to the status quo.[32] In short, there is widespread agreement among analysts that the deterioration of Russia's conventional forces has led to a reduction in its threshold for nuclear use in a conflict.[33]

Dima Adamsky describes the reduction in Russia's nuclear threshold for employment as a means of compensating for the inferiority of its conventional forces in several steps: Russia's official 1993 military doctrine abandoned the commitment to "no first use" and tasked nuclear forces to deter "large-scale conventional" wars; in 1998, Russia's leaders tasked the nuclear forces to deter "regional conventional" conflicts, a mission that was subsequently codified in official military doctrine in 2000; in 2003, an important planning document called for maintaining the ability to use nuclear weapons first in a regional conflict; and so on. "Nuclear weapons had acquired a new *regional* mission," Adamsky writes. "The arsenal's mission became to deter, and if deterrence were to fail, to terminate large-scale conventional aggression through a limited nuclear use in the theater of military operations."[34]

Russia's coercive nuclear escalation posture is also reflected in the nature of its nuclear arsenal, specifically in the emphasis on tactical nuclear weapons modernization and deployment, the integration of these nuclear forces into regular war-fighting concepts and exercises for deterring and defeating conventional adversaries, and the general trend toward developing greater flexibility in nuclear capabilities and the means to fight limited nuclear war. Tactical nuclear weapons play a large role in Russia's strategy to offset NATO's superior conventional forces, including naval capabilities (e.g., cruise missiles, antisubmarine weapons, antiaircraft missiles), tactical air-delivered weapons (gravity bombs and stand-off cruise missiles), air- and missile-defense interceptors, and short-range ballistic missiles.[35] Moreover, Russian military exercises regularly simulate nuclear weapons use against NATO countries and forces.[36] Russian planners have also discussed a new generation of nuclear weapons that would capitalize on low-yield detonations in order to minimize collateral damage, a clear sign that Russia's escalation strategy is meant to be calibrated to coerce a halt to conflict without provoking a NATO nuclear response.[37] As a member of the Russian parliament and former secretary of Russia's Security Council notes, "The principal trend has consistently been in the direction of reducing yield and enhancing accuracy of warheads . . . [and] developing various concepts of limited nuclear war and different controlled nuclear conflicts."[38]

PAKISTAN

Pakistan's nuclear posture clearly reflects the adoption of a coercive nuclear strategy. Pakistan's nuclear weapons arsenal, deployment of forces, and command-and-control system are all geared toward credibly threatening a nuclear response to an Indian conventional invasion of Pakistan's territory; indeed, most experts believe Pakistan would launch nuclear strikes against advancing Indian forces.[39]

The strategic conditions that would make a CNE strategy appealing are precisely those that face Pakistan. On the one hand, Pakistan is a large country with a big population, and India has no desire to conquer and rule over 180 million Pakistani Muslims. On the other hand, most of Pakistan's largest cities—including Karachi, Lahore, Faisalabad, Rawalpindi, and its capital Islamabad—are all within approximately 100 miles of the border with India. (Lahore is about 15 miles from the border.) The most likely Indian attack corridors—across the plains and deserts in the provinces of Punjab and Sindh—would be difficult to defend.[40] Moreover, India is widely considered to have two to three times as much conventional military power as Pakistan.[41] Pakistan's leaders reasonably worry that a major conventional war could lead to the destruction of its conventional forces and India's seizure or isolation of major Pakistani cities unless Pakistan can use nuclear escalatory threats to prevent this outcome.

Pakistan's nuclear posture is structured to deter a conventional invasion by India. If deterrence fails, the goal is to use tactical nuclear weapons against Indian forces in order to forestall what would be a disastrous conventional defeat.[42] Although government officials refer to Pakistan's nuclear doctrine as one of "credible minimum deterrence," experts more accurately describe it as a "proactive" or "aggressive" escalation posture, which "threatens the first use of nuclear weapons against Indian forces in order to deter its conventionally superior neighbor."[43] Pakistan officials have also made clear that the employment of nuclear weapons in the event of conventional attack is the core of its operational nuclear doctrine.[44]

In more concrete terms, the evidence that Pakistan has adopted a coercive nuclear escalation posture is reflected in the composition of its nuclear arsenal and nature of its nuclear doctrine—which, taken together, indicate the pursuit of a flexible, resiliently survivable, and usable nuclear force. Pakistani nuclear weapons have clearly been operationalized as "usable war-fighting instruments" on the battlefield.[45] The arsenal itself, which is estimated to include 140 to 150 warheads, consists of multiple kinds of nuclear weapons and delivery systems geared toward survivability and tactical use, including road-mobile missiles protected by underground facilities, as well as missiles with low-yield options.[46] Warheads and missiles are reportedly stored at six to twelve secret military locations, with survivability enhanced by the use of decoy sites and underground facilities and tunnels.[47]

The twin goals of nuclear survivability and flexibility in wartime are also reflected in Pakistan's command structure and processes. As Narang and others have described, the development of Pakistan's command-and-control architecture—particularly since the 1999 Kargil conflict with India—appears to be driven by the need to rapidly deploy and use nuclear weapons in the early phases of a conflict. The overriding goal has been to ensure that the Pakistani military can quickly assemble, mobilize, and disperse nuclear weapons in a crisis, and be able to deliver these nuclear weapons early in a conventional conflict no matter how chaotic the operational environment.[48] The Pakistani military already maintains strict military control over all of the nuclear components, which are stored on military bases, and has placed a heavy emphasis on getting nuclear weapons into the hands of theater command-ers as quickly as possible. Some analysts believe that theater commanders have already been predelegated launch authority in case communication is severed in the fog and friction of war.[49]

Finally, Pakistan is in the midst of a significant expansion of its arsenal, including the building of more warheads and new delivery systems, which directly or indirectly contributes to the survivability and flexibility neces-sary for a CNE strategy.[50] For example, the military recently tested a new nuclear-capable submarine-launched cruise missile, the Babur-3. The second-strike capability of a submarine leg of the nuclear arsenal could help reduce the likelihood of an Indian preemptive strike on Pakistan's tactical land-based nuclear weapons, thereby strengthening the credibility of its CNE threat.[51] Similarly, the test firing of a new MIRV-capable surface-to-surface ballistic missile (the Ababeel) was accompanied by an official Pakistani statement that the missile's development is "aimed at ensuring the survivability of Pakistan's ballistic missiles in the growing regional Ballistic Missile Defence (BMD) environment," and that the missile could "defeat hostile [Indian] radars."[52]

NORTH KOREA

North Korea has not publicly articulated an explicit nuclear doctrine, but Pyongyang has overtly and frequently threatened to use nuclear weapons against South Korea, Japan, and the United States to ensure the survival of the regime if it were attacked. The document that comes closest to an offi-cial doctrine, which was published by North Korea in 2013, states that nu-clear weapons would be employed in response to an attack with conventional weapons.[53] Experts generally agree that North Korea's "theory of victory" in a conventional war against its most likely adversaries would almost cer-tainly rest on a strategy of nuclear blackmail and brinksmanship.[54] Never-theless, because of the lack of clear evidence on North Korean thinking, doctrine, plans, and capabilities, we refrain from fully coding North Korea as having a CNE posture.

North Korea's likely resort to nuclear weapons stems from its conventional inferiority compared to the United States and South Korea, and the dire im-plications of conventional defeat for the survival of the North Korean regime. If war erupted, the North Korean army, short on training and armed with decrepit equipment, would prove no match for the U.S.–South Korean Com-bined Forces Command. Seoul would suffer some damage, but a conven-tional war would be a rout of North Korea, and CFC forces could quickly cross the border and head north toward Pyongyang. In such a scenario, the prospects for regime survival are virtually zero, and the best that North Korea's leaders can hope for is a "golden parachute" in the form of an offer, most likely from China, to provide a lifelong sanctuary if they keep nuclear weapons holstered. Indeed, North Korea publicly noted the fate of leaders in Iraq and Libya after those leaders renounced nuclear weapons: they were attacked and killed. Given the massive asymmetry in conventional power and the dire fate that would attend defeat, North Korea faces huge incentives to escalate to nuclear use in order to coerce a military stalemate.

The logic behind a North Korean coercive nuclear escalation strategy is compelling, but we cannot confidently ascribe that strategy to the country, given the limited publicly-available information about its nuclear capabilities. North Korea conducted nuclear tests in 2006, 2009, 2012, and 2016, and claims to have nuclear-capable ballistic missiles, but it is unclear whether the country has produced deliverable warheads. Experts conservatively estimate that North Korea has enough fissile material to build thirty to sixty nuclear weapons and might have assembled ten to twenty warheads.[55] In short, North Korea faces huge incentives to adopt CNE, but we cannot point to enough good evidence to suggest that its nuclear arsenal is being structured for resilient survivability and flexibility.

ISRAEL

Israel provides mixed evidence for our argument about those countries most likely to adopt coercive nuclear escalation strategies. On the one hand, Israel acquired its nuclear arsenal as an insurance policy against defeat in a conventional war against its Arab adversaries. This strategy made sense when Israel faced a plausible prospect of defeat in conventional war, and when the consequences of such a defeat would have been catastrophic for the country. Israel explicitly manipulated the risk of nuclear escalation prior to the 1967 Six-Day War and during the 1973 Yom Kippur War, although this strategy appears to have been aimed at compelling the United States to support Israel rather than coercing Israel's enemies to stop fighting.[56]

On the other hand, the best indicators of a CNE posture—dedicated efforts to build a nuclear arsenal that is resiliently survivable and flexible for coercive use during war—are absent or unknown in the Israel case. Israel has long had nuclear-capable aircraft and land-based ballistic missiles, and in the late 1990s it acquired its first submarine capable of launching nuclear cruise missiles. But there is no available evidence to suggest that Israel has developed tactical nuclear weapons for limited escalation on the battlefield, integrated nuclear weapons into its conventional force posture, or developed command-and-control structures and processes tailored for intrawar survivability, much less built multiple and dispersed hardened shelters or trained its forces for limited nuclear escalation on the battlefield.[57] Indeed, such steps make less sense in a world in which Israel retains conventional superiority over its enemies. Ultimately, there is simply not enough information available about Israel's nuclear arsenal and doctrine to make definitive conclusions about its strategy for nuclear employment.

CHINA

China does not appear to have adopted a coercive nuclear strategy or posture, despite the fact that it would likely lose a conventional conflict with the United States and that such a defeat would likely threaten the survival of the ruling regime. As discussed above, even if the United States sought neither to conquer the Chinese mainland (which is implausible) nor to attack China's leadership or other vital targets in Beijing (which seems unlikely), almost any kind of conventional defeat in East Asia or the Western Pacific would be seen as a terrible blow to China's national interests, might provoke a nationalistic backlash and possible uprising, and could lead to an internal coup. China's official nuclear policy is based on a no-first-use pledge and the maintenance of a "minimum deterrent"—meaning the minimal amount of capability necessary to ensure a survivable second-strike capability.

Although Chinese leaders have traditionally espoused assured retaliation as the exclusive objective of China's nuclear posture, there are signs that Chinese military strategists have sought to expand the role for nuclear weapons. Recent Chinese doctrinal writings suggest an ongoing internal debate about the need to "lower the nuclear deterrence threshold" and "adjust nuclear policy" in response to conventional strategic strikes.[58] Based on these writings, some Western experts have questioned the conditionality of China's no-first-use pledge, the range of circumstances that might trigger a Chinese nuclear response (including a response to nonnuclear U.S. military actions), and the strength of the supposed firebreak between conventional and nuclear war in Chinese strategy.[59] Any evolution in China's policy away from strategic retaliation (for the purpose of deterring nuclear attack) toward limited retaliation for the purpose of de-escalating a conflict would mark an important move in the CNE direction.

Nevertheless, for the purpose of coding a country's nuclear posture, the current Chinese approach cannot be classified as CNE. To be sure, a war with the United States could well escalate to China's initial use of nuclear weapons in order to deter and defeat conventional attacks that pose a threat to vital interests and regime survival, but the Chinese arsenal lacks the characteristics of resilient survivability and employment flexibility that would signify such a plan. China is modernizing its nuclear force, having recently deployed new mobile ballistic missiles, for example, but it appears to lack tactical nuclear weapons; it reportedly keeps warheads stored separately from missiles; and it does not behave as if it is concerned with the need to launch precision or low-yield nuclear strikes as part of a wartime escalation strategy.[60] In short, despite concerns about the ambiguity of China's no-first-use pledge, experts on Chinese nuclear strategy see little evidence that China plans to use nuclear weapons to compensate for conventional inferiority or coerce a stalemate in the midst of a conventional conflict.[61]

117

The history and contemporary evidence suggest that the nuclear-weapon states that worry most about calamitous military defeat tend to develop coercive nuclear doctrines and postures to give them the capability to stalemate their most threatening adversary. Coercive nuclear escalation not only makes sense logically, but also appears to be reflected in the behavior of precisely those states that should be expected to adopt such a strategy. Whereas proponents of the theory of the nuclear revolution see the development of robust CNE forces as illogical and motivated by nonstrategic causes, the evidence suggests that the strategic dynamics of international politics are driving states to build robust nuclear capabilities and compete intensely, even in the nuclear age.

This chapter argues that deterring conventional attacks using nuclear weapons is a difficult mission. It explains why countries that face powerful adversaries are not satisfied with modest and simple nuclear forces. Instead, they seek to build arsenals optimized for wartime coercive nuclear escalation—that is, arsenals that can be employed flexibly and can ride out conventional and nuclear-disarming strikes. We also explain why countries that face adversaries that adopt a CNE posture will be driven to invest in counterforce capabilities—to deter adversary escalation and mitigate the consequences if escalation occurs. Finally, the chapter provides evidence that countries actually follow this harsh logic. We demonstrate that there is a clear pattern to which states develop CNE postures and which do not, rather than the random distribution of nuclear doctrines one would expect if such decisions were driven by leaders' misperceptions or organizational pathologies or some other similar explanation.

Our findings provide another major explanation for the puzzle of continued competition in international relations in the nuclear age. In order to reap the deterrent benefits of nuclear weapons, leaders feel compelled to build the type of nuclear arsenals that might otherwise seem unnecessary—that is, large, flexible, and usable forces. What is most striking about this finding is how unanimous leaders are about their need for usable nuclear options. Whether one focuses on U.S. and Soviet views during the Cold War, or Russian, Pakistani, and North Korean views today, the answer is the same: nuclear-armed countries that believe they are outgunned in conventional forces tend to tailor their nuclear forces for coercive nuclear escalation. Viewed this way, many of the behaviors that some analysts find so anomalous are not anomalous at all. The nuclear age remains competitive because building a nuclear arsenal that can thwart an overwhelming conventional attack by a sophisticated enemy is difficult and expensive. Ensuring that such an arsenal will have resilient survivability is an ongoing challenge.

Another implication of this chapter is that recent efforts by China, Russia, Pakistan, and North Korea to enhance their nuclear capabilities are understandable, and thus likely to continue. All four of those countries face enemies that can defeat them on the conventional battlefield. We should not be surprised by their efforts to increase their nuclear options or the wartime survivability of their arsenals. Nor should we be surprised that their conventionally stronger adversaries are working hard to negate the survivability of those countries' deterrent forces. U.S. and South Korean leaders understand that a truly survivable (and deliverable) North Korean nuclear arsenal would pose enormous problems for leaders in Seoul and Washington if war erupted on the Korean Peninsula, because North Korea would likely use that arsenal to stalemate the conventional battle. Thus, the United States and South Korea are developing a range of capabilities to target Pyongyang's arsenal. Likewise, India understands that Pakistan plans to use its arsenal to neutralize India's conventional military might. India is responding by enhancing its counterforce capabilities.[62]

For nuclear weapons to function as the greatest tool of deterrence, they must be usable in response to a major conventional attack. Yet, to make nuclear weapons usable, countries need to build larger, more flexible, and more survivable arsenals than what might otherwise be necessary or wise under conditions of nuclear stalemate. The ultimate result is the persistence of intense security competition, which nuclear weapons seemingly should have banished.

Conclusion

Solving the Nuclear Puzzle

International politics have long been marked by fear, rivalry, and war. Without a world government to protect them, countries have had to provide for their own security. The result, as history shows, was intense geopolitical competition. Countries feared the rise of potential adversaries, engaged in expensive arms races, encircled each other with alliances, and sought to control strategic territory and scarce resources. Even when peace prevailed, rivalry was intense, and conflict simmered below the surface.

The creation of nuclear weapons promised to end this grim reality. Now countries could ensure their core security by simply arming themselves with nuclear weapons. After all, nuclear weapons tend to create stalemate—the condition in which neither side can win a major conflict without suffering unacceptable damage. By largely solving the most serious problem stemming from the absence of a world government, the fear of conquest by a powerful rival, nuclear weapons appear to let countries abandon the costly and dangerous geopolitical playbook used throughout history. Nuclear weapons appear to make not only major war obsolete, but also the strategies countries have long relied on to deter or prepare for conflict. Nuclear weapons seem to promise not just a more peaceful world but a far less competitive one, as well.

The logic of a nuclear revolution is compelling, but it leads to a central puzzle. If nuclear weapons are such powerful instruments of deterrence then why do so many aspects of international competition in the nuclear age resemble those of the prenuclear era? Why do nuclear powers continue to fear rising powers, strive for superior weaponry, build entangling allies, and covet strategically advantageous territory? If nuclear-armed countries are fundamentally secure from attack, why don't they act like it? Although the nuclear era has been free of war between the major powers, the most powerful countries continue to think and act as if large-scale conflict is a looming possibility.

Our explanation for this puzzle lies in the nature of stalemate. The distinguishing feature of the nuclear age is, in fact, the stalemate that these weapons tend to create. But analysts have paid too little attention to the challenges of creating nuclear stalemate, the possibility of escaping stalemate, and the difficulty of deterring conventional attacks under stalemate.

We argue that nuclear weapons are the most effective instruments of deterrence ever invented. Yet, little else about the dynamics of nuclear strategy is simple. Acquiring a robust deterrent arsenal is a dangerous and challenging process. Countries facing powerful adversaries need to build highly survivable arsenals to create a robust deterrent—one which will not merely deter a motivated enemy in peace, but even in crises or wars. Building a survivable nuclear deterrent may take many years, trigger arms racing, and tempt adversaries to strike preemptively. There is also a good reason to expect competition to endure after the emergence of stalemate, because stalemate is reversible. Countries will worry that technological or other developments will allow adversaries to break the shackles of stalemate by developing disarming-strike capabilities. Countries may be tempted to do the same, for the purpose of either coercing adversaries or limiting damage to themselves if war occurs. In either case, intense arms competition will likely result. Finally, if countries wish to use nuclear threats to deter conventional attack as well as nuclear attack, they will feel compelled to build more than simple retaliatory arsenals; they will likely seek sophisticated capabilities suitable for nuclear use in wartime. For these reasons, the dynamics of geopolitical competition have not vanished in the nuclear age.

Chapters 2, 3, and 4 explained the persistence of intense international security competition through an analysis of the nature of nuclear stalemate. These chapters demonstrate the struggle entailed to produce stalemate, the incentives to escape it, and the challenge of deterring conventional attack under it.

Chapter 2 sought to identify the threshold for generating stalemate. How large and survivable does a country's arsenal need to be to deter an adversary nuclear attack in peacetime or wartime? Will only a few weapons do the trick? Or is a more robust arsenal required? The persistence of intense international security competition in the nuclear age remains a puzzle only if stalemate is relatively easy to generate. That is, if the answer to "how much is enough?" is "not much," then the nuclear arms competitions of the past and present are confounding. If, on the other hand, deterrence depends on states building arsenals that are truly survivable—no matter what the enemy throws at them—then intense competition in the nuclear age is no longer puzzling. Such behavior will result from the drive to build enough nuclear capability to make retaliation truly assured, combined with the potential attacker's interest in keeping the other side vulnerable to a disarming strike. Stated differently, if "assured retaliation" (or "assured destruction") is required for robust deterrence, then maintaining a sufficient deterrent is a competitive process—and the arms racing, alliance building, territory seizing behavior of the nuclear age is not a surprise at all.

To answer the question about the requirements of stalemate, chapter 2 examined perhaps the most important case of nuclear deterrence in history, the Cold War conflict between the United States and the Soviet Union. We first analyzed the balance of nuclear power between the superpowers, focusing on the growth of the Soviet arsenal through several key stages in the 1950s and 1960s, from the earliest years when the Soviets had only an existential or minimal deterrent arsenal (that was vulnerable to a U.S. disarming strike) to the later years when the Soviets had an assured retaliatory force. We then evaluated the impact of the growing Soviet arsenal on the U.S.-led alliance's strategic posture, identifying the level of Soviet capabilities that caused NATO to reject nuclear-disarming strikes as its strategy for deterring and winning war. In short, we sought to determine how much was enough to force NATO to recognize the existence of stalemate, the condition in which winning a nuclear war by disarming the Soviet Union was impossible.

The evidence shows that neither the small and vulnerable Soviet arsenal in the early 1950s nor the large and still vulnerable arsenal of the late 1950s was enough to force NATO to abandon its plans to win a major war in Europe through massive nuclear-disarming strikes. Neither existential nor minimal deterrence postures were enough to convince NATO that victory was impossible. In fact, it appears that the initial stages of Soviet nuclear weapons acquisition actually undermined Soviet security by leading U.S. planners to greatly expand the number of Soviet targets that would have been destroyed in the initial phase of any conflict. NATO's strategic posture changed only as the Soviet Union deployed a nuclear arsenal large and robust enough to almost certainly survive such an attack. The Soviet acquisition of such an assured retaliatory capability compelled NATO to accept (for the time being) that winning a major nuclear war was not possible, and to develop options other than a disarming strike against the Russian arsenal. The creation of stalemate between the United States and the Soviet Union was neither quick nor easy. It took plenty to deter.

Chapter 3 tackled another crucial question about the nature of stalemate: its degree of permanence or variability. Regardless of the ease or difficulty of creating stalemate, once adversaries find themselves living under conditions of mutual assured destruction, is that condition reversible? Can nuclear retaliatory forces that have been made survivable become vulnerable again? Can stalemate be broken? The persistence of intense competition in the nuclear age remains a puzzle only if stalemate is irreversible. If the nature of nuclear weaponry and technology make it implausible that adversaries can develop new strategies or capabilities for successful disarming strikes, then countries with survivable arsenals can feel safe and secure. They can be relaxed about any adversary military or economic growth, research and development program, or changes in conventional or nuclear deployments. They need not respond to such behavior because they will always be able to absorb an enemy's first strike and retaliate with nuclear weapons. In such a case, nuclear weapons create stalemate, and stalemate is a one-way street.

However, if stalemate is reversible depending on technological change and the efforts of adversaries to develop new counterforce capabilities, countries will feel compelled to arms race to ensure that their deterrent forces remain survivable in the face of such advances. They will worry about relative gains, because a rich and powerful adversary will have more resources to invest in technology and military forces. They will value allies, which help contribute resources and valuable territory. Moreover, countries may be enticed to develop their own counterforce capabilities in order to disarm adversaries or limit the damage those adversaries can inflict in case of war. In short, if nuclear stalemate can be broken, one should expect countries to act as they always have when faced with military threats, by trying to exploit new technologies and strategies for destroying adversary capabilities. Continued geopolitical competition would not be puzzling.

Chapter 3 sought to answer this question about the relative permanence or variability of stalemate by exploring the strategies that countries employ to protect their nuclear arsenals, and then examining how technology can undermine those strategies. We found that developments rooted in the computer revolution are making nuclear forces around the world far more vulnerable than before. The superpower nuclear arsenals seemed robustly survivable for the latter half of the Cold War, when each side deployed large and dispersed forces, but the foundations of stalemate are being eroded today by vast improvements in weapons accuracy, sensing technology, data processing, communication, and artificial intelligence. The task of securing nuclear arsenals against attack is becoming more challenging. Not surprisingly, nuclear-armed states continue to compete for advantage, track each other's capabilities carefully, invest in counterforce as well as arsenal survivability, and prepare for the possibility that stalemate between them and key rivals may end. Just as the superpowers competed intensely throughout the Cold War because they understood that technological developments were unpredictable, nuclear-armed countries today are no less concerned about the future. Geopolitical rivalry continues in the nuclear age because stalemate is reversible.

Finally, chapter 4 explored the challenge of deterring conventional war under nuclear stalemate. Nuclear stalemate is the condition in which no adversary can launch a nuclear-disarming attack against another and escape devastating nuclear retaliation; it is the heart of nuclear deterrence theory. But using nuclear threats to deter conventional war, not just nuclear war, is a more complicated challenge because it requires the potential victim of conventional attack to credibly threaten to use nuclear weapons against an attacker that can retaliate in kind. How can the threat of nuclear use deter conventional attack by nuclear-armed enemies? What kinds of nuclear forces and postures are necessary to credibly support such nuclear threats?

The persistence of intense international security competition in the nuclear age remains a puzzle if nuclear threats deter conventional war relatively easily. If conventional deterrence with nuclear weapons is fairly easy and straightforward, then security competition among states should be greatly ameliorated. However, if deterring conventional war with nuclear threats requires greater military effort—for example, if conventional deterrence relies on the development of usable tactical nuclear options—then many of the competitive behaviors of the prenuclear age should remain rampant in the nuclear era as well. Nuclear-armed countries facing major conventional threats should be expected to build large, diverse, flexible, and resilient nuclear forces in order to make the threat of nuclear escalation credible. At the same time, adversaries should strive to develop counterforce capabilities to neutralize those countries' wartime escalation strategies. The collective result should be the familiar dynamics of international politics: arms racing, relative-gains concerns, and competition for alliances and other sources of power and security.

Chapter 4 thus explored the strategic incentives that nuclear-armed countries face under nuclear stalemate, when they use nuclear threats to deter powerful conventional adversaries. The core issue concerned the degree to which countries that face overwhelming conventional attacks feel compelled to make their nuclear options usable and credible. We first identified the conditions under which states would be most likely to rely on nuclear threats to deter conventional attacks; we then sorted nuclear-armed countries according to those conditions; and finally we determined whether those states that relied on nuclear threats to deter conventional attacks created flexible, usable nuclear options.

The logic and evidence presented in chapter 4 suggests that much of the competitive behavior we see in the nuclear age is driven by the challenge of deterring conventional attack under the condition of stalemate. The nuclear-weapon countries that worry most about calamitous military defeat tend to develop coercive nuclear doctrines and postures to give them the capability to stalemate their most threatening adversaries. Coercive nuclear escalation not only makes sense logically but also appears to be reflected in the behavior of precisely those states that should be expected to adopt such a strategy. Conventionally weaker states desire to have both survivable and usable nuclear options in order to credibly deter their relatively stronger adversaries. Moreover, the evidence explains why stronger countries that face these escalatory postures strive for counterforce to undermine or counteract those postures. The resulting strategic competition is not puzzling.

Broader Theoretical Implications

Our findings about the nature of deterrence and strategy in the nuclear age have broader theoretical implications beyond the core findings of chapters 2, 3, and 4. First, our book undermines a widely held theory about international politics in the nuclear era: the theory of the nuclear revolution. That school of thought emerged as many U.S. scholars became vocal about what they viewed as unnecessary and dangerous nuclear policies adopted by American leaders during the Cold War. Two of the most prominent scholars in the discipline, Kenneth Waltz and Robert Jervis, repeatedly criticized U.S. policies in the 1970s and 1980s for being rooted in outdated assumptions from the prenuclear era. Specifically, because nuclear weapons made winning wars nearly impossible, the old geopolitical playbook was obsolete, yet according to Waltz, Jervis, and others, leaders in the United States and the Soviet Union were ignoring the implications of nuclear stalemate. Proponents of the nuclear revolution school criticized the size of the superpowers' arsenals, the extent to which each side sought first-strike or damage-limitation capabilities, and the effort by the United States to attain escalation dominance over their Russian nuclear rivals. Some analysts in the theory of the nuclear revolution camp argued more broadly that the global balance of power no longer mattered, that alliances were far less valuable, and that nuclear-armed countries no longer needed to worry much about their security.[1]

Today, many of the common critiques of U.S. nuclear and conventional military modernization owe a great measure of credit to the arguments originally laid out by proponents of the theory of the nuclear revolution. More broadly, major debates about contemporary great power relations—such as whether instability and conflict lie ahead with China's continued rise or Russia's renewed assertiveness—turn implicitly or explicitly on nuclear revolution arguments. According to the logic of the theory, since war cannot be won, geopolitical competition is senseless; in turn, countries need not compete intensely for power and security.

But nuclear weapons have not revolutionized international relations. International security competition is alive and well. Although nuclear weapons are a great tool of deterrence, nuclear-armed countries have continued to engage in arms races, build alliances, pursue relative gains, fear shifts in the balance of power against them, and covet and protect strategic territory. To explain this anomaly, proponents of the theory of the nuclear revolution rely on arguments about persistent misperceptions, powerful arms lobbies, renegade military organizations, or some other perversion of rational decision making.

This book offers a simpler explanation for the persistence of power politics in the nuclear era. The answer lies in a better understanding of the nature of nuclear stalemate. Stalemate emerges through a highly competitive process in which countries must work hard, and often against the determined efforts of their adversaries, to build truly survivable retaliatory arsenals. Countries continue to compete while they are locked in stalemate, because stalemate is reversible. And even when stalemate exists, countries seek flexible capabilities—conventional and nuclear—to deter or respond to nonexistential threats. The thrust of seven decades of theorizing about nuclear weapons is thus only half-right. They are, indeed, the best instruments of deterrence ever created. They have not, however, solved the problems of international anarchy or revolutionized international politics.

This book also serves as a warning against technologically deterministic theories of international politics. The theory of the nuclear revolution is just one prominent example of an explanation that looks to technological developments to predict fundamental change in international behavior. Of course, there is nothing inherently wrong—and much of great utility—in exploring the stabilizing or destabilizing impact of new and emerging technologies (as we do in chapter 3), but scholars often overstate the degree to which technology shapes politics. National leaders and military planners are rarely confident enough in their understandings of how weapons and prevailing technologies will interact during war to be moved to radically alter their basic security strategies, much less their core political objectives. Leaders are highly resistant to abandoning the pursuit of military advantage (or the avoidance of disadvantage) based on the purported "objective" requirements of prevailing technologies. Weapons are tools of war, and thus instruments of policy; they do not merit the kind of independent causal properties often assigned to them. While technological change can shift the balance of power, as well as the strategies that countries pursue in order to improve their own security, it has never been a salve or solution to geopolitics.

Finally, we hope that our analysis in this book will help generate new research and scholarship on the nature of international politics in the nuclear era. For example, many scholars tend to treat nuclear weapons possession as a binary variable; they assume that if two adversaries have nuclear weapons, then those countries are locked in stalemate. In reality, there is substantial variation in the nuclear balance of power across dyads and across time. Our book draws attention to the need for more nuanced assessments of the nuclear balance of power. Such analyses may help explain a wide range of international behaviors throughout the nuclear age (for example, why and when countries arms race, or which allies they choose to protect or trust to provide protection) and provide new hypotheses about the processes within states that generate nuclear policies. Because scholars have often assumed that nuclear weapons create stalemate through a simple process, they have too easily gravitated to explanations for arms races that were rooted in nonstrategic behavior (for example, misperceptions, delusional leaders, renegade militaries, or other explanations stemming from pathological decision making). More broadly, freed of the notion that the nuclear realm of geopolitics is something altogether separate and different from a world of traditional military competition, analysts should be able to see contemporary affairs in a new, but familiar, light.

Policy Implications

These findings also have important implications for contemporary international politics. First, the future of nuclear arms reductions looks bleak. In particular, efforts to reduce the size of nuclear arsenals would need to overcome a major conundrum posed by trends in technology and strategic context. Historically, potential adversaries have agreed to nuclear arms cuts when they did not undermine strategic stability—that is, when the cuts did not raise the danger that either side could launch a disarming first strike. During the Cold War, for example, these goals—nuclear arsenal reductions and strategic stability—seemed compatible because the United States and the Soviet Union had such large and robustly survivable arsenals that substantial cuts did not appear to endanger stalemate. Whether right or wrong in the past, however, the assumption that arms cuts and deterrence stability go hand in hand is increasingly dubious today.[2] Indeed, these are becoming rival goals in light of the growing vulnerability of nuclear arsenals, which stems from technological advances in the areas of nuclear and conventional strike, intelligence and surveillance, missile defense, and cyber operations, among many others.

The fact that today's nuclear powers have far smaller nuclear arsenals to start with than the United States and the Soviet Union did in the Cold War only exacerbates the problem of arms reductions. Back then, bilateral arms cuts left strategic stalemate intact; although cuts reduced the number of nuclear targets that would need to be destroyed in a disarming strike, they also eliminated many of the nuclear weapons that could carry out a strike. Stalemate was preserved because the remaining targets were safe from the diminished pool of shooters. Today, however, countries with growing nonnuclear capabilities to destroy nuclear targets would face an easier disarming mission. The problem is stark: arms-control agreements that cut nuclear weapons reduce the number of targets that must be destroyed in a disarming strike, and all the while, the nonnuclear forces that aim at those targets grow in number and capability.

A second major policy implication of our analysis—the flip side of the difficulty of nuclear arms reductions—is that one should expect to see serious arms racing among nuclear adversaries. In some cases, countries will work hard to create truly survivable retaliatory forces, while their rivals will strive to hone counterforce capabilities to keep those retaliatory forces vulnerable. For example, we expect that China will continue to add significant nuclear capabilities (such as new mobile missiles) to its arsenal, as well as bolster its command-and-control capabilities—all part of a traditional path to deploying a secure, survivable second-strike force. In turn, the United States will continue to modernize its nuclear arsenal and develop offensive (e.g., long-range precision conventional strike systems) and defensive (e.g., missile defense) means to counter Chinese retaliatory capabilities. Counterforce will be attractive to the United States not only for deterring Chinese escalation in a serious conflict but also for assuring allies protected by the U.S. nuclear "umbrella," as well as for mitigating the damage if China were to escalate to nuclear use. In other cases, countries that have had secure nuclear retaliatory arsenals will struggle against adversary efforts to escape stalemate. For example, Russia and the United States are likely to engage in nuclear and conventional arms racing as Russia seeks to respond to U.S. advances in the realm of counterforce.

Another type of arms race, pitting nuclear-armed but conventionally asymmetric adversaries, will be marked by both rapid qualitative and quantitative advances in weaponry, which may increase risks of conventional war and nuclear escalation. Conventionally weaker powers—for example, Pakistan vis-à-vis India—will continue to build and deploy usable nuclear options in order to deter a conventional attack and, if deterrence fails, to coerce a halt to such a conflict before suffering a catastrophic defeat. Pakistan, for example, will need to make these forces—and the command-and-control structure necessary for managing these forces—resiliently survivable under wartime conditions. It will need to do so because India will face powerful incentives to build and deploy nuclear and conventional counterforce capabilities. Stronger conventional powers will see these capabilities as a necessary means to degrade or neutralize the enemy's escalatory strategy, thus locking in the advantages of their conventional superiority.

A third major policy implication pertains to the process of nuclear proliferation and efforts to stop such proliferation. The decision to acquire nuclear weapons is fraught with danger because adversaries have incentives to strike militarily before countries can join the nuclear club.[3] The United States considered preventive action against the Soviet Union early in the Cold War; both U.S. and Russian leaders explored the preventive war option against China in the early 1960s; Israel struck Iraq's nuclear reactor in 1981 to eliminate its path to building the bomb; the United States went to war in 2003 in large part to keep nuclear weapons out of the hands of Iraq's leader; and military threats surely influenced Iran's decision to freeze its nuclear program at least temporarily in 2015. The list of cases is longer than this and is likely to grow, but our analysis reinforces the basic lesson: proliferation is a dangerous game.

New dangers accompany the decision to acquire nuclear weapons, and the main benefit of joining the nuclear club—deterrence—does not accrue instantaneously or automatically. As we saw with the early Soviet arsenal, the initial deployment of nuclear weapons can make a country more vulnerable than before if it causes an adversary to ramp up its targeting and attack plans. As Thomas Schelling once warned, "A fine deterrent can make a superb target."[4] Our research shows that the threshold at which a nuclear arsenal truly stops being a "target" and starts to be only a "deterrent" appears far higher than many analysts assume. Countries that seek to acquire nuclear weapons for compelling strategic reasons—to deter attack—should understand that they will likely need highly survivable delivery systems in order to feel secure. Finally, our research suggests that new nuclear powers will likely have to grapple with enemies that have very potent counterforce capabilities. Those enemies are unlikely to give up the strategic competition, accept those countries as nuclear equals, and embrace the stability of nuclear stalemate. In short, would-be nuclear proliferators face a long road to security, paved with the dangers of preventive attack, preemptive strike, conventional war, and a relentless struggle to maintain a survivable arsenal in an age of rapid, dramatic, and often unpredictable technological change.

Our analysis of the role of nuclear weapons in international relations bears directly on a broader enduring debate about the wisdom of global nuclear disarmament and abolition. The contours of this debate were set immediately after the first atomic bombs were used by the United States against Japan in 1945. Although the bombings ended World War II, the most destructive war in history, and some observers felt that nuclear deterrence might prevent the outbreak of international conflict in the future, many others viewed these weapons as a dangerous scourge of civilization. Prominent scientists, scholars, and politicians pushed for international cooperation to rid the globe of these weapons, often casting the choice as one between atomic abolition or inevitable destruction.[5] The view that nuclear weapons pose an existential threat to mankind was stated in the starkest terms at the start of the nuclear age, and is often repeated today.[6] So, it seems worth asking: Would the world be better off without nuclear weapons?

This book offers significant ammunition for advocates of nuclear abolition. If we had found that even small nuclear arsenals reliably produce stalemate (in chapter 2), or that nuclear stalemate could not be broken (in chapter 3), or that even simple nuclear arsenals can be counted on to deter conventional attacks (in chapter 4), then the case for nuclear weapons as a solution to the problems of international anarchy would be strong. Instead, we found the reverse. Since nuclear weapons have not rendered intense geopolitical competition obsolete, there is a strong case to be made that the deterrence benefits of living in a nuclear world are outweighed by the inherent risks.

Nevertheless, abolition is a deeply misguided goal. In fact, even if the core of the abolitionist argument were correct—that the dangers of a nuclear-armed world outweigh the deterrent benefits those weapons offer—the effort to abolish nuclear weapons would likely have terrible unintended consequences.

First, a successful abolition campaign would not only lead to more conventional wars; it would also likely trigger dangerous nuclear rearmament races during crises and conflicts. "A 'world without nuclear weapons,'" writes

Schelling, "would be a world in which the United States, Russia, Israel, China, and half a dozen or a dozen other countries would have hair-trigger mobilization plans to rebuild nuclear weapons and mobilize or commandeer delivery systems, and would have prepared targets to preempt other nations' nuclear facilities, all in a high-alert status, with practice drills and secure emergency communications. Every crisis would be a nuclear crisis, any war could become a nuclear war. The urge to preempt would dominate; whoever gets the first few weapons will coerce or preempt. It would be a nervous world."[7]

In essence, abolitionists present a false choice: between the world of conventional conflict that existed before 1945 and the world of nuclear dangers we inhabit today. But abolition, if successful, would create a third, more dangerous situation: a world of conventional wars and nuclear know-how, in which adversaries teetered on the brink of a rearmament race and faced real incentives to preempt once they reacquired nuclear weapons during a crisis.

Second, the likely result of the abolition movement is not global elimination but rather incremental progress toward disarmament, a result that would create dangerous deterrence dynamics. All else being equal, smaller nuclear arsenals mean more vulnerable nuclear arsenals. And given long-term trends in technology that are making nuclear forces increasingly vulnerable to conventional attacks, deep multilateral nuclear cuts are likely to create mutual vulnerability to disarming strikes. The arms-control community has often raised the alarm when nuclear-armed states deploy new offensive capabilities (nuclear and conventional) that could undermine deterrence. But the risks to deterrence created by arms reductions—the stepping-stones toward abolition—have been largely ignored in those circles.

In short, no country should aspire to have "just barely enough" nuclear deterrence. The benefit of nuclear weapons—to the countries that possess them and more generally to the world, which has not seen great power war for seventy-five years—stems from the *certainty* they can create in the minds of aggressors that victory is impossible. Chipping away at that certainty through arms cuts is potentially dangerous and counterproductive.

We conclude with one positive note and one caveat. Because this book explains why intense competition endures in the nuclear age, some readers will inevitably take away a gloomy view of the future. That is not our intent. In reality, nuclear weapons have made the world a better place. The nuclear age is a boon to the strongest powers, which for centuries routinely fought large and costly wars against each other. It is also a boon to weaker countries, which for most of history were forced to bend the knee to stronger adversaries.

Our caveat is that nuclear deterrence is serious business. Nothing about strategic stalemate is automatic. If a country is going to acquire nuclear weapons, it will need enough of them to guarantee stalemate, and historically, for countries facing committed adversaries, that has meant building robust and survivable forces. The benefits of nuclear stalemate depend on countries having properly trained forces, clearly defined missions, and secure warheads and delivery systems. They depend on smart civilian officials and military leaders developing realistic nuclear strategies and doctrines. For democracies in particular, maintaining political support for the nuclear mission depends on a vigorous and well-informed public debate about foreign policy objectives and the capabilities that are necessary for pursuing those ends. All of this is tougher to do than it sounds, but it is possible, even as power politics endure in the nuclear age.

Notes

Introduction

1. See John J. Mearsheimer, *The Tragedy of Great Power Politics* (New York: W. W. Norton, 2001); Kenneth N. Waltz, *Theory of International Politics* (Reading, MA: Addison-Wesley, 1979); Robert Jervis, "Cooperation under the Security Dilemma," *World Politics* 30, no. 2 (1978): 167–214.

2. Robert Jervis, *The Meaning of the Nuclear Revolution: Statecraft and the Prospect of Armageddon* (Ithaca, NY: Cornell University Press, 1989).

3. John Lewis Gaddis, *The Long Peace: Inquiries into the History of the Cold War* (New York: Oxford University Press, 1987). The biggest conflict between nuclear-armed states to date is the 1999 Kargil clash between India and Pakistan, which likely resulted in over one thousand troops killed.

4. John Mueller argues that policymakers did not need nuclear weapons to reinforce their desire to avoid war after the catastrophe of World War II. "The nuclear-deterrence-saved-the-world theory is predicated on the notion that policymakers after 1945 were so stupid, incompetent, or reckless that, but for visions of mushroom clouds, they would have plunged the great powers back into war." John Mueller, "Nuclear Weapons Don't Matter: But Nuclear Hysteria Does," *Foreign Affairs* 97, no. 6 (November–December 2018): 10–15.

5. Among the classic works are Kenneth N. Waltz, *The Spread of Nuclear Weapons: More May Be Better*, Adelphi Paper no. 171 (London: International Institute of Strategic Studies, 1981); Robert Jervis, *The Illogic of American Nuclear Strategy* (Ithaca, NY: Cornell University Press, 1984); Jervis, *Meaning of the Nuclear Revolution*; and Kenneth N. Waltz, "Nuclear Myths and Political Realities," *American Political Science Review* 84, no. 3 (September 1990): 731–745.

6. As Jervis wrote, U.S. nuclear strategy had led to "many inconsistencies, incoherences, and contradictions because it seeks to repeal the nuclear revolution rather than coming to grips with [it]." Jervis, *Illogic of American Nuclear Strategy*, 147. Jervis's broader argument that the behavior of nuclear-armed countries contradicts theoretical expectations also runs through his 1989 book (*The Meaning of the Nuclear Revolution*), although there he also describes some factors that he believes are consistent with the nuclear revolution—such as leaders' desire to maintain the status quo and behave cautiously in crises, the relative paucity of crises once the superpowers acquired sufficient nuclear forces, and the importance of credibility and the balance of resolve in the presence of nuclear weapons. Among many others who agree with Jervis (that the pacifying effect of nuclear weapons has not been fully appreciated by policymakers) are Bernard

Brodie, ed., *The Absolute Weapon: Atomic Power and World Order* (New York: Harcourt, Brace, 1946); Waltz, "Nuclear Myths"; Charles L. Glaser, *Analyzing Strategic Nuclear Policy* (Princeton, NJ: Princeton University Press, 1990); and Charles L. Glaser and Steven Fetter, "National Missile Defense and the Future of U.S. Nuclear Weapons Policy," *International Security* 26, no. 1 (Summer 2001): 40–92.

7. See Waltz, "Nuclear Myths"; and Waltz, *Spread of Nuclear Weapons.*

8. Indeed, many historians believe that Soviet fears about the deteriorating balance of power led them to concede the Cold War—a decision that should further puzzle proponents of the theory of the nuclear revolution. Although the Soviet economy could not support a full-scale nuclear arms race with the United States, it could indefinitely support a modest nuclear arsenal. And although the Soviet economy was overtaxed by the costs of the Soviet-era Red Army, the Soviet economy could have supported a greatly reduced military, sized and structured to deter or suppress rebellions within the Warsaw Pact or Soviet republics. Ironically, nuclear revolution proponents may not have focused on this anomaly (Soviet surrender) because the theory also fails to explain what strategic goals the Soviets were seeking to accomplish in the Cold War; after all, from the nuclear revolution perspective, conquering Western Europe was impossible as long as NATO was a nuclear alliance, and maintaining a security buffer in Eastern Europe was unnecessary.

9. See, for example, Eric Heginbotham et al., *The U.S.-China Military Scorecard: Forces, Geography, and the Evolving Balance of Power, 1996–2017* (Santa Monica, CA: RAND Corporation, 2015); and Michael Beckley, "The Emerging Military Balance in East Asia: How China's Neighbors Can Check Chinese Naval Expansion," *International Security* 42, no. 2 (Fall 2017): 78–119.

10. The United States values its global network of military bases for the same reason that Russia values its Mediterranean port in Syria, and China seeks bases in the Horn of Africa and South Asia: to help project conventional military power far from the homeland.

11. Proponents most often attribute the problem to "unit-level" explanations, such as misguided leaders, bureaucratic pathologies, or dysfunctional domestic politics. A thorough discussion of this set of "defensive realist" arguments can be found in Stephen Van Evera, *Causes of War: Power and the Roots of Conflict* (Ithaca, NY: Cornell University Press, 1999). Scholars—some working in the theory of the nuclear revolution tradition and others not—have offered a wide range of explanations for behavior that contradicted the meaning of the nuclear revolution, especially the intensity of the superpower competition. Some argued that the nuclear arms race was largely the result of misunderstanding—specifically, that leaders simply did not comprehend the logic of the nuclear revolution. Others focused on misperceptions rooted in cognitive and emotional distortions; for example, human brains have become hardwired to overestimate the aggressiveness of potential enemies. On cognitive and motivated biases, see Robert Jervis, *Perception and Misperception in International Politics* (Princeton, NJ: Princeton University Press, 1976); Richard Ned Lebow, *Between Peace and War* (Baltimore, MD: Johns Hopkins University Press, 1981); and Robert Jervis, Richard Ned Lebow, and Janice Gross Stein, *Psychology and Deterrence* (Baltimore, MD: Johns Hopkins University Press, 1985). Some emphasized how policies were distorted by powerful military organizations, which lobbied for excessively strong and offensively oriented forces. Jack Snyder, "Civil-Military Relations and the Cult of the Offensive, 1914 and 1984," *International Security* 9, no. 1 (Summer 1984): 108–146; Barry R. Posen, *The Sources of Military Doctrine* (Ithaca, NY: Cornell University Press, 1984); Stephen Van Evera, "The Cult of the Offensive and the Origins of the First World War," *International Security* 9, no. 1 (Summer 1984): 58–107; Scott D. Sagan, "The Origins of the Pacific War," *Journal of Interdisciplinary History* 18, no. 4 (Spring 1988): 893–922; and Lynn Eden, *Whole World on Fire: Organizations, Knowledge, and Nuclear Weapons Devastation* (Ithaca, NY: Cornell University Press, 2004). Others pinned the blame on powerful commercial lobbies—part of the so-called military industrial complex—that captured policymakers and stoked an arms race for profit. And some saw the problem as the deep human predisposition to violence, or male predisposition to symbolic competitions in power and dominance. For example, see Stephen Peter Rosen, *War and Human Nature* (Princeton, NJ: Princeton University Press, 2005); and Bradley A. Thayer, "Bringing in Darwin: Evolutionary Theory, Realism, and International Politics," *International Security* 25, no. 2 (Fall 2000): 124–151. A common thread in many of these works is that the Cold War competi-

tion seemed more intense than necessary, thus requiring further explanation. Few scholars saw evidence in the Cold War—or in the decades since—that nuclear-armed countries have felt fundamentally secure.

12. The best example of the latter is Charles L. Glaser, *Rational Theory of International Politics: The Logic of Competition and Cooperation* (Princeton, NJ: Princeton University Press, 2010).

13. It was clear to Bernard Brodie and others even at the dawn of the nuclear age that these weapons brought a terrifying clarity and simplicity to strategic calculations: nuclear war could not be won in any meaningful sense, so it could not be started.

1. Power Politics in the Nuclear Age

1. Among the classic works on the role of nuclear weapons in deterring war, see Bernard Brodie, ed., *The Absolute Weapon: Atomic Power and World Order* (New York: Harcourt, Brace, 1946); Bernard Brodie, *Strategy in the Missile Age* (Princeton, NJ: Princeton University Press, 1959); Thomas C. Schelling, *The Strategy of Conflict* (Cambridge, MA: Harvard University Press, 1960); Glenn H. Snyder, *Deterrence and Defense: Toward a Theory of National Security* (Princeton, NJ: Princeton University Press, 1961); Thomas C. Schelling, *Arms and Influence* (New Haven, CT: Yale University Press, 1966); Kenneth N. Waltz, *The Spread of Nuclear Weapons: More May Be Better*, Adelphi Paper no. 171 (London: International Institute of Strategic Studies, 1981); Robert Jervis, *The Illogic of American Nuclear Strategy* (Ithaca, NY: Cornell University Press, 1984); Kenneth N. Waltz, "Nuclear Myths and Political Realities," *American Political Science Review* 84, no. 3, (September 1990); and Robert Jervis, *The Meaning of the Nuclear Revolution: Statecraft and the Prospect of Armageddon* (Ithaca, NY: Cornell University Press, 1989).

2. In addition to destructiveness and stalemate, which are discussed here, the speed at which nuclear destruction can occur is sometimes highlighted as a key unique characteristic of nuclear weapons. See Robert Jervis, "The Political Effects of Nuclear Weapons: A Comment," *International Security* 13, no. 2 (Autumn 1988): 80–90.

3. At the dawn of the atomic age, the most powerful conventional bombs exploded with the force of roughly 7 tons of TNT. The atom bomb that destroyed Hiroshima released as much energy as 15,000 tons of TNT, and the 1950s-vintage Mk-15 thermonuclear weapon was designed to explode with the power of 2 million tons of TNT (or 2 megatons). The lethal radius of the Hiroshima bomb was roughly 1 mile, corresponding to a lethal area of just over 3 square miles. Because nuclear weapons effects increase with yield to the one-third power, the lethal radius of an Mk-15 was roughly 5 miles, resulting in a lethal area of approximately 75 square miles.

4. Scott D. Sagan and Kenneth N. Waltz, *The Spread of Nuclear Weapons: A Debate Renewed* (New York: W. W. Norton, 2003), 9.

5. See Philip G. Dower and Lyndall Ryan, eds., *Theatres of Violence: Massacre, Mass Killing, and Atrocity throughout History* (New York: Berghahn Books, 2012).

6. Thucydides, *History of the Peloponnesian War* (New York: Penguin, 1954), 408.

7. Brian Bosworth, "Massacre in the Peloponnesian War," in Dower and Ryan, *Theatres of Violence*, 17–26.

8. Hans van Wees, "Genocide in the Ancient World," in *The Oxford Handbook of Genocide Studies*, ed. Donald Bloxham and A. Dirk Moses (Oxford: Oxford University Press, 2010), 239–258.

9. One study—covering a more contemporary time period—finds that leaders who suffered military defeat were four times as likely to be exiled, jailed, or killed as those who managed to achieve a stalemate. Even this telling statistic hardly conveys the cost of trading power and privilege for jail and often death. See Giacomo Chiozza and H. E. Goemans, *Leaders and International Conflict* (Cambridge: Cambridge University Press, 2011), 56–57. For more on leaders and war outcomes, see Alexandre Debs and H. E. Goemans, "Regime Type, the Fate of Leaders, and War," *American Political Science Review* 104, no. 3 (August 2010): 430–445; and Giacomo Chiozza and H. E. Goemans, "International Conflict and the Tenure of Leaders: Is War Still 'Ex Post' Inefficient?" *American Journal of Political Science* 48, no. 3 (July 2004): 604–619.

10. Perhaps there is some other dimension to the destructiveness of nuclear weapons, distinct from even the worst consequences of total conventional war, that is the key to robust deterrence, such as the speed with which devastation can occur. Or perhaps it is the fact that large-scale nuclear war would threaten the survival of human civilization. Yet, this fate-of-the-earth explanation posits that would-be conquerors are willing to wager their own fates and risk the torture of their families and the ruin of their people, but are paralyzed by the thought of imperiling human civilization. This casts them as having more empathy for humanity than seems plausible.

11. See Jervis, citing Bernard Brodie and Thomas Schelling, in Jervis, "Political Effects," 83.

12. Germany overreached and invaded the Soviet Union, bringing about its eventual ruin. But Germany very nearly prevailed in its effort to conquer the Soviet Union, too. Had Germany knocked the Soviets out of the war in 1941 or 1942, it would have controlled territory from the Urals to the English Channel. Having no organized Eastern Front to contend with, it could have sent scores of divisions from the east to reinforce the west, precluding a D-Day–style invasion. See Richard Overy, *Why the Allies Won* (New York: W. W. Norton, 1995).

13. For example, the nuclear bombs in the current U.S. arsenal are roughly twelve feet long. A standard missile "reentry vehicle," the conical assembly that sits atop a ballistic missile and includes the "physics package" as well as the fuse, is approximately four feet tall.

14. For this reason, proponents of the nuclear revolution argue that smaller nuclear powers do not need large arsenals. As Waltz writes, "Lesser nuclear states may deploy, say, ten real weapons and ten dummies, while permitting other countries to infer that numbers are larger. An adversary need only believe that some warheads may survive its attack and be visited on it. That belief is not hard to create. Sagan and Waltz, *Debate Renewed*, 20–21.

15. The simple reason, as Jervis and others note, is that "military victory is not possible." Jervis, *Meaning of the Nuclear Revolution*, 23; Waltz, *Spread of Nuclear Weapons*; and Stephen Van Evera, *Causes of War: Power and the Roots of Conflict* (Ithaca, NY: Cornell University Press, 1999), 240–247.

16. Kenneth N. Waltz, "The Origins of War in Neorealist Theory," *Journal of Interdisciplinary History* 18, no. 4 (Spring 1988): 627.

17. Brodie, *Absolute Weapon*, 73.

18. Jervis, *Meaning of the Nuclear Revolution*, 19–23.

19. Waltz, *Spread of Nuclear Weapons*, 6. Elsewhere, Waltz writes, "The accumulation of significant power through conquest, even if only conventional weapons are used, is no longer possible in the world of nuclear powers." Waltz, "Origins of War," 625.

20. Jervis, *Meaning of the Nuclear Revolution*, 8. Van Evera writes that a world of deterrable states with second-strike forces is "profoundly peaceful." He continues: "In such a world MAD erases major causes of past war. States fight far less than in the pre-nuclear era." Van Evera, *Causes of War*, 242. Elsewhere, Van Evera writes, "The nuclear revolution has made conquest among great powers impossible." Stephen Van Evera, "A Farewell to Geopolitics," in *To Lead the World: American Strategy after the Bush Doctrine*, ed. Melvyn P. Leffler and Jeffrey W. Legro (Oxford: Oxford University Press, 2008), 11.

21. We consider a major war to be one in which either side sought to seize large tracts of territory or compel capitulation. The only war between nuclear armed states is the 1999 conflict between Pakistan and India in Kargil. Roughly one thousand soldiers were killed. This is an important data point that undermines the claim that countries will be too cautious to launch even limited attacks on nuclear-armed adversaries, but it also remains an outlier.

22. The five great power wars were the Crimean War (1853–56), the Franco-Prussian War (1870–71), the Russo-Japanese War (1904–5), World War I (1914–18), and World War II (1939–45). The list could also include the Austro-Prussian War (1866) and the Soviet-Japanese War (1939).

23. Some scholars dispute whether nuclear weapons played a major role in deterring a U.S.-Soviet war. For example, see John Mueller, *Retreat from Doomsday: The Obsolescence of Major War* (New York: Basic Books, 1989); and Richard Ned Lebow and Janice G. Stein, *We All Lost the Cold War* (Princeton, NJ: Princeton University Press, 1994). We know that during several crises, however, U.S. leaders considered using military force but were seemingly dissuaded by the prospect of nuclear war.

24. Argentina's willingness to seize territory that the United Kingdom claimed as its own raises another question about the assertion that nuclear weapons will reliably deter limited attacks on nuclear weapon states. The conflict over Argentina imposed significant costs on the United Kingdom: in addition to nine hundred fatalities, it lost four major British warships and more than one hundred aircraft.

25. Tellingly, China's leader, Mao Zedong, specifically discussed the possibility of American retaliation in his October 2, 1950, telegram to Soviet leader Josef Stalin. Mao wrote, "We must be prepared [for the fact] that the United States may, at a minimum, use its air force to bomb many major cities and industrial centers in China." See Thomas J. Christensen, *Useful Adversaries: Grand Strategy, Domestic Mobilization, and Sino-American Conflict, 1947–1958* (Princeton, NJ: Princeton University Press, 1996), 163–165, 271.

26. For a detailed accounts of the 1973 war and the threats the initial attacks posed to Israel, see Trevor N. Dupuy, *Elusive Victory: The Arab-Israeli Wars, 1947–1974* (New York: Harper and Row, 1978); Michael B. Oren, *Six Days of War: June 1967 and the Making of the Modern Middle East* (New York: Presidio Press, 2003); and Abraham Rabinovich, *The Yom Kippur War: The Epic Encounter That Transformed the Middle East* (New York: Schocken Books, 2004).

27. Indeed, as Jervis notes, the title of one of the first books on the subject was *The Absolute Weapon* (referring to Brodie's edited volume). Jervis, *Meaning of the Nuclear Revolution*, 18, note 48.

28. Kenneth N. Waltz, "The Emerging Structure of International Politics," *International Security* 18, no. 2 (Fall 1993): 73. Elsewhere he writes, "Nuclear weapons can carry out their deterrent task no matter what other countries do." Waltz, "Nuclear Myths," 732.

29. McGeorge Bundy, *Danger and Survival* (New York: Random House, 1988).

30. Jervis, *Meaning of the Nuclear Revolution*, 42.

31. According to Van Evera, "States cannot mistake what their military forces can and cannot do [in the nuclear age]. . . . They can annihilate the other's society and cannot protect their own society from annihilation. . . . The calculus of relative capabilities drops from the calculus of war." Van Evera, *Causes of War*, 244. Elsewhere he writes, "Any state with a secure nuclear deterrent is secure from conquest, as it could annihilate any attacker. And a secure deterrent is far easier to maintain than to threaten, so superpowers can defend themselves even against states with many times their economic power." Van Evera, "Farewell to Geopolitics," 14.

32. Marc Trachtenberg, "A 'Wasting Asset': American Strategy and the Shifting Nuclear Balance, 1949–1954," *International Security* 13 (Winter 1988–1989); Russell D. Buhite and William Christopher Hamel, "War and Peace: The Question of an American Preventive War against the Soviet Union, 1945–1955," *Diplomatic History* 14 (Summer 1990): 367–384. U.S. preventive war deliberations occurred before the Soviet Union had acquired a secure second-strike nuclear capability, and those considerations faded as the Soviet arsenal grew, but the fact remains that the United States pursued and built counterforce capabilities throughout the Cold War—and, of course, never stopped caring about the relative power balance.

33. Marc Trachtenberg, "Assessing Soviet Economic Performance in the Cold War: A Failure of Intelligence," *Texas National Security Review* 1, no. 2 (February 2018).

34. Trachtenberg, "Assessing Soviet Economic Performance."

35. See Stephen G. Brooks and William C. Wohlforth, "Power, Globalization, and the End of the Cold War," *International Security* 25, no. 3 (Winter 2000/1): 5–53.

36. Paul Kennedy's famous book *The Rise and Fall of the Great Powers* was published in the midst of this heightened concern about Japanese growth, contributing to the book's popularity. Paul Kennedy, *The Rise and Fall of the Great Powers: Economic Change and Military Conflict from 1500 to 2000* (New York: Random House, 1987).

37. Waltz, "Nuclear Myths," 741.

38. Sagan and Waltz, *A Debate Renewed*, 143. Waltz also writes, "Deterrent forces are quite cheap to build and maintain" (30).

39. Robert Jervis, "Why Nuclear Superiority Doesn't Matter," *Political Science Quarterly* 94 (Winter 1979/80): 618.

40. Charles L. Glaser, "Realists as Optimists: Cooperation as Self-Help," *International Security* 19, no. 3 (Winter 1994/95): 87.

41. See Brendan R. Green and Austin Long, "The MAD Who Wasn't There: Soviet Reactions to the Late Cold War Nuclear Balance," *Security Studies* 26, no. 4 (July 2017): 606–641.

42. Chinese officials have even justified Beijing's more restrained approach to nuclear arms competition with arguments about the robustness of nuclear deterrence. See Liping Xia, "China's Nuclear Evolution: Debates and Evolution," Carnegie Endowment for International Peace, June 30, 2016, https://carnegieendowment.org/2016/06/30/china-s-nuclear-doctrine-debates -and-evolution-pub-63967; Jeffrey G. Lewis, "Minimum Deterrence," *Bulletin of Atomic Scientists* 64, no. 3 (July–August 2008); Jeffrey G. Lewis, *The Minimum Means of Reprisal: China's Search for Security in the Nuclear Age* (Cambridge, MA: MIT Press, 2007).

43. Eric Heginbotham et al., *China's Evolving Nuclear Deterrent: Major Drivers and Issues for the United States* (Santa Monica, CA: RAND Corporation, 2017); Hans M. Kristensen and Robert S. Norris, "Chinese Nuclear Forces, 2018," *Bulletin of the Atomic Scientists* 74, no. 4 (2018): 289–295; Hans M. Kristensen and Robert S. Norris, "Pakistani Nuclear Forces, 2018," *Bulletin of the Atomic Scientists* 74, no. 5 (2018): 348–358; and Hans M. Kristensen and Robert S. Norris, "Indian Nuclear Forces, 2017," *Bulletin of the Atomic Scientists* 73, no. 4 (2017): 205–209. Vipin Narang suggests we are seeing a "decoupling" of India's nuclear strategy toward Pakistan and China, and the forces India needs to threaten retaliation against China may allow it to adopt a more aggressive nuclear strategy against Pakistan. As cited in Kristensen and Norris, "Indian Nuclear Forces, 2017," 205.

44. Eric Heginbotham et al., *The U.S.-China Military Scorecard: Forces, Geography, and the Evolving Balance of Power, 1996–2017* (Santa Monica, CA: RAND Corporation, 2015).

45. On entrapment and abandonment—the two perennial risks associated with alliances— see Glenn H. Snyder, "The Security Dilemma in Alliance Politics," *World Politics* 36, no. 4 (July 1984): 461–495. Other problems with alliances include highly inefficient pooling of resources. In the military domain, this can lead to disastrously ineffective multinational military operations.

46. Waltz, "Emerging Structure," 73.

47. According to Jervis, national security is ensured by retaliatory nuclear capabilities, so nuclear countries no longer need to pool resources. Jervis, *Meaning of the Nuclear Revolution*, 35–36. In addition to reducing the need for alliances, nuclear weapons may also make them less useful—because of the difficulty of credibly committing to engage in nuclear war to defend an ally. For a discussion of those concerns in the context of Cold War France, see Philip H. Gordon, "Charles de Gaulle and the Nuclear Revolution," in *Cold War Statesmen Confront the Bomb: Nuclear Diplomacy Since 1945*, ed. John Gaddis, Philip Gordon, Ernest May, and Jonathan Rosenberg (Oxford: Oxford University Press, 1999), 226–227.

48. Russian president Vladimir Putin and his allies may also fear NATO for political as well as strategic reasons; that is, they may fear that the growing democratic alliance could undermine the authority and legitimacy of the Russian regime.

49. See, for example, Alexander Gabuev, "Why Russia and China Are Strengthening Security Ties: Is the U.S. Driving Them Closer Together?," *Foreign Affairs*, September 24, 2018, https:// www.foreignaffairs.com/articles/china/2018-09-24/why-russia-and-china-are-strengthening -security-ties?cid=int-fls&pgtype=hpg; and Dave Majumdar, "Russia and China Are Sending Their Navies to the Baltic Sea: Is a Formal Alliance Next?" *National Interest*, July 25, 2017, https:// nationalinterest.org/blog/the-buzz/russia-china-are-sending-their-navies-the-baltic-sea -formal-21669.

50. Van Evera, *Causes of War*, 245.

51. On the lack of importance of strategic depth in a nuclear world, see Klaus Knorr, *On the Uses of Military Power in the Nuclear Age* (Princeton, NJ: Princeton University Press, 1966), 86–87.

52. Van Evera, *Causes of War*, 245.

53. Barry R. Posen and Stephen Van Evera, "Defense Policy and the Reagan Administration: Departure from Containment," *International Security* 8 (Summer 1983): 33.

54. As Jervis argues, the United States "should not have felt menaced by Soviet gains in the third world." Robert Jervis, "Was the Cold War a Security Dilemma?" *Journal of Cold War Studies* 3 (Winter 2001): 54.

55. Not all competition during the Cold War in the so-called Third World was about the value of territory. In Vietnam, for example, the United States sought to prevent the spread of Com-

munist, pro-Soviet governments. But the location of many of the Cold War struggles was driven by the strategic location of the territory.

56. Whether one believes that international anarchy causes countries to compete intensely or merely permits them to do so, the creation of a weapon that deters major acts of aggression should substantially reduce competition.

57. Many prominent nuclear deterrence analysts argue that deterrence will be robust even if arsenals are far less than perfectly survivable. See, for example, Kenneth Waltz's discussion of the requirements of deterrence in Sagan and Waltz, *Debate Renewed*, 20–21, 142–43; McGeorge Bundy, "Strategic Deterrence Thirty Years Later: What Has Changed?" in *The Future of Strategic Deterrence: Part I*, Adelphi Paper no. 160 (London: International Institute for Strategic Studies, 1980); Avery Goldstein, *Deterrence and Security in the 21st Century: China, Britain, France, and the Enduring Legacy of the Nuclear Revolution* (Stanford, CA: Stanford University Press, 2000), esp. 44–46; Lewis, *Minimum Means of Reprisal*. The view that even vulnerable arsenals create a robust deterrent, which we sort into the theoretical categories of "existential deterrence" and "minimum deterrence," is discussed in chapter 2.

58. An even more demanding version of this view—"assured destruction"—holds that retaliation must be not only assured but also truly devastating. Both views are discussed in chapter 2.

59. The competitive process described here matches the current dynamics on the Korean Peninsula, as North Korea seeks to create a survivable nuclear arsenal and the United States and South Korea race to keep it vulnerable (through improved sensors, conventional strike systems, missile defense, and other approaches). Elements of this process were evident in the early days of China's nuclear arsenal, and both the Soviet Union and the United States considered launching preventive attacks to stop China's development of a survivable nuclear force. As chapter 2 reveals, these dynamics fueled the major nuclear arms race of the 1950s, as the United States sought to maintain its disarming strike capabilities while the Soviets struggled to create stalemate.

60. On the key role of allies in providing deterrence while nuclear arsenals are vulnerable, see Alexandre Debs and Nuno P. Monteiro, *Nuclear Politics: The Strategic Causes of Proliferation* (New York: Cambridge University Press, 2017).

61. The assumption that mutual vulnerability cannot be reversed is explicit in the writings of nuclear revolution proponents; for instance, Jervis acknowledges in his book on the nuclear revolution that if a state could protect itself against nuclear retaliation (through, for example, the development of a defensive shield, or by gaining the ability to destroy all of an adversary's nuclear forces in a first strike), then "the analysis presented here would be negated." Jervis, *Meaning of the Nuclear Revolution*, 9–10. Similarly, Waltz refers to the invulnerability of nuclear arsenals "both now and as far into the future as anyone can see." Waltz, "Nuclear Myths," 732.

62. The challenge of using nuclear threats to deter conventional attacks on one's *allies* is even greater, given the mismatch between risk (high) and interests (protecting someone else's country).

63. As Jervis writes, nuclear weapons deter conventional attack because "escalation can occur although no one wants it to." Jervis, *Meaning of the Nuclear Revolution*, 21–22. Waltz adds, "Anyone—political leader or man in the street—can see that catastrophe lurks if events spiral out of control and nuclear warheads begin to fly." Waltz, "Nuclear Myths," 734.

2. Getting to Stalemate

1. On the key role of allies in providing deterrence while nuclear arsenals are vulnerable, see Alexandre Debs and Nuno P. Monteiro, *Nuclear Politics: The Strategic Causes of Proliferation* (New York: Cambridge University Press, 2017).

2. A recent example of the first approach is Campbell Craig and Sergey Radchenko, "MAD, Not Marx: Khrushchev and the Nuclear Revolution," *Journal of Strategic Studies* 41, nos. 1–2 (2017): 208–233.

3. See Gregory Mitrovich, *Undermining the Kremlin: America's Strategy to Subvert the Soviet Bloc, 1947–1956* (Ithaca, NY: Cornell University Press, 2000).

4. One might add a fifth school of thought, "war-fighting." For the argument that robust deterrence requires the ability to fight and win, see Colin Gray, "War-Fighting for Deterrence," *Journal of Strategic Studies* 7 (March 1984): 5–28; and Caspar W. Weinberger, Secretary of Defense, *Annual Report to the Congress, Fiscal Year 1984* (Washington,DC: USGPO, February 1, 1983), 51.

5. Bernard Brodie, ed., *The Absolute Weapon: Atomic Power and World Order* (New York: Harcourt, Brace, 1946), 52. Although Brodie may have provided the essential observation for the existential deterrence school, his arguments seem to fall more squarely in the assured retaliation school.

6. Herman Kahn as quoted in Robert Jervis, *The Meaning of the Nuclear Revolution: Statecraft and the Prospect of Armageddon* (Ithaca, NY: Cornell University Press, 1989), 23n63. Kahn was summarizing the existential deterrence school, of which he was a staunch critic.

7. Leon Wieseltier, *Nuclear War, Nuclear Peace* (New York: Holt, Rinehart and Winston, 1983), 38. From an existential deterrence view, as Robert Tucker writes, "deterrence is not only an inherent property of nuclear weapons, it is very nearly a self-sufficient property." Robert Tucker, "The Nuclear Debate," *Foreign Affairs* 63 (1984/85): 3. For a critique of the existential deterrence school, see Lawrence Freedman, "I Exist; Therefore I Deter," *International Security* 13, no. 1 (Summer 1988): 177–195.

8. McGeorge Bundy, "The Bishops and the Bomb," *New York Review of Books* 30, no. 10 (June 16, 1983): 3.

9. McGeorge Bundy, "Strategic Deterrence Thirty Years Later: What Has Changed?" in *The Future of Strategic Deterrence: Part I*, Adelphi Paper no. 160 (London: International Institute for Strategic Studies, 1980), 11. Similarly, journalist and *New Yorker* columnist Richard Rovere wrote: "If the Russians had ten thousand warheads and a missile for each, and we had ten hydrogen bombs and ten obsolete bombers . . . aggression would still be a folly that would appeal only to an insane adventurer." Quoted in Albert Wohlstetter, "The Delicate Balance of Terror," *Foreign Affairs* 37, no. 2 (January 1959) 213.

10. Bundy, "Strategic Deterrence Thirty Years Later," 11. At times, however, Bundy seemed to emphasize that survivable retaliatory forces—not just the mere existence of weapons—were necessary for reliable deterrence. For example: "As long as each side has thermonuclear weapons that could be used against the opponent, *even after the strongest possible preemptive attack*, existential deterrence is strong and it rests on uncertainty about what could happen." Bundy, "Existential Deterrence and Its Consequences," in *The Security Gamble: Deterrence Dilemmas in the Nuclear Age*, ed. Douglas MacLean (Totowa, NJ: Rowman and Allanheld, 1984), 8–9 (emphasis in original).

11. James H. Lebovic, *Deadly Dilemmas: Deterrence in U.S. Nuclear Strategy* (New York: Columbia University Press, 1990), 193.

12. Hedley Bull, "Future Conditions of Strategic Deterrence," in *Future of Strategic Deterrence*, 17.

13. Michael J. Mazarr, *Nuclear Weapons in a Transformed World: The Challenge of Virtual Nuclear Arsenals* (New York: St. Martin's Press, 1997); Jonathan Schell, *The Abolition* (1984) reprinted in Schell, *The Fate of the Earth and the Abolition* (Stanford, CA: Stanford University Press, 2000).

14. Michael Howard, "Nuclear Danger and Nuclear History," *International Security* 14, no. 1 (Summer 1989): 181 (emphasis in original).

15. Scott D. Sagan and Kenneth N. Waltz, *The Spread of Nuclear Weapons: A Debate Renewed*, 20–21 (emphasis added). Waltz also wrote, "Even with numbers immensely disproportionate, a small force strongly inhibits the use of a large one." Kenneth N. Waltz, "Nuclear Myths and Political Realities," *American Political Science Review* 84, no. 3 (September 1990): 734. Also, "It does not take much to deter" (Sagan and Waltz, *A Debate Renewed*, 142), and "Numbers are not very important. To have second-strike forces, states do not need large numbers of weapons. Small numbers do quite nicely. . . . The requirements of second-strike deterrence have been widely and wildly exaggerated" (143). Or, as Lebow and Stein write, "A little deterrence goes a long way." Richard Ned Lebow and Janice G. Stein, *We All Lost the Cold War* (Princeton, NJ: Princeton University Press, 1994), 361.

16. As Goldstein describes it, unless a "nuclear power can be disarmed with virtual 100% certainty, the onus of initiating an unpredictable, possibly disastrous chain of events that could

entail absorbing a nuclear retaliatory strike, falls to the aggressor. In even the most lopsided nuclear pairs, this unavoidable worry exerts a powerfully dissuasive effect." Avery Goldstein, "Why Nukes Still Trump: Deterrence and Security in the 21st Century," Foreign Policy Research Institute E-Notes, November 2000, 5.

17. Waltz, "Nuclear Myths," 734.

18. William W. Kaufmann, "The Requirements of Deterrence," in *Military Policy and National Security*, ed. William W. Kaufmann (Princeton, NJ: Princeton University Press, 1956), 19. The preceding sentences are: "Potential as against actual capability cannot be regarded as a convincing instrument of deterrence in the present state of affairs. Nor is it enough simply to have a certain number of planes supplied with fission and fusion bombs."

19. Avery Goldstein, *Deterrence and Security in the 21st Century: China, Britain, France, and the Enduring Legacy of the Nuclear Revolution* (Stanford, CA: Stanford University Press, 2000), 44–46. See also Devin Hagerty, *The Consequences of Nuclear Proliferation: Lessons from South Asia* (Cambridge, MA: MIT Press, 1998), esp. 3, 26, 46–47, 184–185.

20. Waltz, "Nuclear Myths," 734. Waltz frequently refers to "second-strike" forces (e.g., in Sagan and Waltz, *Debate Renewed*, 143), which suggests he should fall in the assured retaliation school, not the minimal deterrence one. Waltz's fundamental position, however, is that almost any kind of nuclear arsenal is an awesome deterrent. He argued that the large superpower arsenals deterred, but so did the smaller and more vulnerable forces possessed by China, Pakistan, and North Korea. He argued that if Ukraine had kept its nuclear weapons, they would have deterred. And he argued that if Iran were to acquire nuclear weapons, that arsenal, too, would deter. Most revealing about Waltz's view is that he reaches these conclusions without conducting any force-on-force analysis aimed at determining second-strike arsenal survivability. Waltz rejected the need for such an approach because, in his view, such calculations mistakenly implied an unnecessarily high threshold for robust deterrence. Waltz thought that virtually all arsenals deter because he believed that deterrence does not really depend on assured survivability. His analysis falls squarely in the minimum deterrence school.

21. For example, China arguably possessed an existential deterrent toward the United States from its initial nuclear test in 1964 until it deployed its first intercontinental-range ballistic missiles in 1981. For the next two decades, China fielded an arsenal of long-range missiles that could reach the U.S. homeland, but these were few in number and stored in fixed silos, and thus highly vulnerable to a preemptive strike. Beijing's development of mobile long-range missiles reflects its movement toward a posture of assured retaliation (as described below).

22. Assured retaliation has been the most popular view in the international security analytic community. For example, see the works of George Quester, Stephen Van Evera, Charles Glaser, Shai Feldman, and Jack Snyder, among others.

23. Robert Jervis, *The Illogic of American Nuclear Strategy* (Ithaca, NY: Cornell University Press, 1984); and Jervis, *Meaning of the Nuclear Revolution*.

24. Robert Jervis, "Why Nuclear Superiority Doesn't Matter," *Political Science Quarterly* 94 (Winter 1979/80): 617–618. Jervis uses the term *assured destruction* to describe this school of thought, but his discussion better accords with our category of assured retaliation. Jervis himself never sharply distinguished between the two.

25. In the 1970s, analysts often stressed the need for a secure enough force so that a "clever briefer" could not make a compelling case for attacking. See Morton H. Halperin, "Clever Briefers, Crazy Leaders and Myopic Analysts," *Washington Monthly*, September 1974, 42–49.

26. Robert Jervis, "Deterrence Theory Revisited," *World Politics* 31, no. 2 (January 1979): 299.

27. Bernard Brodie is often identified with the existential deterrence school, but the bulk of his work suggests that deterrence rests on the concrete capability to retaliate in kind after a nuclear attack, which cannot be taken for granted simply because a state possesses nuclear weapons. As Brodie explained, "The preparation of such retaliation must occupy a decisive place in any over-all policy of protection against the atomic danger." Brodie, *Absolute Weapon*, 134.

28. Robert Jervis is closely associated with both the assured retaliation school and the view that nuclear weapons ought to transform international politics. Nevertheless, as we argue below, the logics of the former and the latter are in tension. Specifically, if countries need an assured retaliatory capability to have a truly robust deterrent, then the degree of effort and vigilance

required to reach and maintain that force posture will generate more competition than can be reconciled with the pacific relations predicted by a nuclear revolution. The history of the strategic arms race from 1950 to 1960, described in detail below, demonstrates exactly this dynamic: that is, how the Soviet Union's long, drawn-out efforts to build a truly secure retaliatory force, and U.S. efforts to prevent that, energized a decade-long arms race and intense competition. The "assured retaliation" threshold also opens the door wider for the development of counterforce capabilities to push an adversary back below that threshold, a dynamic discussed in chapter 3.

29. As prospect theory suggests, desperate leaders facing certain losses are much more likely to take such great risks.

30. For a good discussion of the balance of power at the start of the Cold War, and the challenges inherent in measuring the aggregate balance of power, see William C. Wohlforth, "The Stability of a Unipolar World," *International Security* 24, no. 1 (Summer 1999): 9–22.

31. The United States suffered approximately 418,000 military and civilian deaths. Japan lost approximately 3 million, Germany 6.5 million, and the Soviet Union 23 million (conservatively estimated).

32. See Melvyn P. Leffler, *A Preponderance of Power: National Security, the Truman Administration, and the Cold War* (Palo Alto, CA: Stanford University Press, 1992); John Lewis Gaddis, *Strategies of Containment* (New York: Oxford University Press, 1982); and Marc Trachtenberg, *A Constructed Peace: The Making of the European Settlement, 1945–1963* (Princeton, NJ: Princeton University Press, 1999).

33. Harry R. Borowski, "A Narrow Victory: The Berlin Blockade and the American Military Response," *Air University Review* 32, no. 5 (July–August 1981): 1–2; and Steven T. Ross, *American War Plans, 1945–1950* (London: Frank Cass, 1996), 86.

34. Ross, *American War Plans*, 86.

35. The term *atomic bomb* typically refers to a fission weapon, which generates its destructive power by splitting atomic nuclei. This was the type of bomb used at Hiroshima and Nagasaki. Fusion weapons, which generate much of their destructive power by fusing together atomic nuclei, are generally referred to as "nuclear" or "thermonuclear" weapons—and they can create vastly more destructive power than atomic weapons.

36. Ross, *American War Plans*, 12–13; Borowski, "Narrow Victory," 1–2. U.S. long-range atomic bombers in this period were still B-29s, the same type of aircraft that dropped the atomic bombs on Japan.

37. See Ross, *American War Plans*, 84.

38. By 1949 the United States had trained three more atom bomb assembly crews, increasing its assembly rate to 3.5 bombs per day. Ross, *American War Plans*, 12.

39. Borowski, "Narrow Victory," 5. He cites General Hoyt Vandenberg to Commanding General, HQ Strategic Air Command, July 13, 1948, Air Force OPD A/AE 381 (Atomic Weapons Test), and Memorandum for General Schlattter from William E. Kennedy, Office Assistant Operations for Atomic Energy, August 27, 1948, AF OPD A/AE 381 (Harrow).

40. Moreover, bomber crew training had declined precipitously since the war, raising questions about whether the crews could achieve the average World War II "miss distance," especially at night over unfamiliar territory.

41. Ross, *American War Plans*, 12–15. "Whether or not these aircraft in the absence of full fighter cover and complete target information could in fact have delivered their weapons in the face of fierce Soviet fighter attacks, anti-aircraft fire, and electronic countermeasures is perhaps a question that may happily remain unanswered" (13). In 1949, the Harmon Committee report argued that a successful strategic bombing campaign would have killed millions of Soviet people and reduced Soviet industrial capacity by a third or more, but would not stop the advance of Soviet forces in Europe, Asia, or the Middle East. As David Holloway summarizes the report, "An atomic attack could not by itself defeat the Soviet Union." David Holloway, *Stalin and the Bomb: The Soviet Union and Atomic Energy, 1939–1956* (New Haven, CT: Yale University Press, 1954), 229. The U.S. Air Force refused to pass along the report's findings to President Truman.

42. The Soviets had five fission bombs by March 1950, fifty by 1952, and 150 in 1954. In August 1953 they tested a "boosted" fission weapon, but their first "true" thermonuclear test

employing a two-stage fusion device did not occur until November 1955. They deployed their first fusion bomb the following year. Michael Kort, *The Columbia Guide to the Cold War* (New York: Columbia University Press, 1998), 187.

43. Although 847 Tu-4s were eventually produced, only some (the Tu-4As) were made nuclear-capable. Moreover, very few of the Tu-4As received any kind of range-extension improvements. See "Tu-4 (Bull)," Globalsecurity.org, accessed July 14, 2019, https://www.globalsecurity.org/wmd/world/russia/tu-4.htm; and Pavel Podvig, ed., *Russian Strategic Nuclear Forces* (Cambridge, MA: MIT Press, 2001), 366–370. In theory, the Soviets could have tried to launch some bombers on one-way suicide missions against some cities in the northern United States by flying directly from bases in northern Russia and Siberia (weather permitting). But they would have had to fly at high altitudes in order to save fuel and along a direct path from their air bases to U.S. cities, which would have greatly simplified the task for Canadian and U.S. air defenses and fighter aircraft. Podvig, *Russian Strategic Nuclear Forces*, 347.

44. Data on U.S. strategic capabilities in this period are derived from a declassified U.S. air force report, Richard D. Little, "Expansion of the Strategic Atomic Striking Force," in *A History of the Air Force Atomic Energy Program, 1943–1953*, vol. 3, pt. 1, sec. 1: *Building an Atomic Air Force, 1949–1953* (U.S. Air Force Historical Division, 1959), Digital National Security Archive; and Thomas C. Cochran, William M. Arkin, Robert S. Norris, Milton M. Hoenig, *Nuclear Weapons Data Book*, vol. 2: *U.S. Nuclear Warhead Production* (Cambridge, MA: NRDC/Ballinger, 1987).

45. A fusion, thermonuclear, or hydrogen bomb (the terms are interchangeable) fuses together two hydrogen isotopes to produce its nuclear effects. The first U.S. thermonuclear weapon, the Mk-17, was preceded by three "emergency capability" weapons (the EC-14, -16, and -17), but those were prototypes.

46. The destructive power of nuclear weapons does not scale directly with explosive yield. Specifically, the radius of destruction increases as a function of yield to the one-third power—meaning that a doubling of the lethal radius requires multiplying yield by a factor of eight.

47. Little, *History of the Air Force Atomic Energy Program*; and Cochran et al., *Nuclear Weapons Data Book*. Our count of U.S. aircraft includes all heavy and medium nuclear bombers designated as "primary authorized aircraft" (PAA); that is, those that were assigned to operational units and combat-ready for SAC's atomic offensive in the emergency war plan. All figures here and below indicate totals at end of the fiscal year (June 30) unless otherwise indicated. The bombers include nuclear modified B-36s, B-29s, B-47s, and B-50s. Warhead totals represent the number of warheads that would be carried by PAA aircraft. From 1953 through 1955 B-47 bombers had an average of 1.5 bombs per aircraft. There were 206 B-47s in the force in 1953 and 405 in 1954. All other aircraft carried one bomb.

48. The refueling bases had to be in the Arctic because the shortest route between most parts of the Soviet Union and the United States went over the pole. Soviet bombers, therefore, would need to refuel in the Arctic, then proceed north over the pole, and then south over Canada, before reaching the United States.

49. The U.S. arsenal was not similarly vulnerable to a Soviet disarming strike. In 1957, soon after the Soviets deployed their first bombers that could reach the United States, the U.S. Strategic Air Command established a "ground alert" to keep a portion of the B-52 bomber force armed and ready to take off at first warning of a Soviet attack. Henry M. Narducci, *Strategic Air Command and the Alert Program: A Brief History* (Offutt Air Force Base, NE: Headquarters Strategic Air Command, 1988). By 1959, new U.S. radar sites would provide three to four hours of warning of an incoming strike before Soviet bombers could reach SAC bases in the middle of the United States—enough time to launch four hundred nuclear-armed bombers. And starting in 1960, in anticipation of the deployment of the first Soviet intercontinental ballistic missiles (ICBMs), SAC made its requirements for its "alert force" more stringent: "One-third of SAC achieved 15 minute ground alert status by August 1960," meaning that 150 (out of 450) nuclear-armed B-52s would be in the air before Soviet ICBMs could strike SAC airfields. See Memorandum, Lawrence C. McQuade to Paul Nitze, May 31, 1963 ("But Where Did the Missile Gap Go?"), Digital National Security Archive, 12. The same memorandum notes that the U.S. Defense Department estimated that a disarming attack on the United States would require at least 270

Soviet ICBMs in 1960, and at least 440 missiles in 1961. The Soviets had less than 1 percent of the required forces in 1960, and less than 3 percent in 1961.

50. The holes in Soviet radar networks are mentioned in Carl Kaysen, "Strategic Air Planning and Berlin," Memorandum to General Maxwell, September 6, 1961; Carl Kaysen, "Thoughts on Berlin," Memorandum, August 22, 1961; Carl Kaysen, "Annex A: An Alternative to SIOP-62."

51. Podvig, *Russian Strategic Nuclear Forces*, 363; Marc Trachtenberg, *History and Strategy* (Princeton, NJ: Princeton University Press, 1991), 29–31. Moreover, there were few bases overall, some of which were undefended with air defenses.

52. Scott D. Sagan, "SIOP-62: The Nuclear War Plan Briefing to President Kennedy," *International Security* 12, no. 1 (Summer 1987): 29, 29n23; Podvig, *Russian Strategic Nuclear Forces*, 237; and "629 Golf," Globalsecurity.org, accessed July 14, 2019, https://www.globalsecurity.org/wmd /world/russia/629.htm.

53. Podvig, *Russian Strategic Nuclear Forces*, 312. The Soviets deployed Zulu and Golf submarines in 1958 and 1959 with nuclear-capable ballistic missiles onboard, but the warheads were stored on shore. Beginning in 1960, U.S. cities were targeted by several types of Soviet submarine with nuclear warheads on board: converted Whiskey-class subs starting in 1960, and Golf- and Hotel-class subs, which began nuclear-armed patrols in 1961. The Whiskeys that were deployed in 1960 had two nuclear missiles each. The Golf- and Hotel-class subs had three missiles each.

54. Podvig, *Russian Strategic Nuclear Forces*, 121–126, 172–173, 181. Soviet ICBMs all had single warheads in this period. The Soviets deployed two SS-6 missiles in 1960, and four more in 1961. It deployed six SS-7 missiles in 1961. "R-7/SS-6 SAPWOOD," Federation of American Scientists, July 29, 2000, https://fas.org/nuke/guide/russia/icbm/r-7.htm.

55. U.S. naval forces would have scoured the ocean for any Soviet submarines that survived a U.S. attack on Soviet ports, but antisubmarine warfare (ASW), especially in this period, was far from a sure thing. See Austin Long and Brendan Rittenhouse Green, "Stalking the Secure Second Strike: Intelligence, Counterforce, and Nuclear Strategy," *Journal of Strategic Studies* 38, nos. 1–2 (2015): 38–73.

56. The new missiles were modified SS-6s and SS-7s. Podvig, *Russian Strategic Nuclear Forces*.

57. This data on U.S. nuclear forces includes only America's long-range nuclear attack forces; the United States also had medium-range bombers and ballistic missiles stationed abroad. Had the United States decided to launch a nuclear first strike on the Soviet Union during this period, however, it is likely that it would have relied solely on the forces deployed in the United States and at sea in order to achieve a high level of surprise. On triad numbers, see Memorandum, Lawrence C. McQuade to Paul Nitze, "But Where Did the Missile Gap Go?," May 31, 1963.

58. For a remarkably detailed description of U.S. nuclear war planning at the time, see "Memorandum for General Maxwell Taylor," September 5, 1961, esp. Annex A and its appendix, in William Burr, ed., "First Strike Options and the Berlin Crisis, September 1961: New Documents from the Kennedy Administration," National Security Archive Electronic Briefing Book no. 56, September 25, 2001, http://www.gwu.edu/~nsarchiv/NSAEBB/NSAEBB56/.

59. Sagan, "SIOP-62," 32–33.

60. The Soviets deployed five submarines in the Caribbean during the crisis "to support Soviet naval operations." Despite U.S. efforts, the submarines "were not detected until they encountered American quarantine forces in the region. . . . The sub-air barrier off Argentia [Newfoundland] that was established after the quarantine began therefore missed them." Owen Coté Jr., *The Third Battle: Innovation in the U.S. Navy's Silent Cold War Struggle with Soviet Submarines* (Newport, RI: U.S. Naval War College, 2003), 46. See also Sagan, "SIOP-62," 34–35.

61. The Soviet ICBM force included six SS-6s and thirty-two SS-7s in 1962. The SS-6s required twenty-four hours to fuel and prepare to launch, making them very vulnerable to a U.S. first strike. But SS-7s could be launched within a few hours of warning. If previously alerted, SS-7s could be launched in less than an hour. See Podvig, *Russian Strategic Nuclear Forces*, 179–181, 189–190.

62. "Memorandum for General Maxwell Taylor"; Sagan, "SIOP-62," 32–35.

63. On the possibility of spotters, see Stephen M. Meyer, "Soviet Nuclear Operations," in *Managing Nuclear Operations*, ed. Ashton B. Carter, John D. Steinbruner and Charles A. Zraket (Washington, DC: Brookings Institution, 1987), 488.

64. Major parts of this section are drawn from Daryl G. Press, *Calculating Credibility: How Leaders Assess Military Threats* (Ithaca, NY: Cornell University Press, 2007).

65. For U.S. assessments of Soviet capabilities across this period, see NIE-3; SE-10; SE-14; NIE-64; NSC 140/1; SE-36/1; SNIE 11-2-54; NIE 11-5-54; and NIE 11-3-55. See also JCS report in David Alan Rosenberg, "The Origins of Overkill: Nuclear Weapons and American Strategy, 1945–1960," *International Security* 7, no. 4 (Spring 1983): 23n68.

66. NIE 11-56, "Soviet Gross Capabilities for Attack on the US and Key Overseas Installations and Forces through Mid-1959," March 6, 1956, 8; SNIE 11-6-57, "Soviet Gross Capabilities for Attack on the Continental United States in Mid-1960," January 15, 1957, 9, 19; SNIE 11-8-57, "Evaluation of Evidence concerning Soviet ICBM Flight Tests," September 18, 1957, 4–6; NIE 11-8-59, "Soviet Capabilities for Strategic Attack through Mid-1964," February 9, 1960, 7; and NIE 11-8-61, "Strength and Deployment of Soviet Long Range Ballistic Missile Forces," June 7, 1961, 6–10. Note the care with which the United States monitored those facilities.

67. NIE 11-8-60, "Soviet Capabilities for Long Range Attack through Mid-1965," August 1, 1960, 22; NIE 11-8-61, 18.

68. NIE 11-8/1-61, "Strength and Deployment of Soviet Long Range Ballistic Missile Forces," June 7, 1961, 9.

69. On early worries about Soviet nuclear retaliatory capability, see Richard K. Betts, *Nuclear Blackmail and Nuclear Balance* (Washington, DC: Brookings Institution, 1987), 144–161.

70. An earlier study—the February 1955 report of the Technological Capabilities Panel (the Killian report)—warned that the United States could expect to maintain its strategic superiority for three to five years. Rosenberg, "Origins of Overkill," 38. Similarly, on May 24, 1956, Army Chief of Staff General Maxwell Taylor argued to Eisenhower that by 1960, "a situation of mutual deterrence must be envisaged." Memorandum of Conference with the President, May 24, 1956, Digital National Security Archive.

71. Memorandum of Discussion at the 364th Meeting of the National Security Council, May 1, 1958, Document 23, in *FRUS*, 1958–1960, vol. 3, *National Security Policy, Arms Control and Disarmament*, 80–96. See also Peter J. Roman, *Eisenhower and the Missile Gap* (Ithaca, NY: Cornell University Press, 1996), 64–77.

72. Trachtenberg, *History and Strategy*, 42.

73. Trachtenberg, *History and Strategy*, 191.

74. See Burr, "First Strike Options and the Berlin Crisis."

75. "Memorandum for General Maxwell Taylor."

76. "Evaluation of Strategic Offensive Weapons Systems," WSEG Report No. 50, December 27, 1960 [DNSA].

77. "Reactions to DOD Study on Conventional Forces," May 12, 1961.

78. In 1961 the chairman explained, however, that "under any circumstances—even a pre-emptive attack by the U.S.—it would be expected that some portion of the Soviet long-range nuclear force would strike the United States." Scott D. Sagan, *Moving Targets: Nuclear Strategy and National Security* (Princeton, NJ: Princeton University Press, 1989), 25–26; and Sagan, "SIOP-62," 30. The quotation is from General Lemnitzer's briefing notes for President Kennedy. For the change in 1963, see Trachtenberg, *Constructed Peace*, 182–183; and Francis J. Gavin, "The Myth of Flexible Response: United States Strategy in Europe during the 1960s," *International History Review* 23, no. 4 (December 2001): 853.

79. Memorandum for the President from McGeorge Bundy, "Net Evaluation Subcommittee Report 1963," September 12, 1963.

80. Summary Record of the 517th Meeting of the National Security Council, Washington, September 12, 1963, 11 a.m., https://history.state.gov/historicaldocuments/frus1961-63v08/d141.

81. James G. Blight and David A. Welch, *On the Brink: Americans and Soviets Reexamine the Cuban Missile Crisis* (New York: Hill and Wang, 1989), 29–30, 33, 52, 90–91.

82. The memo is dated November 21, 1962. Sagan, "SIOP-62," 30. John Lewis Gaddis agrees with this description of McNamara's views during the crisis. Gaddis, *We Now Know: Rethinking*

Cold War History (New York: Oxford University Press, 1997), 268. McGeorge Bundy, Kennedy's national security advisor, appears to have shared McNamara's views about the nuclear balance of power at the time. See McGeorge Bundy, *Danger and Survival* (New York: Random House, 1988), 448; and Comments of Colonel Lawrence J. Legere, Assistant to the President's Military Representative, cited in editorial note 127, *FRUS*, 1961-1963, Vol. VIII, 463.

83. Trachtenberg, *Constructed Peace*, 293–297, 318.

84. Even though the Soviet Union enjoyed conventional military superiority in Europe in 1948, and even though a U.S. atomic offensive, as described below, would have required months to grind down Soviet industry, the prospects of suffering a months-long U.S. atomic campaign was presumably horrifying to Soviet leaders. In hindsight, it is hard to understand why U.S. leaders were not sufficiently confident in their overall military advantage in 1948 to adopt a hard-line position on Berlin and force the Soviets to back down. In this sense, the airlift operation was the "prudent"—not aggressive—course of action.

85. An excellent source on U.S. war plans during the late 1940s is Ross, *American War Plans*.

86. See the discussion of emergency war plans Halfmoon-Fleetwood (for 1948) and Trojan (for 1949). Ross, *American War Plans*, xx; David M. Kunsman and Douglas B. Lawson, *A Primer on U.S. Strategic Nuclear Policy* (Albuquerque, NM: Sandia National Laboratories, 2001), 23; and Scott D. Sagan, "Change and Continuity in U.S. Nuclear Strategy," in *America's Defense*, ed. Michael Mandelbaum (New York: Holmes and Meier, 1989), 283–284. By 1949 the United States had trained three more atom bomb assembly crews, increasing its assembly rate to 3.5 bombs per day. Ross, *American War Plans*, 12, 84–91; and Borowski, "Narrow Victory," 3–5.

87. Ross, *American War Plans*, 108–110.

88. The direction for U.S. defense plans for years to come was formalized in September 1948, in NSC-30, which directed that the "National Military Establishment must be ready to utilize promptly and effectively all appropriate means available, including atomic weapons, in the interest of national security and must therefore plan accordingly." Cited in Sagan, "Change and Continuity," 238.

89. Nina Tannenwald, *The Nuclear Taboo: The United States and the Non-use of Nuclear Weapons since 1945* (New York: Cambridge University Press, 2007), chap. 4; and T. V. Paul, *The Tradition of Non-use of Nuclear Weapons* (Stanford, CA: Stanford University Press, 2009), 55–57.

90. Gaddis, *We Now Know*, 105–107; and John Lewis Gaddis, *The Cold War: A New History* (New York: Penguin, 2005), 56–58.

91. Within a year, the JCS had established three principal categories for targets in the "Sino-Soviet bloc"—Bravo (nuclear forces), Delta (industry and governmental control), and Romeo (conventional forces). Bravo targets were given the highest priority. David A. Rosenberg, "Reality and Responsibility: Power and Process in the Making of United States Nuclear Strategy, 1945–1968," *Journal of Strategic Studies* 9, no. 1 (March 1986): 39–40; Sagan, "Change and Continuity," 288–289; and Ross, *American War Plans*, 119–131.

92. David A. Rosenberg, "A Smoking Radiating, Ruin at the End of Two Hours': Documents on American Plans for Nuclear War with the Soviet Union, 1954–1955," *International Security* 6, no. 3 (Winter 1981/82): 3–38; Rosenberg, "Origins of Overkill," 39; and Sagan, "Change and Continuity," 287–288. NATO military plans in the early 1950s closely mirrored U.S. strategic concepts, with the main difference being that early Alliance documents were less transparent about NATO's inability to halt the Red Army. The first NATO plan, DC 13 (adopted in 1950), called for NATO to "delay and arrest the enemy advance . . . as far to the East as possible" to "gain time for reinforcements to arrive and for the cumulative effect of the strategic [atomic] air offensive to be felt." But stopping the Soviet Army's advance was an aspirational objective. As DC 13 tacitly admitted, the alliance would need ninety divisions to accomplish such military objectives, an entirely implausible ground force given the political and resource constraints at the time. Actual U.S. and NATO plans were in sync, since everyone understood that the phrase "as far to the East as possible" in DC 13 meant the English Channel. Gregory W. Pedlow, "The Evolution of NATO Strategy, 1949–69," in *NATO Strategy Documents, 1949–1969*, ed. Gregory W. Pedlow (Brussels: NATO, 1999).

93. The need to strike rapidly was fully understood at the highest levels of the U.S. government. Each year a subcommittee of the National Security Council, the Net Evaluation Sub-

commmittee (NESC), produced a top secret estimate for the president and his top advisors on the expected outcome of a nuclear war. In 1957 the NESC proposed to examine the survivability of U.S. nuclear forces in a scenario in which the U.S. had sufficient warning of an Soviet attack to put the Strategic Air Command (SAC) on high alert. Eisenhower rejected that scenario for its "unrealism" and asked NESC to study, instead, a scenario in which the Soviets put their arsenal on alert and the United States launched a massive preemptive strike. See the discussion of Eisenhower's rejection of the "full alert" scenario in General Nathan Twining to Robert Cutler, "Recommended Changes to Paragraph 3 of NSC 5605," November 20, 1957; and Dwight D. Eisenhower, "Directive on a Net Evaluation Subcommittee," NSC 5728, December 24, 1957.

94. General Maxwell Taylor to Lemnitzer, September 19, 1961. Though Kennedy was clearly interested in exploring the possibility of a small strike on the Soviets—which would maximize the odds of destroying all Soviet long-range nuclear systems at the expense of leaving unscathed the medium-range systems that threatened Europe—he was not indifferent to the fate of Europe. He also asked General Power, in the same memo: "A surprise attack aimed at destroying the long-range striking power of the USSR would leave a sizeable number of MRBMs facing Europe. a. Would the inclusion of these MRBMs in the initial attack so enlarge the target list as to preclude tactical surprise? b. If so, is it possible to plan an immediate follow-on attack which would strike these targets before the first attack was completed?"

95. See Gavin, "Myth of Flexible Response"; William Burr, "The Nixon Administration, the 'Horror Strategy,' and the Search for Limited Nuclear Options, 1969–72," *Journal of Cold War Studies* 7, no. 3 (Summer 2005): 34–78; and Sagan, *Moving Targets*.

96. The debates within the Eisenhower administration at this time, which frequently saw Eisenhower (who insisted on sticking with massive retaliation) pitted against his national security advisor and secretary of state (who argued for moving away from massive retaliation), are well summarized in Roman, *Eisenhower and the Missile Gap*, 68–74; Campbell Craig, *Destroying the Village: Eisenhower and Thermonuclear War* (New York: Columbia University Press, 1998), 53–89; and Trachtenberg, *Constructed Peace*, 179–193.

97. Memorandum of Discussion at the 364th Meeting of the National Security Council, May 1, 1958, 80–96.

98. Roman, *Eisenhower and the Missile Gap*, 68–70.

99. Cited in Kunsman and Lawson, *Primer on U.S. Strategic Nuclear Policy*, 38.

100. Cited in Roman, *Eisenhower and the Missile Gap*, 78. On several occasions, U.S. political and military leaders suggested to Eisenhower that he might want to develop a range of plans to give him options during a crisis or a war. He repeatedly rejected those suggestions, insisting that there only be one plan: winning by "hitting the Russians as hard as we could." As Eisenhower explained, "They . . . will have started the war, we will finish it. That is all the policy [I have]" (82–84).

101. Gavin, "Myth of Flexible Response," 851; and Burr, "Nixon Administration," 34–78.

102. For two accounts that focus on elements of U.S. efforts to escape from stalemate, see Peter Sasgen, *Stalking the Red Bear: The True Story of a U.S. Cold War Submarine's Covert Operations against the Soviet Union* (New York: St. Martin's Press, 2009); and Benjamin B. Fischer, "CANOPY WING: The U.S. War Plan That Gave the East Germans Goose Bumps," *International Journal of Intelligence and Counterintelligence* 27, no. 3 (2014): 431–464. For an article that puts the various efforts to escape stalemate into strategic context, see Long and Green, "Stalking the Secure Second Strike." Note that during the 1960s, the United States grew increasingly concerned that U.S. nuclear command and control was vulnerable to the first waves of a Soviet nuclear strike, and that a well-designed Soviet attack could prevent the United States from executing its nuclear war plans. It is likely that the United States had developed offensive options based on a similar observation about Soviet command-and-control (C2) vulnerabilities. In March 1970, Kissinger, who was then national security advisor, received briefings at SAC headquarters on U.S. nuclear options "both within and outside of the SIOP," the latter referring to the theater nuclear options discussed below. The commander of SAC, Bruce Holloway, later noted that "certain aspects of the SIOP . . . were deliberately not gone into" in the briefing for Kissinger. According to Burr, "some features of the SIOP were too sensitive to share even with the president's chief

security advisor." See Burr, "Nixon Administration," 61–62. Those "aspects of the SIOP" that could not be shared with Kissinger could refer to counter-C2 capabilities, antisubmarine capabilities, or something else.

103. Descriptions of the war plan and the available options are in Burr, "Nixon Administration," 42–45, with ninety withholds described on p. 59.

104. Gavin, "Myth of Flexible Response."

105. See the description of the BERCON plans—which were contingency plans for a Berlin conflict—in SHAPE to Chairman, Standing Group, NATO, "Berlin Contingency Planning," March 24, 1962; and the discussion of those and other plans in Sean M. Maloney, "Berlin Contingency Planning: Prelude to Flexible Response, 1958–1963," *Journal of Strategic Studies* 25, no. 1 (March 2002): 99–134. After much debate, NATO approved these plans—not as a pathway they had agreed to execute, but as a set of options from which they could select during a conflict—i.e., exactly as "flexible response" advocates would desire.

106. See the discussion of NATO nuclear options in Sean M. Maloney, *Learning to Love the Bomb: Canada's Nuclear Weapons during the Cold War* (Washington, DC: Potomac Books, 2007), especially chap. 13. See the mention of these options as an alternative to developing more limited options within the SIOP, cited in Burr, "Nixon Administration," 51.

107. Maloney, "Berlin Contingency Planning," 116–21.

108. Interestingly, the United States appears to have developed its own parallel plans for graduated escalation and tactical nuclear employment in the theater, separate from NATO's options, though the details of the U.S. options (called POODLE BLANKET) remain classified. These plans may have provided a way for the United States to conduct theater nuclear attacks even if NATO did not authorize NATO nuclear operations, but such conclusions must await eventual declassification. The escalatory steps in POODLE BLANKET are described in Maloney, "Berlin Contingency Planning," 114–115.

109. For example, as Michael Desch has shown, the German and French military plans formulated in peacetime prior to World War I and II were substantially changed as war approached. Michael C. Desch, "Planning War in Peacetime," *Joint Forces Quarterly* 30, no. 3 (Spring 2002): 94–104.

110. Burr, "First Strike Options."

111. See Campbell Craig and Sergey Radchenko, *The Atomic Bomb and the Origins of the Cold War* (New Haven, CT: Yale University Press, 2008), 94, 111, 117.

112. See, for example, Bruce G. Blair, *The Logic of Accidental Nuclear War* (Washington, DC: Brookings Institution, 1993), 46–49; and Trachtenberg, *Constructed Peace*, 146–178.

113. In fact, one of the key differences between U.S. "strategic posture" in the first decade of the Cold War and in all subsequent decades was the singular nature of U.S. plans for fighting World War III. Clearly the Eisenhower administration did not want war, but the president's detailed engagement with the plans and satisfaction with the existence of a single military option suggest that the U.S. administration knew how it would respond to a Soviet invasion of Europe. By contrast, starting in the 1960s, U.S. civilian leaders asked the military to produce an ever-expanding set of options for waging war in Europe precisely because all the options were bad, and because U.S. leaders did not know what they would do if war erupted. With only one option, we can say with some confidence that had war erupted in 1959 the United States would have launched the massive SAC campaign against the Warsaw Pact that was outlined in U.S. war plans—and that conclusion is enough to cast great doubt on both the existential and minimal deterrent views. We cannot say what the United States would have done had war erupted in the mid-1960s or later—because U.S. leaders themselves did not know. But we attribute that change—from a period of near-certain strategic nuclear offensive to a period of options and uncertainty—to the growth of Soviet nuclear capabilities.

114. Mitrovich, *Undermining the Kremlin.*

115. Schelling was referring to Japan's decision to attack Pearl Harbor, lamenting that U.S. leaders had forgotten that a deterrent could still be a target. Thomas C. Schelling, Foreword to *Pearl Harbor: Warning and Decision*, by Robert Wohlstetter (Stanford, CA: Stanford University Press, 1962), viii.

3. Escaping Stalemate

1. See Robert Jervis, *The Meaning of the Nuclear Revolution: Statecraft and the Prospect of Armageddon* (Ithaca, NY: Cornell University Press, 1989), 10; Spurgeon M. Keeny Jr. and Wolfgang K. H. Panofsky, "Nuclear Weapons in the 1980s: MAD vs. NUTS," *Foreign Affairs* 60, no. 2 (Winter 1981/82): 287–304; Harold Feiveson and Frank von Hippel, "The Freeze and the Counterforce Race," *Physics Today* 36, no. 1 (January 1983): 36–49; Robert Jervis, *The Illogic of American Nuclear Strategy* (Ithaca, NY: Cornell University Press, 1984); Charles L. Glaser, "Why Do Strategists Disagree about the Requirements of Strategic Nuclear Deterrence?" in *Nuclear Arguments: Understanding the Strategic Nuclear Arms and Arms Control Debates*, ed. Lynn Eden and Steven E. Miller (Ithaca, NY: Cornell University Press, 1989), 109–171, esp. 134–142; and Michael Salman, Kevin J. Sullivan, and Stephen Van Evera, "Analysis or Propaganda? Measuring American Strategic Nuclear Capability, 1969–88," in Eden and Miller, *Nuclear Arguments*, 172–263.

2. Kenneth Waltz argued that survivable retaliatory arsenals were very easy to build, deploy, and maintain. See, for example, Scott D. Sagan and Kenneth N. Waltz, *The Spread of Nuclear Weapons: A Debate Renewed* (New York: W. W. Norton, 2003), 20–23, 142–143. Other analysts have been more conservative about the requirements, but nonetheless expressed confidence that the development of first-strike capabilities was impossible, and would remain so for the foreseeable future. See Jervis, *Meaning of the Nuclear Revolution*, 10; Jervis, *Illogic of American Nuclear Strategy*; Charles L. Glaser, *Analyzing Strategic Nuclear Policy* (Princeton, NJ: Princeton University Press, 1990); and Charles L. Glaser and Steve Fetter, "Should the United States Reject MAD? Damage Limitation and U.S. Nuclear Strategy toward China," *International Security* 41, no. 1 (Summer 2016): 49–98.

3. Keir A. Lieber and Daryl G. Press, "The Next Korean War," *Foreign Affairs*, April 1, 2013, https://www.foreignaffairs.com/articles/north-korea/2013-04-01/next-korean-war. For a more general discussion of wartime escalation risks, see Keir A. Lieber and Daryl G. Press, *Coercive Nuclear Campaigns in the 21st Century: Understanding Adversary Incentives and Options for Nuclear Escalation*, Project on Advanced Systems and Concepts for Countering Weapons of Mass Destruction (PASCC) Report no. 2013-001 (Monterey, CA: Naval Postgraduate School, 2013); and Caitlin Talmadge, "Too Much of a Good Thing? Conventional Military Effectiveness and the Dangers of Nuclear Escalation," in *The Sword's Other Edge: Trade-offs in the Pursuit of Military Effectiveness*, ed. Dan Reiter (New York: Cambridge University Press, 2017), 197–226.

4. Chinese planners assume that their underground nuclear sites have been discovered by the United States because digging is difficult to hide, and because Chinese planners know that the United States is using a wide range of surveillance tools to find the sites. See Wu Riqiang, "Certainty of Uncertainty: Nuclear Strategy with Chinese Characteristics," *Journal of Strategic Studies* 36, no. 4 (July–August 2013): 586–587; Li Bin, "Tracking Chinese Strategic Mobile Missiles," *Science and Global Security* 15, no. 1 (2007): 5; Zhang Yuliang, ed., *Zhanyi xue* [The science of campaigns] (Beijing: National Defense University Press, 2006), 635, 637; and Yu Jixun, ed., *Di'er pao bing zhanyi xue* [The science of Second Artillery campaigns] (Beijing: PLA Press, 2004), 302.

5. New historical evidence reveals that technological breakthroughs and innovative naval operations allowed the United States to trail Soviet ballistic missile submarines during periods of the Cold War. The Soviets were unaware of the extent of the vulnerability of their submarines for several years. See Austin Long and Brendan Rittenhouse Green, "Stalking the Secure Second Strike: Intelligence, Counterforce, and Nuclear Strategy," *Journal of Strategic Studies* 38, nos. 1–2 (2015): 38–73; Owen R. Coté Jr., *The Third Battle: Innovation in the U.S. Navy's Silent Cold War Struggle with Soviet Submarines* (Newport, RI: U.S. Naval War College, 2003); and Peter Sasgen, *Stalking the Red Bear: The True Story of a U.S. Cold War Submarine's Covert Operations against the Soviet Union* (New York: St. Martin's Press, 2009).

6. Wu, "Certainty of Uncertainty," 586–587; Li, "Tracking Chinese Strategic Mobile Missiles," 7–11; Hans M. Kristensen, Robert S. Norris, and Matthew G. McKinzie, *Chinese Nuclear Forces and U.S. Nuclear War Planning* (Washington, DC: Federation of American Scientists/Natural Resources Defense Council, November 2006), 51; and Yu, *Di'er pao bing zhanyi xue*.

7. Redundancy involves trade-offs, too. Building additional command sites, warning systems, or communication systems is expensive and therefore comes at the cost of deploying additional weapons. Furthermore, redundancy may promote complacency, thus undermining survivability.

8. Both global and U.S. nuclear weapons stockpiles have declined about 80 percent since the end of the Cold War and 85 percent from peak levels in the Cold War. See U.S. Bureau of Arms Control, Verification, and Compliance, "Fact Sheet: Transparency in the U.S. Nuclear Weapons Stockpile" (Washington, DC: U.S. Department of State, April 29, 2014); Hans M. Kristensen and Matt Korda, "Nuclear Notebook: Nuclear Arsenals of the World," *Bulletin of the Atomic Scientists*, accessed July 14, 2019, http://thebulletin.org/nuclear-notebook-multimedia; Hans M. Kristensen and Robert S. Norris, "United States Nuclear Forces, 2016," *Bulletin of the Atomic Scientists* 72, no. 2 (March 2016): 63–73; and Shannon N. Kile and Hans M. Kristensen, *Trends in World Nuclear Forces, 2016* (Stockholm: Stockholm International Peace Research Institute, June 2016), 2.

9. For an earlier analysis of the consequences of technological trends in the United States–Russia case, see Keir A. Lieber and Daryl G. Press, "The End of MAD? The Nuclear Dimension of U.S. Primacy," *International Security* 30, no. 4 (Spring 2006): 7–44; and Keir A. Lieber and Daryl G. Press, "The Rise of U.S. Nuclear Primacy," *Foreign Affairs* 85, no. 2 (March–April 2006): 42–54.

10. See Brendan R. Green and Austin Long, "The MAD Who Wasn't There: Soviet Reactions to the Late Cold War Nuclear Balance," *Security Studies* 26, no. 4 (2017): 606–641; Long and Green, "Stalking the Secure Second Strike"; and Brendan Rittenhouse Green, *The Meaning of the Nuclear Counterrevolution: Arms Competition and Arms Control after MAD* (New York: Cambridge University Press, 2020).

11. Green and Long, "MAD Who Wasn't There."

12. See Lieber and Press, "End of MAD?"; Lieber and Press, "Rise of U.S. Nuclear Primacy"; Keir A. Lieber and Daryl G. Press, "U.S. Nuclear Primacy and the Future of the Chinese Nuclear Deterrent," *China Security Quarterly* 5 (Winter 2006/7): 66–89; Wu "Certainty of Uncertainty," 586–587; and Li Bin, "Tracking Chinese Strategic Mobile Missiles," 1–30.

13. See Michael Russell Rip and James M. Hasik, *The Precision Revolution: GPS and the Future of Aerial Warfare* (Annapolis, MD: Naval Institute Press, 2002), 14–67.

14. For example, the first U.S. intercontinental ballistic missiles (ICBMs) had a median miss distance (called circular error probable, or CEP) that was two or three times worse than that of contemporary bombers. See David Miller, *The Cold War: A Military History* (New York: Thomas Dunne, 1998), appendix 7; and Duncan Lennox, *IHS Jane's Weapons: Strategic 2012/2013* (London: IHS, 2012).

15. Before submarines used global positioning system (GPS) navigation, ballistic missile accuracy was measured in kilometers. See Rip and Hasik, *Precision Revolution*, 63, 66.

16. Currently, the two main technologies underlying smart weapons are laser- and GPS-guidance. In the former, a laser is trained on the target, and a computer in the bomb adjusts the tail fins to guide the weapon toward the laser's reflection. In a GPS-guided bomb, a computer on the munition uses GPS to repeatedly assess its location as it falls; the bomb adjusts its tail fins to guide it to a predetermined aimpoint.

17. We focus on U.S. capabilities, but recent versions of Israel's Jericho, India's Agni, Pakistan's Hatf, and Russia's Iskander nuclear-capable missiles employ advanced guidance systems that may outperform even the best contemporary U.S. ballistic missiles described here. See Hans M. Kristensen and Robert S. Norris, "Israeli Nuclear Weapons, 2014," *Bulletin of the Atomic Scientists* 70, no. 6 (November 2014): 97–115; "Quiet Leap," *Aviation Week & Space Technology* 175, no. 26 (July 2013): 1; Hans M. Kristensen and Matt Korda, "Indian Nuclear Forces, 2018," *Bulletin of the Atomic Scientists* 74, no. 6 (November 2018): 361–366; James C. O'Halloran, *IHS Jane's Weapons: Strategic* (London: IHS, 2015), 33; Hans M. Kristensen, Robert S. Norris, and Julia Diamond, "Pakistani Nuclear Forces, 2018," *Bulletin of the Atomic Scientists* 74, no. 5 (September 2018): 348–358; and "SS-26 (Iskander)," MissileThreat (CSIS Missile Defense Project), September 27, 2016, https://missilethreat.csis.org/missile/ss-26/; and Hans M. Kristensen and Matt Korda, "Russian Nuclear Forces, 2019," *Bulletin of the Atomic Scientists* 75, no. 2 (March 2019): 73–84.

18. See the online appendix at http://dx/doi.org/10.7910/DVN/NKZIVT. The seminal unclassified work on the effects of nuclear weapons is Samuel Glasstone and Philip J. Dolan, *The*

Effects of Nuclear Weapons (Washington, DC: U.S. Government Printing Office, 1977). See also Lynn E. Davis and Warner R. Schilling, "All You Ever Wanted to Know about MIRV and ICBM Calculations But Were Not Cleared to Ask," *Journal of Conflict Resolution* 17, no. 2 (June 1973): 207–242. These formulas and calculations are also discussed in Lieber and Press, "End of Mad?" 7–44, and appendix 1.

19. On nuclear fratricide, see John D. Steinbruner and Thomas M. Garwin, "Strategic Vulnerability: The Balance between Prudence and Paranoia," *International Security* 1, no. 1 (Summer 1976): 138–181; and Bruce W. Bennett, *How to Assess the Survivability of U.S. ICBMs* (Santa Monica, CA: RAND Corporation, 1980), with appendices. For an excellent nontechnical discussion of nuclear fratricide, see Andrew Cockburn and Alexander Cockburn, "The Myth of Missile Accuracy," *New York Review of Books*, November 20, 1980, http://www.nybooks.com /articles/1980/11/20/the-myth-of-missile-accuracy/.

20. A four-second buffer would separate warheads by approximately 10 kilometers. For an analysis of the targeting issues involved with spacing out warheads, including time of arrival uncertainty, see Bennett, "How to Assess the Survivability," appendix E, 34–39.

21. John Steinbruner and Thomas Garwin estimate that a reentry vehicle (RV) would collide, on average, with five to ten particles in the range of 3 to 10 grams as it passed through a typical dust cloud—any one of which would destroy the RV. See Steinbruner and Garwin, "Strategic Vulnerability," Appendix C, 178.

22. For a Cold War example, see Salman et al., "Analysis or Propaganda?" For a contemporary analysis that makes the same assumption, see Lauren Caston et al., *The Future of the U.S. Intercontinental Ballistic Missile Force* (Santa Monica, CA: RAND Corporation, 2014), 36, 36n16.

23. Debris clouds around silos would not prevent missiles in those silos from launching. At the relatively slow speeds of early "boost phase," missiles could ascend through particles in the debris cloud.

24. The consequences of the fading problem of fratricide for counterforce are illustrated in table 3.1.

25. U.S. ICBMs launched at Russia or China—or vice versa—would take a polar route to their targets. As a result, critical sites could be shielded from ICBMs by locating them on the south side of steep mountains. SLBMs can strike targets from a wide range of launch locations, thwarting efforts to shield them.

26. See the online appendix; Theodore Postol, "Monte Carlo Simulations of Burst-Height Fuse Kill Probabilities," unpublished presentation, July 28, 2015; Donald A. Price and Charles A. Louis, "Burst Height Compensation," United States Patent US4456202 A, June 26, 1984; Sandia National Laboratories, "Defense Programs," *Sandia Weapon Review Bulletin*, Autumn 1992, 4–5; Hans M. Kristensen, "Small Fuze, Big Effect," *Strategic Security* (blog), Federation of American Scientists, March 14, 2007, https://fas.org/blogs/security/2007/03/small_fuze_-_big_effect/; and Hans M. Kristensen, Matthew McKinzie, and Theodore A. Postol, "How U.S. Nuclear Force Modernization is Undermining Strategic Stability: The Burst-Height Compensating Super-Fuze," *Bulletin of the Atomic Scientists*, https://thebulletin.org/2017/03/how-us-nuclear-force -modernization-is-undermining-strategic-stability-the-burst-height-compensating-super-fuze/. The compensating fuse is reportedly now deployed on all SLBMs with Mk-5 RVs (i.e., those armed with W88 warheads) and Mk-4A RVs (i.e., those armed with the recently upgraded W76-1 warheads). See Aaron Mehta, "Work Completed on Navy's Upgraded Nuclear Warhead," *Defense News*, January 23, 2019; Hans M. Kristensen and Matt Korda, "United States Nuclear Forces, 2019," *Bulletin of the Atomic Scientists* 75, no. 3 (May 2019): 122–134.

27. Compensating fuses may also enhance the capability of SLBMs to conduct "depressed trajectory" strikes, in which a missile flies along a flatter trajectory, thereby reducing its flight time (and hence the target's warning). In the past, the benefit of depressed trajectory for counterforce strikes was mitigated because flat trajectories eroded accuracy. Compensating fuses, however, allow planners to minimize the deleterious effects of depressed trajectories and thus allow SLBMs to strike hard targets with little warning.

28. Writing in 1976, Steinbrunner and Garwin argued that the threats to U.S. ICBMs were overblown, but they cautioned that if the Soviets developed highly accurate delivery systems

(i.e., systems less accurate than U.S. missiles today) and utilized reprogramming, ICBM fields would be highly vulnerable. The technological conditions that they feared have come to pass. Steinbrunner and Garwin, "Strategic Vulnerability," 151–155, 159–168.

29. On the Air Force's Rapid Execution and Combat Targeting (REACT) system and the Navy's SLBM Retargeting System (SRS), see Amy E. Woolf, *U.S. Strategic Nuclear Forces: Background, Development, and Issues* (Washington, DC: Congressional Research Service, March 10, 2016), 14; Hans M. Kristensen, "U.S. Strategic War Planning after 9/11," *Nonproliferation Review* 14, no. 2 (July 2007): 382; Andrew S. Kovich, "ICBM Strike Planning," *Association of Air Force Missileers (AAFM) Newsletter* 15, no. 2 (June 2007): 6–11; and William M. Arkin, "The Six-Hundred Million Dollar Mouse," *Bulletin of the Atomic Scientists* 52, no. 6 (November–December 1996): 68.

30. Reprogramming creates complications for war planners. For example, ballistic missile strike plans are orchestrated to prevent incoming weapons from interfering with each other. A plan that fully employed reprogramming to negate missile failures would need to establish two (or more) temporal windows for reentry vehicles to safely approach their targets—one for the warheads on the initial missile assigned to a target and one for the warheads on reserve missiles if the initial missile failed. Planners might also need to employ lofted trajectories for reserve missiles to clear the dust clouds shielding targets that were already struck.

31. Bruce Blair, a former missile launch control officer, testified to the U.S. Congress nearly two decades ago that Russia could reprogram its silo-based missiles in ten seconds. See *Hearing Before the House Committee on National Security, Subcommittee on Military Research and Development*, 105th Cong., 1st sess. (March 17, 1997) (testimony of Bruce Blair).

32. One hundred moderately hard targets is a plausible estimate of the number of targets that the United States might strike in a disarming attack against North Korea (to hit possible missile shelters, weapon storage, and command-and-control sites) or in a limited strike on China. Two hundred hardened silos roughly correspond to Russia's fixed ICBM force. See Hans M. Kristensen and Matt Korda, "Russian Nuclear Forces, 2019," 74; Hans M. Kristensen and Matt Korda, "Chinese Nuclear Forces, 2019," *Bulletin of the Atomic Scientists* 75, no. 4 (July 2019): 177–178; and Office of the Secretary of Defense, *Annual Report to Congress: Military and Security Developments Involving the People's Republic of China* (Washington, DC: U.S. Department of Defense, 2019).

33. A group of engineers and scientists with relevant expertise advised us that our 80 percent baseline figure for missile reliability is too low. Indeed, the Trident II boasts a 96 percent success rate. See "Navy's Trident II D5 Missile Marks 155 Successful Test Flights," press release (Bethesda, MD: Lockheed Martin, February 23, 2015); and "Trident D-5," *Encyclopedia Astronautica*, accessed July 17, 2019, http://www.astronautix.com/t/tridentd-5.html. The former commander of Russia's Strategic Rocket Forces claims a 92 percent launch success rate for Russian missiles throughout the Cold War; the U.S. Central Intelligence Agency (CIA) estimates the success rate to be slightly higher. On Russia claims and tests, see Pavel Podvig, "History of Missile Launches and Reliability," Russianforces.org, January 6, 2005, http://russianforces.org/blog/2005/01/history_of_missile_launches_an.shtml. For CIA estimates, see CIA, "Russian Expectations," February 1, 1993, document 0000382541, CIA FOIA Electronic Reading Room, 9–10, https://www.cia.gov/library/readingroom/docs/DOC_0000382541.pdf. Tests cannot simulate the conditions of a wartime missile launch, but a 90 percent reliability figure—which we employ in rows 4 to 7 of table 3.1—seems reasonable given this evidence and expert opinion.

34. In an important respect, our model substantially understates the vulnerability of hard targets, because it does not capture the growing contribution of nonnuclear forces to counterforce missions.

35. See, for example, Julian Borger, "America's New, More 'Usable,' Nuclear Bomb in Europe," *Guardian*, November 10, 2015, https://www.theguardian.com/world/julian-borger-global-security-blog/2015/nov/10/americas-new-more-usable-nuclear-bomb-in-europe. As U.S. senator Dianne Feinstein recently stated, "The so-called improvements to this weapon [the long-range nuclear cruise missile] seemed to be designed candidly to make it more usable, to help us fight and win a limited nuclear war. I find that a shocking concept. I think this is really unthinkable." Cited in Hans M. Kristensen, "Flawed Pentagon Nuclear Cruise Missile Advocacy," *Strategic Security* (blog), Federation of American Scientists, June 10, 2016, https://fas.org/blogs/security/2016/06/dod-lrso-letter/.

36. If counterforce targets are located outside cities (as most are), targeters can select aim-points, yields, and heights of burst to minimize the fire and overpressure consequences for civilians. For a study that illustrates the potentially vast consequences of fallout in strategic strikes, see William Daugherty, Barbara Levi, and Frank von Hippel, "The Consequences of 'Limited' Nuclear Attacks on the United States," *International Security* 10, no. 4 (Spring 1986): 3–45. On the large-scale consequences of fire and blast, see Lynn Eden, *Whole World on Fire: Organizations, Knowledge, and Nuclear Weapons Devastation* (Ithaca, NY: Cornell University Press, 2004).

37. For example, targeters cannot reliably predict whether wind speed and direction will blow fallout over an unpopulated region or a city.

38. Glasstone and Dolan, *Effects of Nuclear Weapons*, 36–38; and Office of Technology Assessment, *The Effects of Nuclear War* (Washington, DC: U.S. Government Printing Office, 1979), 18, 22–24, 35.

39. See the online appendix for the calculations underpinning these claims and figure 3.2.

40. See the online appendix.

41. The B61-12 is a guided munition that is said to be similar to a conventional Joint Direct Attack Munition (JDAM). JDAMs use inertial navigation and GPS in tandem to guide the bomb to the target. If a JDAM has a clear GPS signal all the way to the target, the CEP is approximately 5 meters. If the GPS signal is not available, accuracy is approximately 30 meters. If the B61-12 uses inertial navigation with in-flight updates from some external source (perhaps GPS), it should have accuracy comparable to that of the JDAM. In fact, in a recent test drop the B61-12 appears to have landed within 15 meters of the aimpoint. See Hans M. Kristensen and Matthew McKinzie, "Video Shows Earth-Penetrating Capability of B61-12 Nuclear Bomb," *Strategic Security* (blog), Federation of American Scientists, January 14, 2016, https://fas.org/blogs/security /2016/01/b61-12_earth-penetration/; and Hans M. Kristensen, "B61 LEP: Increasing NATO Capability and Precision Low-Yield Strikes," *Strategic Security* (blog), Federation of American Scientists, June 15, 2011, https://fas.org/blogs/security/2011/06/b61-12/.

42. See the online appendix for these calculations.

43. Several nuclear-armed countries have deployed short- and medium-range ballistic missiles with approximately 50-meter CEP. Although (according to open source data) no intercontinental-range ballistic missiles can achieve 50-meter CEP, compensating fuses may allow existing missiles (with primary-only options) to destroy hardened sites from above the fallout threshold.

44. HPAC allows the user to select the number, yield, altitude, location, date, and time of simulated nuclear detonations, then estimates the amount and pattern of fallout that would likely be generated by the strikes.

45. Countries may respond to these advances by putting some counterforce targets in urban areas, denying their adversaries the option of low-fatality nuclear strikes. Doing so, however, would exacerbate the vulnerability of those targets in other ways. For example, mobile missiles deployed in or near cities would be exposed to surveillance techniques that would be more difficult to employ if the launchers were deployed in rural areas. It is easier to surreptitiously emplace sensors and tracking systems in urban areas. Protection from low-fatality nuclear strikes would thus come at the cost of concealment, and if target intelligence improved sufficiently, those city-based weapons would be more vulnerable to conventional strikes.

46. For an overview of modern remote-sensing capabilities, see Thomas L. Lillesand, Ralph W. Kiefer, and Jonathan W. Chipman, *Remote Sensing and Image Interpretation*, 7th ed. (Hoboken, NJ: Wiley, 2015). For an excellent discussion of the military implications of advanced remote-sensing technology—written in the context of capabilities as they were in 2001—see Alan J. Vick et al., *Aerospace Operations against Elusive Ground Targets* (Santa Monica, CA: RAND Corporation, 2001).

47. See Vick et al., *Aerospace Operations*, appendix A; and Gordon Corera, *Cyberspies: The Secret History of Surveillance, Hacking, and Digital Espionage* (New York: Pegasus, 2015).

48. For a discussion of some of these advances, see Defense Advanced Research Projects Agency (DARPA), *Breakthrough Technologies for National Security* (Arlington, VA: DARPA, 2015).

49. Richard Hollingham, "Inside the Google Earth Satellite Factory," BBC News, February 11, 2014, http://www.bbc.com/future/story/20140211-inside-the-google-earth-sat-lab; and

DigitalGlobe, "WorldView-4," Data Sheet, https://web.archive.org/web/20160424030451/https://dg-cms-uploads-production.s3.amazonaws.com/uploads/document/file/196/DG_WorldView4_DS_11-15_Web.pdf.

50. Among journalistic accounts, which are based on interviews with ASW operators, see Sasgen, *Stalking the Red Bear*; and Sherry Sontag and Christopher Drew, with Annette Lawrence Drew, *Blind Man's Bluff: The Untold Story of American Submarine Espionage* (New York: Public Affairs, 1998). For academic analyses, see Coté, *Third Battle*; Long and Green, "Stalking the Secure Second Strike"; and Brendan Rittenhouse Green and Austin Long, "The Role of Clandestine Capabilities in World Politics" (paper presented at the annual meeting of the American Political Science Association, Philadelphia, September 1–4, 2016).

51. Coté, *Third Battle*; Long and Green, "Stalking the Secure Second Strike"; and Green and Long, "Role of Clandestine Capabilities."

52. As quoted in Long and Green, "Stalking the Secure Second Strike," 51.

53. Although U.S. Cold War ASW successes rested heavily on technical breakthroughs in acoustics and data processing, well-trained operators and intelligence analysts were essential to the success.

54. The main Soviet countermeasures included deploying longer-range SLBMs, which permitted Soviet submarines to target the U.S. homeland from well-defended bastions near the Soviet coast, and developing quieter Soviet SSBNs and SSNs to elude detection and threaten the submarine hunters. It appears that Soviet countermeasures significantly reduced the U.S. undersea advantage, but this judgment (like the Cold War assumptions that the United States was not tracking Soviet SSBNs) is tentative given that relevant documents remain classified.

55. See Bryan Clark, *The Emerging Era in Undersea Warfare* (Washington, DC: Center for Strategic and Budgetary Affairs, 2015): 8–17; James Holmes, "Sea Changes: The Future of Nuclear Deterrence," *Bulletin of the Atomic Scientists* 72, no. 4 (July 2016): 229–230; Bryan Clark, "Undersea Cables and the Future of Submarine Competition," *Bulletin of the Atomic Scientists* 72, no. 4 (July 2016): 235–237; and Elizabeth Mendenhall, "Fluid Foundations: Ocean Transparency, Submarine Opacity, and Strategic Nuclear Stability," *Journal of Military and Strategic Studies* 19, no. 1 (2018): 119–158.

56. This scenario is salient because if conventional war erupts on the Korean Peninsula, the United States and South Korea may feel compelled to destroy North Korea's nuclear capabilities. See Lieber and Press, "Coercive Nuclear Campaigns"; Lieber and Press, "Next Korean War"; and Talmadge, "Too Much of a Good Thing?"

57. Unlike the Soviet Union, which conducted armed peacetime deterrent patrols, most countries with nuclear-armed mobile forces appear to keep their TELs in hardened facilities during peacetime (and even during crises). On China's doctrine, see Li, "Tracking Chinese Strategic Mobile Missiles," 7–11; and Wu, "Certainty of Uncertainty," 586–587. On Israeli basing, see "Beit Zachariah/Zekharyeh," Globalsecurity.org, accessed July 15, 2019, http://www.globalsecurity.org/wmd/world/israel/sedot_mikha.htm.

58. The IPB framework for elusive targets is reflected in Vick et al., *Aerospace Operations*, especially chap. 4 and appendix B. Some sensing platforms carry sensors for both detection and identification. For example, the RQ-4 Global Hawk drone has a ground moving target indicator (GMTI) radar that can scan a wide area and then switch to "spot" mode to look more closely at an identified target.

59. For natural aperture radars, image resolution is constrained by the size of the antenna, and operating very large antennas in space is currently impractical. As a result, satellites employ synthetic aperture radars, which use the movement of the satellite to simulate the function of a larger antenna, allowing satellites to generate images at higher resolution than their antenna size would normally permit. Until recently, however, SAR systems could not image moving targets. See Joseph Post and Michael Bennett, *Alternatives for Military Space Radar* (Washington, DC: Congressional Budget Office, January 2007).

60. For one of the earliest papers on using SAR for tracking mobile targets, see R. P. Perry, R. C. DiPietro, and R. L. Fante, "SAR Imaging of Moving Targets," *IIEEE Transactions on Aerospace and Electronic Systems* 35, no. 1 (January 1999): 188–200. For a recent study that employs a

civilian radar satellite to identify the location and velocity of cars and trucks, see Christoph H. Gierull, Ishuwa Sikaneta, and Delphine Cerutti-Maori, "Two-Step Detector for RADARSAT-2's Experimental GMTI Mode," *IEEE Transactions on Geoscience and Remote Sensing* 51, no. 1 (January 2013): 436-454.

61. One 2015 study used RADARSAT-2 data to scour 150-kilometer-wide swaths of sea, locating and characterizing the velocity of moving vessels. See Louis-Philippe Rousseau, Christoph Gierull, and Jean-Yves Chouinard, "First Results from an Experimental ScanSAR-GMTI Mode on RADARSAT-2," *IEEE Journal of Selected Topics in Applied Earth Observations and Remote Sensing* 8, no. 11 (November 2015): 1-13. One of the authors of that paper confirmed via personal communication that the technique that the authors employed and the large swath widths that they used should be applicable to truck-sized vehicles on the ground.

62. Using the experimental "High-Resolution-Wide-Swath" mode, SAR satellites may be able to generate swaths 300 to 500 kilometers wide with sufficient resolution to track truck-sized moving targets. See Stefan V. Baumgartner and Gerhard Krieger, "Simultaneous High-Resolution Wide-Swath SAR Imaging and Ground Moving Target Indication: Processing Approaches and System Concepts," *IEEE Journal of Selected Topics in Applied Earth Observations and Remote Sensing* 8, no. 11 (November 2015): 1-15.

63. With a 150-kilometer-wide swath, the terrain within 75 kilometers of either side of the garrison would be within the zone covered by the radar. A typical TEL can move approximately 40 kilometers per hour. Given that roads in North Korea are not perfectly straight, the actual driving time to escape a 75-kilometer-wide swath (on either side of the garrison) would be at least two hours.

64. See the online appendix.

65. These two factors are linked. If North Korea's topography is sufficiently problematic that only satellites in a narrow orbital band (i.e., almost directly overhead) can see over the mountains, then there will be fewer usable passes each day (and hence a longer interval between passes). On the other hand, if even satellite passes that are far from North Korea can see the roads, then there will be many usable passes per day.

66. See the online appendix for details on all three steps in the analysis.

67. The United States may or may not have agreements and technology in place to rapidly share sensitive satellite imagery, even with its closest military partners. From the perspective of North Korean missile commanders, however, a German or Japanese SAR satellite pass overhead poses a major threat.

68. The major military and intelligence radar satellites operated by the United States and key allies include Lacrosse 3-5 and Topaz 1-3 (United States); SAR-Lupe 1-5 (Germany); COSMO A-D (Italy); IGS 7a, IGS 8a, and a third satellite with name unclear (Japan); and OFEQ 8 and OFEQ 10 (Israel). Civilian radar satellites operated by allied countries include TerraSAR-X and TanDEM-X (Germany); Copernicus Sentinel-1 and -3 (European Union); KOMPSat-5 (South Korea); ALOS-2 (Japan); PAZ (Spain); and RADARSAT-2 (Canada). See "Synthetic Aperture Radar (SAR) Satellites," UNAVCO, August 7, 2015, https://www.unavco.org/instrumentation/geophysical/imaging/sar-satellites/sar-satellites.html.

69. Although some older satellites on our list may have limited capabilities for this mission (e.g., they may have single-channel receivers), new satellites currently being deployed may supplement those capabilities (e.g., small cube satellites may orbit near an older radar satellite and serve as a second receiver). Most important, as the number of radar satellites continues to grow, U.S. and allied capabilities will exceed those described in table 3.2.

70. See Eric Heginbotham et al., *The U.S.-China Military Scorecard: Forces, Geography, and the Evolving Balance of Power, 1996-2017* (Santa Monica, CA: RAND Corporation, 2015), chap. 10. Of course, the United States is seeking to counter antisatellite weapon technologies.

71. Li, "Tracking Chinese Strategic Mobile Missiles," 7-11, 15-25.

72. Identifying a vehicle as truck-sized might be sufficient for a strike, depending on the context of the conflict. If, during a war, North Korea has employed nuclear weapons, detecting a large vehicle on a road near a North Korean missile garrison may be enough to trigger a strike against the vehicle. The level of identification required to trigger a strike presumably depends on the weapons available to the United States for the strike: the threshold for launching

a conventional weapon at a suspected TEL is presumably lower than the threshold for employing nuclear weapons.

73. A standoff distance of 80 kilometers puts the aircraft outside the range of most North Korean air defenses. We assume a sensor range of 240 kilometers, which was the reported GMTI range of joint surveillance target attack radars during the 1991 Persian Gulf War. Our results are not sensitive to sensor-range assumptions because even at 200 kilometers, the beam is grazing the ground at a shallow angle, allowing the mountainous topography to constrain line of sight.

74. See the online appendix for calculations.

75. Two such stealthy drones are the RQ-170 and RQ-180. See Amy Butler and Bill Sweetman, "Secret New UAS Shows Stealth, Efficiency Advances," *Aviation Week*, December 6, 2013, http://aviationweek.com/defense/secret-new-uas-shows-stealth-efficiency-advances; and John A. Tirpak, "For Those Hard-to-Reach Areas," *Air Force Magazine*, June 10, 2014, http://www.airforcemag.com/DRArchive/Pages/2014/June%202014/June%2010%202014/For-Those-Hard-to-Reach-Areas.aspx.

76. Passive sensors "look" but do not emit. Active sensors (those that emit) generally have longer range, but increase the risk that the UAV will be detected. LPI radars emit but are designed to hinder adversary efforts to detect and locate the emitter.

77. RQ-170s (and probably RQ-180s) are equipped with turbofan engines, implying a flight speed of approximately 800 kilometers per hour. We assume that once cued to identify a target, the UAVs gain altitude, if necessary, to attain line-of-sight to the target.

78. In the five minutes we allow the UAVs to maneuver, they can fly approximately 67 kilometers given 800 kilometer per hour flight speed. Some sources suggest that the Lynx Multimode Radar, currently deployed on some UAVs, can sense a TEL-sized target moving at 11 kilometers per hour out to 25 kilometers. See Sherrill Lingel et al., *Methodologies for Analyzing Remotely Piloted Aircraft in Future Roles and Missions* (Santa Monica, CA: RAND Corporation, 2012), 73. (A TEL moving more quickly would be observable at a longer range.) Our results are not sensitive to modest deviations in sensor range. If the sensor range on U.S. penetrating UAVs were 25 percent less than we estimate (35 kilometers instead of 50 kilometers), one additional minute of flight time would compensate. See Lingel et al., *Methodologies for Analyzing*, 25–27, 73–74.

79. Maintaining four continuous orbits during a conflict would likely require at least twelve UAVs—not accounting for losses from air defenses.

80. The results in the North Korea scenario should not be applied directly to other potential U.S. adversaries—such as China or Russia—because those countries are larger, with different topography, bigger arsenals, and more modern defenses. The sensor revolution is significantly increasing the vulnerability of the Chinese and Russian arsenals as well, but not as quickly as it is undermining North Korea's force.

81. Nuclear weapon states that are weaker than their main rivals typically strive to develop survivable nuclear forces in order to stalemate more powerful foes. Counterforce tends to be the domain of the strong, which have the resources to pursue it and the incentive to negate the stalemating forces of their weaker enemies.

82. Green and Long, "Role of Clandestine Capabilities."

83. The United States had Cold War programs to jam and simulate communications linking Soviet nuclear command and control with deployed forces. See Benjamin B. Fischer, "CANOPY WING: The U.S. War Plan That Gave the East Germans Goose Bumps," *International Journal of Intelligence and Counterintelligence* 27, no. 3 (2014): 431–464.

84. See Wu Riqiang, "Survivability of China's Sea-Based Nuclear Forces," *Science & Global Security* 19, no. 2 (2011): 91–120; and comments by Chinese analysts in "Why Is China Modernizing Its Nuclear Arsenal?," panel session at the Carnegie International Nuclear Policy Conference, March 24, 2015, Washington, DC, http://carnegieendowment.org/files/12-chinanucleararsenal240315wintro-formatted.pdf.

85. See Green and Long, "MAD Who Wasn't There"; Long and Green, "Stalking the Secure Second Strike"; Fischer, "CANOPY WING"; Fred Kaplan, *Dark Territory: The Secret History of Cyber War* (New York: Simon and Schuster, 2016), 12–20; and Gordon Barrass, "Able Archer 83: What Were the Soviets Thinking?," *Survival* 58, no. 6 (2016): 7–30.

86. On the value of effective counterforce, see Keir A. Lieber and Daryl G. Press, "The Nukes We Need: Preserving the American Deterrent," *Foreign Affairs* 88, no. 6 (November–December 2009): 39–51; and Lieber and Press, "Coercive Nuclear Campaigns."

87. For a discussion of the dangers of first-strike capabilities in particular, see Glaser and Fetter, "Should the United States Reject MAD?," 52–53, 92–97.

4. Deterrence under Stalemate

1. Limited attacks do not directly threaten the existence of the defender. This can include conventional attacks against one's territory (if the adversary objectives fall short of conquest), conventional attacks against allies, and—if we push the concept to its logical limits—even nuclear attacks on one's own territory or the territory of allies. The boundary between limited and existential attack is blurry because even geographically limited operations could create existential threats to an adversary's regime. The distinction is important, however, because under nuclear stalemate countries will have difficulty making their threats to escalate credible in response to limited attacks.

2. Glenn Snyder developed the stability-instability paradox in Glenn Snyder, "The Balance of Power and the Balance of Terror," in *The Balance of Power*, ed. Paul Seabury (San Francisco: Chandler, 1965), 184–201. The concept is discussed at greater length later in this chapter.

3. In theory, one could conduct the type of analysis we performed in chapter 2 to learn whether changes in NATO's tactical and theater nuclear capabilities affected Soviet assessment of their adversary's credibility. There are a few problems with this approach. First, the data needed would include very sensitive documents (for example, war plans and discussions among senior political and military leaders about very sensitive matters). Even in the West, some key documents have not been declassified even though fifty years have passed. In modern Russia, these documents will likely never be released, if they exist. Second, there was not much variation in NATO's embrace of flexible options during the period of nuclear stalemate. As a consequence, we cannot compare periods of stalemate (that is, when the stability-instability paradox exists) with and without NATO flexible options.

4. Although his views fit better in the next category of optimistic views, this basic logic appears in Robert Jervis, *The Illogic of American Nuclear Strategy* (Ithaca, NY: Cornell University Press, 1984), 20, 129–140; and Robert Jervis, *The Meaning of the Nuclear Revolution: Statecraft and the Prospect of Armageddon* (Ithaca, NY: Cornell University Press, 1989), 22. As he writes in the latter book, nuclear weapons deter conventional attack because "escalation can occur although no one wants it to" (21–22). See also Thomas C. Schelling, *Arms and Influence* (New Haven, CT: Yale University Press, 1966), 89–99; and Kenneth N. Waltz, "Nuclear Myths and Political Realities," *American Political Science Review* 84, no. 3 (September 1990): 731–745.

5. Waltz, "Nuclear Myths and Political Realities," 734.

6. In fact, Jervis claims that any plan to intentionally escalate would in reality be senseless. As he writes, "A rational strategy for the employment of nuclear weapons is a contradiction in terms." Jervis, *Illogic of American Nuclear Strategy*, 19.

7. Schelling, *Arms and Influence*, chap. 3.

8. Jervis, *Illogic of American Nuclear Strategy*, 134–138.

9. The discrepancy between theory and behavior motivated many of these proponents, including Waltz and Jervis, to criticize U.S. nuclear policies in the Cold War. Proponents typically attribute the discrepancy between theory and practice to nonrational, nonstrategic causes such as leaders who misunderstand or misperceive the strategic consequences of nuclear weapons possession; individual officials, agencies, and interest groups pushing their own agendas as they compete for power and influence; military and other organizations striving to reduce uncertainty and preserve budgets by following standard operating procedures without regard to the unique dynamics of a nuclear world; domestic politics; and so forth.

10. For example, in 1999 Pakistani soldiers and local militants attacked India, sparking the Kargil War. The fighting was limited to isolated regions in the Himalayas, far from the center of Indian political power. In 1982, Argentina seized the Falkland Islands from the United Kingdom.

Although the ensuing conflict claimed four British warships (and two smaller amphibious craft), more than one hundred aircraft, and over nine hundred fatalities, the territories being fought over were far from Great Britain. The 1969 border skirmish between nuclear-armed China and Russia fits this category as well.

11. On Saddam Hussein's confidence that Israel would not strike back with nuclear weapons, see Hal Brands and David Palkki, "Saddam, Israel, and the Bomb: Nuclear Alarmism Justified?," *International Security* 36, no. 1 (Summer 2011): 157–161.

12. Another interpretation of history is that leaders who attacked did not consider the likelihood of escalation at all—which would be even more problematic for the optimistic views.

13. Examples of Cold War–era versions of this view include William R. Van Cleave and Roger W. Barnett, "Strategic Adaptability," *Orbis* 18, no. 3 (Autumn 1974): 655–676; and Peter Stratmann and Rene Hermann, "Limited Options, Escalation, and the Central Region," Laurence Martin, "Flexibility in Tactical Nuclear Response," and other essays in *Beyond Nuclear Deterrence: New Aims, New Arms*, ed. Johan J. Holst and Uwe Nerlich (New York: Crane, Russak, 1977), 239–254, 255–266. Examples of contemporaneous assessments include Morton H. Halperin, *Limited War in the Nuclear Age* (New York: John Wiley and Sons, 1963); Ted Greenwood and Michael L. Nacht, "The New Nuclear Debate: Sense or Nonsense?," *Foreign Affairs* 52, no. 4 (July 1974): 761–780; and Desmond Ball, *Can Nuclear War Be Controlled?*, Adelphi Paper no. 169 (London: IISS, 1981). For recent articulations, see Keir A. Lieber and Daryl G. Press, "The Nukes We Need: Preserving the American Deterrent," *Foreign Affairs* 88, no. 6 (November–December 2009): 39–51; Vipin Narang, "Posturing for Peace? Pakistan's Nuclear Postures and South Asian Stability," *International Security* 34, no. 3 (Winter 2009/10): 38–78; Vipin Narang, *Nuclear Strategy in the Modern Era: Regional Powers and International Conflict* (Princeton, NJ: Princeton University Press, 2014); and several essays in Jeffrey A. Larsen and Kerry M. Kartchner, eds., *On Limited Nuclear War in the 21st Century* (Stanford, CA: Stanford University Press, 2014).

14. To be clear, the goal of such an escalation strategy is to coerce the enemy to back down, not to prevail in full-scale war fighting. Whereas the second pessimistic view (described below) calls for preparations to fight and win at even the top rung of an escalation ladder—that is, in an all-out nuclear war—this view believes that the crucial steps of escalation are at the beginning and intermediate stages, where a country would primarily want usable nuclear capabilities to signal the potential consequences of continued fighting. A coercive escalation strategy seeks to inflict some initial pain and damage while generating the expectation that more pain and damage will be forthcoming unless the adversary backs down.

15. Examples of Cold War–era versions of this view include Herman Kahn, *On Escalation: Metaphors and Scenarios* (New York: Praeger, 1965); Paul H. Nitze, "Assuring Strategic Stability in an Era of Détente," *Foreign Affairs* 54, no. 2 (January 1976): 207–232; Paul H. Nitze, "Deterring Our Deterrent," *Foreign Policy* 25 (Winter 1976/77): 195–210; Carl H. Builder, *The Case for First-Strike Counterforce Capabilities* (Santa Monica, CA: RAND, 1978); Carl H. Builder, *Why Not First-Strike Counterforce Capabilities?* (Santa Monica, CA: RAND, 1979); Walter Slocombe, "The Countervailing Strategy," *International Security* 5, no. 4 (Spring 1981): 18–27; and Colin S. Gray and Keith Payne, "Victory Is Possible," *Foreign Policy* 39 (Summer 1980): 14–27. For recent articulations, see Matthew Kroenig, *The Logic of American Nuclear Strategy: Why Strategic Superiority Matters* (New York: Oxford University Press, 2018); and Elbridge Colby, "If You Want Peace, Prepare for Nuclear War: A Strategy for the New Great-Power Rivalry," *Foreign Affairs* 97, no. 6 (November–December 2018).

16. According to data in Chiozza and Goemans, 47 percent of leaders of countries that lost wars were "punished"—exiled, jailed, or killed—within four years of the conflict; only 13 percent of those who achieved a "draw" were punished. See Giacomo Chiozza and H. E. Goemans, *Leaders and International Conflict* (Cambridge: Cambridge University, 2011), 56–57. For more on leaders and war outcomes, see Alexandre Debs and H. E. Goemans, "Regime Type, the Fate of Leaders, and War," *American Political Science Review* 104, no. 3 (August 2010): 430–445. See also Giacomo Chiozza and H. E. Goemans, "International Conflict and the Tenure of Leaders: Is War Still 'Ex Post' Inefficient?," *American Journal of Political Science* 48, no. 3 (July 2004): 604–619.

17. For example, in the 1991 Gulf War, the United States conducted 203 airstrikes on "government control" targets. In the 2003 war, U.S. aircraft struck 1,799 aim points in the "SR" (regime survival) target set, plus an additional fifty strikes against time-sensitive leadership targets—meaning Saddam Hussein and other senior members of the government. See Eliot A. Cohen, Director, *Gulf War Air Power Survey (GWAPS)*, vol. 5 (Washington, DC: U.S. Government Printing Office, 1993), table 177; and T. Michael Moseley, "Operation Iraqi Freedom—By the Numbers," USCENTAF Assessment and Analysis Division, April 20, 2003, 4, 5, 9.

18. Observers of Chinese politics have noted that the Chinese Communist Party (CCP) no longer bases its legitimacy on communism, but rather on nationalism and the perception that the CCP has made China strong and globally respected—a peer of the Western powers who once victimized China. If the United States inflicted a crushing defeat against the Chinese air force and navy, the leaders of the CCP may question whether their government could survive the political repercussions stemming from popular or military humiliation and anger.

19. For the seminal discussion of "gambling for resurrection," see George W. Downs and David M. Rocke, "Conflict, Agency, and Gambling for Resurrection: The Principal-Agent Problem Goes to War," *American Journal of Political Science* 38, no. 2 (May 1994): 362–380. Note that Downs and Rocke use the phrase to describe what might be rational for individual leaders, not a country as a whole, but the logic is useful in both cases.

20. See Scott D. Sagan, "The Origins of the Pacific War," *Journal of Interdisciplinary History* 18, no. 4 (Spring 1988): 893–922.

21. There are many additional options for coercive nuclear employment. For example, even within the category of "alerting forces," countries seeking to coerce could take a wide range of actions—some of which would be designed to look like a signal (for example, canceling personnel leaves) and others that could look like preparations to strike. Similarly, there are a large number of ways to conduct a nuclear demonstration or even strike with nuclear weapons to either minimize or maximize damage.

22. Some analysts might detect a contradiction in our model of escalation. The effectiveness of any coercive act depends on the threat of future pain if the demands are not met. But then, why would a coercing state ever conduct its final act of nuclear employment? The final act of escalation cannot coerce, because by definition there is no additional pain to come. Furthermore, if the final act of employment is irrational, then so is the second-to-last act. (If targets of coercion do not expect the final employment to occur because it is irrational, they will also not be coerced by the second-to-last employment because it lacks the threat of more pain to come.) By this logic, all of the coercive escalation steps should break down, dissolving the rational foundation of coercive escalation strategies.

One response is that the final act of escalation may be rational, yet not motivated by coercion per se but rather by anger, spite, or revenge. One should note that all theories of strategic nuclear deterrence confront the same puzzle—namely, if one's society has already been destroyed, what is the rational purpose of retaliation? McDermott, Lopez, and Hatemi note that humans share a universal thirst for retaliation out of hatred in the wake of loss. This psychology of revenge can make a seemingly irrational response, such as nuclear retaliation, entirely credible. Rose McDermott, Anthony Lopez, and Peter Hatemi, "'Blunt Not the Heart, Enrage It': The Psychology of Revenge and Deterrence," *Texas National Security Review* 1, no. 1 (November 2017). There is a second potential response to this critique: if neither side knows which act of nuclear employment is the last one, every detonation (even the last) will signal that additional pain may come if the enemy does not give up. For example, if a country's nuclear stockpile is being whittled down during a war through its own employment and enemy strikes against its nuclear forces and command and control, then its leaders may never reach a point at which they are explicitly choosing to use their last warhead. Furthermore, even if the coercer knows a weapon is its last, it is still possible for the final warhead to coerce if the target (mistakenly) believes there are more to come.

23. "Resilient survivability" refers to an arsenal's survivability beyond peacetime—throughout a crisis, the various phases of conventional war, and counterforce strikes. Unclassified analyses of nuclear forces typically examine peacetime survivability—that is, survivability before forces are degraded by conventional attacks, initial nuclear operations, or other operations against

command-and-control and warning systems. See, for example, John D. Steinbruner and Thomas M. Garwin, "Strategic Vulnerability: The Balance between Prudence and Paranoia," *International Security* 1, no. 1 (Summer 1976): 138–181; and Michael Salman, Kevin J. Sullivan, and Stephen Van Evera, "Analysis or Propaganda? Measuring American Strategic Nuclear Capability, 1969–88," in *Nuclear Arguments: Understanding the Strategic Nuclear Arms and Arms Control Debates*, ed. Lynn Eden and Steven E. Miller (Ithaca, NY: Cornell University Press, 1989), 172–263. We know of no unclassified force exchange models that explore how conventional operations might erode survivability, and the consequence of that dynamic on the nuclear balance.

24. Keir A. Lieber and Daryl G. Press, *Preventing Escalation during Conventional Wars*, Project on Advanced Systems and Concepts for Countering Weapons of Mass Destruction (PASCC) Report no. 2015–001 (Monterey, CA: Naval Postgraduate School, 2015); Keir A. Lieber and Daryl G. Press, "The Next Korean War," *Foreign Affairs*, April 1, 2013; and Caitlin Talmadge, "Would China Go Nuclear? Assessing the Risk of Chinese Nuclear Escalation in a Conventional War with the United States," *International Security* 41, no. 4 (Spring 2017): 50–92.

25. As discussed above, firing a country's last weapon (including the only one) even when the coercive demands are ignored can be rational for two reasons: (1) leaders may rationally wish to inflict pain on those who are conquering their country or toppling their government, and (2) the victims of coercion may not know that a given weapon is the only one—hence firing it could be accompanied by a final threat (a bluff) that the next strike will be worse.

26. Narang, "Posturing for Peace?," 41.

27. Critics may object that figures 4.1 and 4.2 should include all states, not merely the nuclear-armed countries. After all, the theory we advance predicts that any state that perceives a high chance of suffering a costly military defeat would be powerfully inclined to adopt a coercive nuclear doctrine—even if doing so required acquiring nuclear weapons as the first step. We agree with this logic up to a point, but the critique goes too far. A large body of evidence suggests that proliferation decisions involve a careful balancing of security concerns with a host of factors. Furthermore, in many cases acquiring nuclear weapons would greatly increase security risks until the arsenal was deployed and large enough to effectively execute CNE. See Nuno P. Monteiro and Alexandre Debs, "The Strategic Logic of Nuclear Proliferation," *International Security* 39, no. 2 (Fall 2014); and Alexandre Debs and Nuno P. Monteiro, *Nuclear Politics: The Strategic Causes of Proliferation* (New York: Cambridge University Press, 2017).

28. In 1948, for example, the U.S. Joint Chiefs of Staff estimated that two (non–combat-ready) U.S. army divisions in Europe would face roughly 235 Soviet and allied army divisions if Russia decided to attack. This probably overstated the imbalance of conventional military power, but clearly Western Europe was tremendously vulnerable to attack by the Red Army—not just in the late 1940s, but also arguably into the 1980s. In case of attack, the likelihood of conventional defeat was very high. Some analysts argued that NATO had a fighting chance to defeat a conventional Warsaw Pact attack in Central Europe by the early 1980s, and more convincing prospects by the late 1980s. Those analyses successfully reframed the debate, from NATO has no chance to NATO could initially thwart an attack if NATO rapidly mobilizes before a war begins. See John J. Mearsheimer, "Why the Soviets Can't Win Quickly in Central Europe," *International Security* 7, no. 1 (Summer 1982): 3–39; Barry R. Posen, "Measuring the European Conventional Balance: Coping with Complexity in Threat Assessment," *International Security* 9, no. 3 (Winter 1984/85): 47–88; John J. Mearsheimer, "Numbers, Strategy, and the European Balance," *International Security* 12, no. 4 (Spring 1988): 174–185.

29. See, for example, J. Michael Legge, *Theater Nuclear Weapons and the NATO Strategy of Flexible Response*, RAND Report R-2964-FF (Santa Monica, CA: RAND, 1983); and Elbridge A. Colby, "The United States and Discriminate Nuclear Options in the Cold War," in Larsen and Kartchner, *On Limited Nuclear War*, 49–79.

30. Recurring statements by acting and retired U.S. officials to justify the ongoing U.S. effort to delegitimize nuclear weapons and work toward global nuclear disarmament note that the United States and its allies have the world's most powerful conventional forces in the world—implicitly acknowledging that these weapons were once useful because NATO and the United States were weak. Those statements gloss over the darker implications: that weak states will

resist efforts to deny them their needed instrument of stalemate as vigorously as NATO rejected Soviet suggestions for a mutual pledge of no first use during the Cold War, and that efforts to delegitimize these weapons may come at the expense of U.S. allies who still feel some risk of catastrophic military defeat (i.e., Israel).

31. Paul I. Bernstein, "The Emerging Nuclear Landscape," in Larsen and Kartchner, *On Limited Nuclear War*, 110; and William Burr and Svetlana Savranskaya, "Previously Classified Interviews with Former Soviet Officials Reveal U.S. Strategic Intelligence Failure Over Decades," National Security Archive Electronic Briefing Book no. 285, September 11, 2009, https://nsarchive2.gwu.edu/nukevault/ebb285/.

32. See Nikolai N. Sokov, "Why Russia Calls a Limited Nuclear Strike 'De-escalation,'" *Bulletin of the Atomic Scientists*, March 13, 2014, https://thebulletin.org/2014/03/why-russia-calls-a-limited-nuclear-strike-de-escalation/. According to Russia's 2014 military doctrine, "The Russian Federation shall reserve for itself the right to employ nuclear weapons . . . in the case of aggression against the Russian Federation with use of conventional weapons when the state's very existence has been threatened." Russian Federation, "The Military Doctrine of the Russian Federation," December 26, 2014. Also see Alexei Arbatov, Vladimir Dvorkin, and Sergey Oznobishchev, *Contemporary Nuclear Doctrines* (Moscow: IMEMO RAM, 2010), 21–27; Keir Giles, "The Military Doctrine of the Russian Federation 2010," *NATO Research Review* (Rome: NATO Defense College, February 2010); and Stephen J. Blank, ed., *Russian Nuclear Weapons: Past, Present, and Future* (Carlisle, PA: Strategic Studies Institute, November 2011); and Mark Schneider, *The Nuclear Forces and Doctrine of the Russian Federation* (Washington, DC: United States Nuclear Strategy Forum, 2006). CNE is implicit in Russian president Vladimir Putin's statement, in the wake of Russian military incursions into Ukraine and rising tensions with NATO, that Moscow does not intend to fight a "large-scale" conventional conflict with the West: "I want to remind you that Russia is one of the most powerful nuclear nations. This is reality, not just words." Greg Botelho and Laura Smith-Spark, "Putin: You Better Not Come After a Nuclear-Armed Russia," CNN, August 30, 2014, https://edition.cnn.com/2014/08/29/world/europe/ukraine-crisis/index.html. Soon after this, Putin announced that Russia would counter NATO's decision to deploy a rapid-reaction conventional force to protect Eastern Europe with the development of new nuclear capabilities. On Russian "pre-nuclear" deterrence, see Andrei Kokoshin, *Ensuring Strategic Stability in the Past and Present: Theoretical and Applied Questions* (Cambridge, MA: Belfer Center for Science and International Affairs, Harvard University, June 2011), 57–58.

33. The 2018 U.S. Nuclear Posture Review contends that Russia "mistakenly assesses that the threat of nuclear escalation or actual first use of nuclear weapons would serve to 'de-escalate' a conflict on terms favorable to Russia." Office of the Secretary of Defense, *Nuclear Posture Review* (Washington, DC: U.S. Department of Defense, February 5, 2018).

34. Dmitry (Dima) Adamsky, "Nuclear Incoherence: Deterrence Theory and Non-strategic Nuclear Weapons in Russia," *Journal of Strategic Studies* 37, no. 1 (2014): 94–95 (emphasis in original). However, Adamsky argues that it remains ambiguous—largely because of classification issues—as to how Russia's coercive nuclear escalation strategy has been translated into concrete operational plans.

35. Kristensen and Korda estimate that Russia has almost two thousand tactical nuclear warheads assigned for delivery by air, naval, and various defensive forces. In terms of short-range missiles, Russia is estimated to have roughly 140 warheads, including both SS-21 (Tochka) and the replacement SS-26 (Iskander-M) missiles. Hans M. Kristensen and Matt Korda, "Russian Nuclear Forces, 2019," *Bulletin of the Atomic Scientists* 75, no. 2 (March 2019): 73–84. Also see Jakob Hedenskog and Carolina Vendil Pallin, eds., *Russian Military Capability in a Ten-Year Perspective, 2013* (Stockholm: Swedish Defence Research Agency, 2013).

36. Hans M. Kristensen and Robert S. Norris, "Russian Nuclear Forces, 2016," *Bulletin of the Atomic Scientists* 72, no. 3 (2016): 125–134; and Brad Roberts, *The Case for U.S. Nuclear Weapons in the 21st Century* (Stanford, CA: Stanford University Press, 2016), 137.

37. See Roberts, *Case for U.S. Nuclear Weapons*, 130–131; and Mark B. Schneider, "Deterring Russian First Use of Low-Yield Nuclear Weapons," RealClearDefense, March 12, 2018, https://www.realcleardefense.com/articles/2018/03/12/deterring_russian_first_use_of_low-yield_nuclear_weapons_113180.html.

38. Kokoshin, *Ensuring Strategic Stability*, 33, 43. Also see the thorough discussion of expert views in Roberts, *Case for U.S. Nuclear Weapons*, 138.

39. For example, see Evan Braden Montgomery and Eric S. Edelman, "Rethinking Stability in South Asia: India, Pakistan, and the Competition for Escalation Dominance," *Journal of Strategic Studies* 38, nos. 1–2 (2015): 159–182; Jaganath Sankaran, "Pakistan's Battlefield Nuclear Policy: A Risky Solution to an Exaggerated Threat," *International Security* 39, no. 3 (Winter 2014/15): 118–151; Narang, "Posturing for Peace?"; and especially Narang, *Nuclear Strategy in the Modern Era*, 76–90.

40. This is similar to NATO's predicament in the Cold War, where the Soviets were expected to attack through lowlands along the intra-German border (e.g., the Fulda Gap and North German Plain). Not surprisingly, Pakistan's nuclear doctrine is thought to be modeled on NATO's flexible response posture.

41. See Narang, *Nuclear Strategy in the Modern Era*, 90 (citing Paul Kapur data). For a dissenting view of the implications of the conventional military balance, see Walter C. Ladwig III, "Could India's Military Really Crush Pakistan?," *National Interest*, July 2, 2015, https://nationalinterest.org/feature/could-indias-military-really-crush-pakistan-13247.

42. Peter Lavoy, "Islamabad's Nuclear Posture: Its Premises and Implementation," in *Pakistan's Nuclear Future: Worries beyond War*, ed. Henry D. Sokolski (Carlisle, PA: Strategic Studies Institute 2008), 134; Montgomery and Edelman, "Rethinking Stability in South Asia," 169–171; and Narang, *Nuclear Strategy in the Modern Era*, 76–90.

43. Narang, *Nuclear Strategy in the Modern Era*, 55, 78–79, 81.

44. As described by military officers and in planning documents, the conditions for nuclear use include the significant loss of territory, destruction of large parts of the army or air force, economic "strangulation," and domestic destabilization. Zachary Keck, "Pakistan Says It's Ready to Use Nuclear Weapons—Should India Worry?," *National Interest*, July 8, 2015, https://nationalinterest.org/blog/the-buzz/pakistan-says-its-ready-use-nuclear-weapons%E2%80%94should-india-23034.

45. Narang, "Posturing for Peace?," 44.

46. The short-range Hatf-9 NASR and Hatf-2 Abdali missiles are designed to deliver low-yield nuclear warheads against invading Indian forces. The Pakistani road-mobile missile force has "undergone significant development and expansion over the past decade": the mobility of the medium-range Hatf-5 Ghauri and Hatf-6 Shaheen-2 missiles improve survivability, and the latter's use of solid fuel helps reduce launch times and thus survivability against Indian conventional targeting. Pakistan's arsenal also includes nuclear bombs deliverable by F-16s and Mirage III/V aircraft and growing cruise missile capabilities. Hans M. Kristensen, Robert S. Norris, and Julia Diamond, "Pakistani Nuclear Forces, 2018," *Bulletin of the Atomic Scientists* 74, no. 5 (September 2018): 348–358.

47. Narang, *Nuclear Strategy in the Modern Era*, 86.

48. Narang, *Nuclear Strategy in the Modern Era*, 66, 83, 86; Bernstein, "Emerging Nuclear Landscape," 107.

49. On predelegation, see T.D. Hoyt, "Pakistani Nuclear Doctrine and the Dangers of Strategic Myopia," *Asian Survey*, Vol. 41, no. 6 (November-December 2001): 956–977; Feroz Hassan Khan, "Nuclear Command-and-Control in South Asia during Peace, Crisis and War," *Contemporary South Asia*, Vol. 14, no. 2 (June 2005): 163-174; and Narang, *Nuclear Strategy in the Modern Era*. As Hoyt writes, "It is apparent that Pakistan's [command and control] procedures are delegative, lean heavily toward the always side of the always/never divide, and probably include both devolution and possibly pre-delegation in order to ensure the use of weapons" (966).

50. Daniel R. Coats, *Worldwide Threat Assessment of the U.S. Intelligence Community* (Washington, DC: Office of the Director of National Intelligence, March 6, 2018), 8. Some analysts think Pakistan could almost double the size of its nuclear warhead stockpile by 2025. Kristensen et al., "Pakistani Nuclear Forces," 348.

51. Ankit Panda and Vipin Narang raise the possibility that a sea leg could potentially reduce Pakistan's "use-it-or-lose-it" fears and thus allow Pakistan to reduce its reliance on the early use of tactical land-based nuclear weapons, although they ultimately reject such optimism about

the impact of nuclear submarines on strategic stability. See Ankit Panda and Vipin Narang, "Pakistan Tests New Sub-Launched Nuclear-Capable Cruise Missile. What Now?," *Diplomat*, January 10, 2017, https://thediplomat.com/2017/01/pakistans-tests-new-sub-launched-nuclear -capable-cruise-missile-what-now/.

52. "Pakistan Conducts First Flight Test of Nuclear-Capable 'Ababeel' Missile," *Indian Express*, January 24, 2017, https://www.newsnation.in/world-news/pakistan-conducts-first-flight -test-of-nuclear-capable-ababeel-missile-article-158984.html.

53. See Léonie Allard, Mathieu Duchâtel, and François Godement, "Pre-Empting Defeat: In Search of North Korea's Nuclear Doctrine," European Council on Foreign Relations, November 2017, 2–3.

54. As former U.S. Deputy Assistant Secretary of Defense for Nuclear and Missile Defense Policy Brad Roberts writes, "Little is known about how North Korea thinks about or plans for armed confrontation with the United States under the nuclear shadow. . . . But the capabilities they have deployed and are developing and deploying enable a bold but risky strategy of nuclear blackmail." Brad Roberts, "On the Strategic Value of Ballistic Missile Defense," IFRI Proliferation Papers no. 50, June 2014, 14; also see 11–18. Roberts further discusses a plausible North Korean theory of victory in Roberts, *Case for U.S. Nuclear Weapons*, 58–80.

55. Hans M. Kristensen and Robert S. Norris, "North Korean Nuclear Capabilities, 2018," *Bulletin of the Atomic Scientists* 74, no. 1 (January 2018): 41–51.

56. See Avner Cohen, *Israel and the Bomb* (New York: Columbia University Press, 1998); Seymour Hersh, *The Samson Option: Israel's Nuclear Arsenal and American Foreign Policy* (New York: Random House, 1991); and Narang, *Nuclear Strategy in the Modern Era*, chap. 7. See also Avner Cohen, "When Israel Stepped Back from the Brink," *New York Times*, October 3, 2013, https:// www.nytimes.com/2013/10/04/opinion/when-israel-stepped-back-from-the-brink.html; and Elbridge Colby et al., *The Israeli 'Nuclear Alert' of 1973: Deterrence and Signaling in Crisis* (Alexandria, VA: Center for Naval Analysis, 2013).

57. See Hans M. Kristensen and Robert S. Norris, "Israeli Nuclear Weapons, 2014," *Bulletin of the Atomic Scientists* 70, no. 6 (2014): 97–115.

58. Roberts, *Case for U.S. Nuclear Weapons*, 169; Bernstein, "Emerging Nuclear Landscape," 111–117.

59. See Bernstein, "Emerging Nuclear Landscape," 111–117; Thomas J. Christensen, "The Meaning of the Nuclear Evolution: China's Strategic Modernization and US-China Security Relations," *Journal of Strategic Studies* 35, no. 4 (August 2012): 474–481; M. Taylor Fravel and Evan S. Medeiros, "China's Search for Assured Retaliation: The Evolution of Chinese Nuclear Strategy and Force Structure," *International Security* 35, no. 2 (Fall 2010): 48–87; and Alastair Iain Johnston, "China's New 'Old Thinking': The Concept of Limited Deterrence," *International Security* 20, no. 3 (Winter 1995/96): 5–42. For a dissenting view that predicts continuity in China's strategic posture, albeit with a move to allow limited ambiguity over the application of China's no-first-use policy, see Fiona S. Cunningham and M. Taylor Fravel, "Assuring Assured Retaliation: China's Nuclear Posture and U.S.-China Strategic Stability," *International Security* 40, no. 2 (Fall 2015): 7–50. Many U.S. government officials, policy analysts, and academics—including those with expertise on China and who have participated in conversations about nuclear doctrine with Chinese officials—believe China's no-first-use pledge should not be interpreted literally. They indicate that discussions with official Chinese delegations about these issues reinforce the impression that China's actual nuclear policy is nuanced, and that China's representatives indicated that a range of nonnuclear U.S. military actions might trigger a Chinese nuclear response.

60. Hans M. Kristensen and Matt Korda, "Chinese Nuclear Forces, 2019," *Bulletin of the Atomic Scientists* 75, no. 4 (July 2019): 171–178. Some PLA officials have reportedly advocated increasing the readiness of nuclear missiles. Gregory Kulacki, "China's Military Calls for Putting Its Nuclear Forces on Alert," Union of Concerned Scientists, January 2016, https://www.ucsusa .org/nuclear-weapons/us-china-relations/china-hair-trigger. Moreover, after the release of the U.S. 2018 Nuclear Posture Review, the Chinese state-run *Global Times* released an op-ed suggesting China might need to respond with a low-yield nuclear program. Ellen Mitchell, "China Pushing New Generation of Nuclear Weapons: Report," *The Hill*, May 28, 2018, https://thehill .com/policy/defense/389628-china-pushing-new-generation-of-nuclear-weapons-report.

61. See Bernstein, "Emerging Nuclear Landscape," 113–114 and sources cited therein. As Bernstein notes, however, some experts on Chinese strategic culture worry about China's willingness to use "sudden, rapid, asymmetrical escalation" to shock the adversary into ending a conflict (116–117).

62. Max Fisher, "India, Long at Odds with Pakistan, May Be Rethinking Nuclear First Strikes," *New York Times*, March 31, 2017, https://www.nytimes.com/2017/03/31/world/asia/india-long-at-odds-with-pakistan-may-be-rethinking-nuclear-first-strikes.html.

Conclusion

1. These arguments and their sources can be found in chapter 1.

2. See Keir A. Lieber and Daryl G. Press, "Why Nuclear Disarmament and Strategic Stability Are Incompatible," in *Nuclear Disarmament: A Critical Assessment*, ed. Bård Nikolas Vik Steen and Olav Njølstad (New York: Routledge, 2019). In the 1980s, Thomas Schelling bemoaned the fact that nuclear arms control talks between the United States and the Soviet Union were concentrating on numbers, not crisis stability. Thomas C. Schelling, "What Went Wrong with Arms Control?," *Foreign Affairs* 64, no. 2 (Winter 1985/86): 219–233.

3. For a recent discussion of the strategic incentives for counterproliferation, and the impact these threats have on decisions to proliferate, see Alexandre Debs and Nuno P. Monteiro, *Nuclear Politics: The Strategic Causes of Proliferation* (New York: Cambridge University Press, 2017), esp. chap. 2.

4. Schelling was referring to Japan's decision to attack Pearl Harbor, lamenting that U.S. leaders had forgotten that a deterrent could still be a target. Thomas C. Schelling, Foreword to *Pearl Harbor: Warning and Decision*, by Robert Wohlstetter (Stanford, CA: Stanford University Press, 1962), viii.

5. For example, see U.S. presidential adviser Bernard Baruch, "The Baruch Plan," presented to the United Nations Atomic Energy Commission, June 14, 1946; and Dexter Masters and Katharine Way, eds., *One World or None: A Report to the Public on the Full Meaning of the Atomic Bomb* (New York: McGraw-Hill, 1946; repr., New Press, 2007); and "Atomic Education Urged by Einstein," *New York Times*, May 25, 1946. The final chapter of *One World or None*, titled "Survival Is at Stake," summarizes the basic premise: "The atomic arms race, which can mean our doom, is in full swing. . . . It is the eloquent and unanswerable argument of this book that [it] will bring death to the society that produced it if we do not adapt ourselves to it. . . . Nations can have atomic energy, and much more. But they cannot have it in a world where war may come." Masters and Way, *One World or None*, 215–220.

6. Starting in 2007, a group of prominent American statesmen—George Shultz, William Perry, Henry Kissinger, and Sam Nunn—sought to galvanize the nuclear disarmament movement, repeating in a series of op-eds that nuclear deterrence is "decreasingly effective and increasingly hazardous" and that U.S. leadership is "required to take the world to the next stage"—reversing reliance on nuclear weapons and "ultimately ending them as a threat to the world." George P. Shultz, William J. Perry, Henry A. Kissinger, and Sam Nunn, "A World Free of Nuclear Weapons," *Wall Street Journal*, January 4, 2007. Follow-up op-eds appeared in 2008, 2010, 2011, and 2013. In 2009, President Obama declared America's commitment to the goal of global nuclear disarmament. Obama stated, if "one nuclear weapon exploded in one city . . . no matter where it happens, there is no end to what the consequences might be—for our global safety, our society, our economy, to our ultimate survival." The White House, Office of the Press Secretary, "Remarks by President Barack Obama," Hradčany Square, Prague, Czech Republic, April 5, 2009.

7. Thomas C. Schelling, "A World without Nuclear Weapons?" *Daedalus* 138, no. 4 (Fall 2009): 127.

Index

Lightning Source UK Ltd.
Milton Keynes UK
UKHW011044271120
374202UK00008B/302/J

9 781501 749292